BANDIT COUNTRY

BANDIT COUNTRY

Brothers, betrayal and murder in the heart of a gambling empire

JAMIE REID

First published in the UK by John Blake Publishing
an imprint of Bonnier Books UK
4th Floor, Victoria House
Bloomsbury Square,
London, WC1B 4DA
England

Owned by Bonnier Books
Sveavägen 56, Stockholm, Sweden

www.facebook.com/johnblakebooks
twitter.com/jblakebooks

First published in paperback in 2023

Paperback ISBN: 978 1 78946 550 1
Ebook ISBN: 978 1 78946 551 8

British Library Cataloguing-in-Publication Data:

A catalogue record for this book is available from the British Library.

Design by www.envydesign.co.uk

Printed and bound in Great Britain by Clays Ltd, Elcograf S.p.A.

1 3 5 7 9 10 8 6 4 2

John Blake Publishing is an imprint of Bonnier Books UK
www.bonnierbooks.co.uk

For Jack and Alex

AUTHOR'S NOTE

This is a story with many names and many faces. To aid the reader, I have included a 'cast of characters' at the back of the book for ease of reference.

'We have whiskey, wine, women, song and slot machines.
I won't deny it and I won't apologise for it. If the majority of
people didn't want them, they wouldn't exist. The fact that they
do exist proves to me that people want them.'
Enoch 'Nucky' Johnson (*Boardwalk Empire*'s Nucky Thompson)
Atlantic City, New Jersey, 1929

'The one-armed bandit man
Came north to fill his boots
Came up from Cockneyland
E-type Jags and flashy suits'
From '5.15 a.m.' by Mark Knopfler

'Sinners interest me more than saints'
Mike Hodges
British Film Institute, 2009

PROLOGUE

THE BODY WAS in the back of a dark-green Jaguar Mark X saloon that had been abandoned beneath a railway bridge in a small Durham mining village sixteen miles south of Newcastle.

The discovery was made by Tom Leak, a shot-firer on his way home after a night shift in the local colliery. For the last eight hours, Leak had been working more than 800 feet underground: his job to safely set and detonate the explosives used to blast the coal from the seam. When his shift finished at 4:45am, he had ridden the cage back up to the top of the shaft, showered, changed and then started walking home along Front Street past Fallowfield Garage and the village school.

It was bitterly cold in South Hetton in the early hours of 5th January, 1967. It had been snowing during the night and an icy wind was blowing in off the North Sea. While he was underground, Leak had been told that the snow had started falling at around 3:15am and the first thing he noticed about the big car badly parked near Pesspool bridge was that it was covered with a light layer of snow, mostly on the boot, but that there was no snow underneath it so it must have been there for some time.

The Jaguar was about fourteen inches from the kerb on the west side of the bridge going towards Easington. It was a dangerous spot where many accidents had occurred and, at first, Leak thought it must have run out of petrol. Such an expensive and powerful car was not an everyday sight in South Hetton and the miner crossed the road to have a closer look. Front Street was brightly lit at night and Leak could see that the Jaguar's rear lights were burning dimly and the rear offside door wasn't properly closed. He also noticed that the driver's side window was wound down and the rear passenger window shattered. The windscreen wipers were broken too but the ignition was still on and the key in place.

When Leak peered in through the nearside front window, he saw nothing but, when he looked in through the back window, which was up, he saw a man's body lying stretched out on the back seat, with its head and shoulders jammed between the driver's seat and the offside door. There was mud on his shirt and a bruise on his forehead, but the short, dark blue, overcoat and expensive looking suit and shoes were not the uniform of an ordinary working man.

Leak opened the door and shook the man's left leg by the calf, which was bare. 'Hey, mate,' he called. 'You can't park there. Hey. Wake up.' But there was no response. He tried again, leaning right in across the smart leather upholstery but the body was cold and there were no signs of life.

Leak, who had spent eight years in the army before going down the mine, knew what a dead body looked like. He shut the car door and was heading to the Post Office kiosk to phone 999 when three other miners came walking up the road from the pithead.

They were led by Leak's friend, Leslie Marshall, who was a colliery supervisor. Leak told them there was a man in the Jaguar who appeared to be dead and they all went over and had a look. There was broken glass on the man's chest and on the back seat. Leslie Marshall attempted to take a pulse. 'There's no beat at the carotid artery,' he said to the others. They went to the back of the car to examine the lights and get the number, and then Tom Leak went to the phone box and called the police.

The village constable, PC Maurice Cluer, arrived soon afterwards, followed by two uniformed traffic officers, driving an Austin Westminster saloon. They were joined by the local GP, Dr John Seymour Hunter, and an official police photographer. At 7am Detective Superintendent Ronald Kell of Durham CID arrived to take charge. He was accompanied by the pathologist, Dr John Ennis, and he was the one who peeled back the dead man's coat to reveal the three bullet holes in his body: two in the left shoulder and one in the chest. By then the area around Pesspool bridge was swarming with uniformed and plain-clothes police. The detectives, eyes watering, smoking cigarettes and turning their coat collars up in the biting wind. The beat coppers stamping their feet and blowing on their hands to keep warm as 'Jack' Ennis began a tentative examination.

By mid-morning, the dead man's identity had been established and DS Kell confirmed that he was now conducting a murder enquiry and had established an HQ in nearby Peterlee police station. 'If it bleeds, it leads' was the old Fleet Street saying and the press fell on the news like bounty hunters stripping booty off an outlaw's corpse. GAMING KING SHOT DEAD proclaimed a banner headline in the *Newcastle Evening Chronicle*. GANG WAR FEAR IN MURDER HUNT.

Like so many homicides, it was a story that would end up destroying a lot more than just the one life. A glittering self-made fortune would be ruined. Marriages and families broken up. And two men, not wholly innocent but not indisputably guilty either, would forever claim that they had been the victims of a shocking miscarriage of justice.

As more details became known over the following days, they formed a dramatic contrast to the image of Newcastle and the north-east being promoted by politicians and property developers who were busy tearing down great chunks of the city in the name of progress. They claimed to be building a better tomorrow but were profiting from corrupt deals and backhanders they were anxious to conceal. The last thing they needed was reporters and television crews digging around for information about the 'One-Armed Bandit Murder', as it became known. But for many others, the killing combined cinematic violence with an underlying visceral thrill. It was the Swinging Sixties. It was the era of free love, dope smoking and social change. But it was also the era of gangsters, of casinos and protection rackets, of plush gambling clubs, rich living and a silver cascade of cash.

What had brought the dead man to such a lonely, out-of-the-way spot in the middle of the night? Was it really true, local people wondered, what some of the journalists were saying? Had the man been the victim of a gangland feud?

And had the Mafia come to Newcastle?

CHAPTER ONE

'TAKE THE MONEY . . . or open the box,' explained the off-screen announcer, Bob Danvers-Walker, as the first ever episode of *Take Your Pick* was broadcast on Independent Television on Friday, 23rd September, 1955.

The game show, produced by Associated-Rediffusion and hosted by its creator, the New Zealand-born Michael Miles, required contestants to answer a series of quick-fire questions without using the words 'Yes' or 'No'. If they qualified for the second round, they had to choose a key, which would open one of ten boxes, each containing a different prize. Miles would offer them cash to give the key back and then they'd have to decide whether to accept it or take their chances of winning something better. One of the boxes might contain the keys to a new car or tickets for a holiday in the sun but others held only booby prizes, like a feather duster or a cup of tea.

The seductive emphasis on material rewards was in evidence again three nights later when ITV's second game show, *Double*

Your Money, made its debut under the stewardship of Hughie Greene. The BBC, which was still in the grip of the high moral tone laid down by its former Director-General, Lord Reith, disdained game shows with cash prizes, insisting it would stick to its official mission statement to 'inform, educate and entertain'. Not that it was above trying to sabotage the new channel's birth by scheduling a sensational episode of *The Archers* on the Light Programme, in which the popular Grace Archer was killed in a stable fire, on the same evening.

The Labour MP Patrick Gordon-Walker complained that ITV's commercial advertising would promote 'false values of material success' and give British people the idea that they could enjoy 'an easy life without effort'. In fact, the new broadcaster's first night was remarkably sober, beginning with live coverage of a banquet at the Guildhall featuring numerous white male bigwigs in white tie and tails. The evening's fare did include twenty-three adverts for items such as Gibbs SR toothpaste, Cadbury's chocolate and Esso, but they were described by *Life* magazine as possessed of such 'excessive gentility that the name of the product almost seemed to be dropped in by accident.'

Within a few months, though, a livelier and more crowd-pleasing tone had emerged, helped by new home-grown productions like *Robin Hood* and *Sunday Night at the London Palladium*, and popular US imports such as *I Love Lucy* and *The Liberace Show*. High-street shops started springing up – Granada, Radio Rentals, Rediffusion – selling and renting new television sets and a TV suddenly became the indispensable accompaniment to a three-piece suite and Cyril Lord carpeting. But if you had already purchased your set before 1955, perhaps to watch the Queen's coronation in 1953, you needed a set-top converter box to enable you to watch the new channel.

When television began in Britain in 1936, it was just the BBC transmitting on Band One within the VHF, or Very High Frequency, part of the electro-magnetic spectrum. The Television Act of 1954 specified that ITV should use a separate TV mast (a situation that persisted for the next ten years) and a group of six channels within the Band Three range of VHF frequencies, allocated by the Postmaster-General. In 1955, only twenty-four per cent of the nation's TV owners had access to independent television but, by 1961, that number would rise to eighty per cent of all households in the land.

The converter was a plain metal box with a dark-brown or black paint finish. The box had an aerial input for Band Three and a bypass for Band One. The two cables from the aerials went into the box and the output from the converter was plugged into the TV set's aerial socket, whereby ITV on Band Three was 'converted' into the same frequency as the BBC channel. In the mid-1950s, the boxes were much in demand, affording a golden opportunity to an enterprising young man like Vincent Luvaglio, who had a franchise to sell converters from a stall in Lewisham market, and a younger brother, Michael, who knew how to fit them.

The Luvaglio brothers, who were both born before World War II – Vincent in 1932 and Michael five years later – shared a quintessential post-war longing to throw off the shackles of austerity and restraint and embrace a more exciting, aspirational life. Their parents, Frank and Maud Luvaglio, devout Catholics and second-generation Italian immigrants, lived in a street of modest semi-detached red-brick houses in Mitcham in south-west London. Frank Luvaglio was a master tailor who worked in the menswear department at the Army and Navy Stores in Victoria before opening a couple of hairdressing shops and the boys were brought up in a comfortable, if not exactly prosperous, home.

A total of 692 high-explosive bombs and 6 parachute mines fell on the London borough of Merton during the Blitz and Mitcham took more than its fair share of damage. A particularly heavy raid in October 1940 destroyed houses and the Methodist church on Upper Green and flattened the General Stores in Inglemere Road. The nearby fire station in Pembroke Road was hit too and twelve firemen lost their lives. But St Peter and St Paul's Roman Catholic church and the Catholic primary school, which the Luvaglios attended, survived and the church still stands today at the junction of St Mark's Road and Baker Lane.

Vincent and Michael were never evacuated and, like other adventurous boys of their age and time, found the bomb sites and rubble an irresistible attraction. Vincent was a strong, self-reliant child and a natural leader and instigator of scrapes, who organised his followers into a *Just William* style gang. Michael was a gentler, more passive character, who always looked up to his older brother and was prepared to follow him anywhere. Michael loved dogs, played the piano and the violin, and excelled at arithmetic. In 1948, he passed the new Eleven Plus exam and won a place at St John Fisher, then a fee-paying Catholic grammar school in Purley, which accepted non-fee-paying pupils by selective entry. In its prospectus, it vowed to nurture 'young Catholic gentlemen aspiring for Academic, Cultural and Sporting Excellence.'

Frank and Maud Luvaglio, like so many other parents in post-war Britain, hoped that the ladder created by RA Butler's 1944 Education Act would offer their sons a chance to acquire professional qualifications and live a life less restrictive than their own. But first they had to do their compulsory National Service, which both boys served in the RAF. Beginning with three months' basic training for twenty-eight shillings a week, home comforts were replaced by a cramped bunk in a Nissen Hut that had previously been used to house German POWs. It was an oppressive and monotonous experience but the Luvaglio boys found ways to get by: Michael, valued for his mathematical and scientific expertise, was deployed as an aircraft loader, calculating the precise weight and fuel capacity of bombers and transport planes. When he came out, he got a job in the printing trade and went back to live with his parents in their house in Mitcham.

Vincent, bigger and more pugnacious, became a corporal in the Military Police, drawing on the amateur boxing skills he'd learned as a teenager in the Repton Club gym, in Bethnal Green. The club grew out of the Repton Boys Club, which was set up by Repton School in the nineteenth century and intended to help under-privileged young men in the East End. 'No Guts, No Glory' proclaims the club's motto over the side entrance to what was once the old men's and women's Bath House on Cheshire Street, E2 – a rallying cry that has inspired many legendary fighters, including Billy Walker, John H Stracey and Maurice Hope. Vincent had the guts – boxing in a few local Amateur Boxing Association bouts as a young man and earning the respect of the club's hard East End trainers – and by the time he left the air force and returned to Civvy Street in 1953, he was yearning for glory too.

Vincent's first official job was as a salesman and trainee manager in a shop selling TV sets in Tooting Broadway. It appeared to offer a solid, if unspectacular, path to a regular income and a secure future. But Vince's quick wits and streetwise brain, much more streetwise than that of his younger brother, told him that staying power, hard work and playing by the rules wouldn't get you very far in those drab early 1950s years. He dreamed of a life where he was his own master, rather than someone else's employee, and, with the help of some of the black-market friends he'd made in and around the boxing ring, he secured the stall in Lewisham market and a franchise of sorts to stock and sell TV converters – cash only – in London and the Kent and Surrey suburbs. Like the spivs and used-car dealers who congregated in Warren Street, he got used to carrying his bank in his pocket and doing business with 'suppliers' in grubby pubs and steamed-up caffs. He was a natural salesman and, as his fortunes rose, he displayed the kind of 'self-conscious impudence' ascribed by Graham Greene to the black marketeer Harry Lime in *The Third Man*, another man possessed of a smile and charm that suggested he thought 'his own well-being made the world's day'.

Not content with marketing TV converters, Vincent also sold second-hand television sets, radios and discount records and, as popular taste began to change, he sensed that the hunger for entertainment, especially among the younger generation, was about to enter a significant new stage.

On 15th September, 1956, thirty-seven people were arrested, six of them juveniles, after a Saturday-night showing of *Rock Around the Clock* at the Gaumont cinema in Lewisham. The American musical, starring Bill Haley and His Comets and featuring their smash hit of the same name, thrilled teenage audiences longing to escape the greyness and conformity of everyday life. Embracing the music and the new dance moves to the point of jumping up and jiving in the aisles, they alarmed and outraged conventional authority figures and over a hundred young cinemagoers were ejected from the Gaumont before the performance had ended. Afterwards, an estimated thousand-strong crowd gathered in the square outside and began to 'chant and sing', as the *Daily Express* reported it, until police intervened. One inspector and two uniformed officers were slightly injured, and one policeman's helmet was damaged. Twenty-four of those arrested ended up being charged with disorderly conduct and one with assaulting the police. The following day, they were hauled up before Greenwich Magistrates Court, where most of them were fined or put on probation, although one sixteen-year-old Teddy Boy was committed to an approved school.

More crowds gathered at the Elephant and Castle, where some bottles and fireworks were thrown, and there were further Bill Haley-inspired rumbles outside the Trocadero in the New Kent Road and in Wallington, Welling and Carshalton. Outside London there were fireworks and a mile-long jive down the main street in Bootle on Merseyside and, at Manchester's Gaiety cinema, the film was temporarily halted as about fifty Teddy Boys threw electric lightbulbs from the balcony into the stalls.

Older people may have felt threatened by the eruption of so much youthful energy but teenagers had arrived and were about to become the dominant market, not just for the new music but also for other emerging fashions and tastes. In 1955, ten years after the end of the war, Anthony Eden's Conservative government finally relaxed import restrictions on luxury goods and, as well as the washing machines and refrigerators beloved of game shows like *Take Your Pick*, the first plane loads of American jukeboxes started arriving in Britain.

The gleaming Wurlitzer and Rock-Ola machines derived their style from the Detroit car industry: all lustrous tail fins and chrome grilles, with each machine capable of holding up to a hundred records. With only offshore stations like Radio Luxembourg playing rock 'n' roll, jukeboxes were one of the few ways teenagers could listen to their favourite music. By the end of 1957, 8,000 jukeboxes had been imported into the UK, most of them destined to be installed in one of the coffee bars that had become the nation's other new fashionable craze.

The coffee bar trend began in 1952 with the opening of the Moka Bar in Frith Street in Soho. It was owned by Pino Riservato, an Italian dental technician who also owned the British concession for Gaggia machines. Others soon followed, like the Las Vegas on Old Brompton Road, the Two 2i's on Old Compton Street, the exotic El Cubano in Knightsbridge, which had sombreros and bullfighting posters on the wall, and the Gondola in Wigmore Street, which had a more ordered and nautical air. All of them were individually owned, rather than part of a chain like the Kardomah, and the work of amateur designers and architects. Essential items included stools instead of chairs, Formica-top tables, glass cups and the hissing, steaming Gaggia coffee machines, which cost between £150 and £400 and served up what was often described outside London as a cup of 'expresso', as opposed to espresso.

One of the big attractions for younger people was that places like the Gondola opened at 10am and, in some cases, stayed open until midnight, enabling their customers to meet and talk and listen to records without being pressed to drink up and leave. Apart from private-members clubs, there was nowhere else where they could socialise so cheaply and so late.

Film producers caught on to the craze and coffee bars provided the backdrop to a series of popular British films of the period, like *The Golden Disc* (1958), *Beat Girl* (1959), starring Adam Faith, and, most famously, *Expresso Bongo* (1959), in which Cliff Richard appeared as a teenage singer called Bert Rudge whose hustler of a manager, Johnny Jackson, played by a chain-smoking Laurence Harvey in a pork pie hat, persuades him to change his name to 'Bongo' Herbert, as a result of which he gets a record deal and an American girlfriend.

The coffee bar trend was deplored by some adults, who contrasted them with the supposedly character-building qualities of church youth clubs run by vicars in cardigans and offering orange squash and table tennis as opposed to espresso and rock 'n' roll. In September 1958, the Lord Mayor of Birmingham, Donald Johnstone, attacked 'aimless café society', as he called it, where teenagers spent 'hour after hour listening to records and feeding pennies into machines because they have nothing better to do.' Johnstone may have disapproved but for bored and benighted youth, especially in provincial towns outside London, a coffee bar – like The Cabana in Sevenoaks, complete with jukebox, glass cups and a pinball machine – was the next best thing to live entertainment. And as the demand grew, enterprising characters like Vincent Luvaglio saw that the potential profits to be made might be even greater than from TVs and television converters.

The big jukebox manufacturers like Wurlitzer and AIM (Automatic Musical Instruments) didn't sell directly to cafés and clubs. They sold to regional distribution companies who, in turn, sold to operators of jukebox 'routes' that contained groups of neighbouring venues. By 1958, Vincent was the overlord of a route from south-west London to the south coast and was supplying jukeboxes to seaside arcades as well as to half-a-dozen coffee bars that he and his brother owned on the urban and suburban border. The money was good and, suddenly, the living was easy and, in a less stratified and class-conscious society, Vincent and Michael's entrepreneurial zeal could have seen them move on to more mainstream financial transactions: stockbroking maybe, or corporate finance. But there was no place for the Luvaglios in the City of London in 1958, other than as messengers or teaboys, and the twenty-four-year-old Vincent had his sights on something much bigger: a characteristic he shared with another larger-than-life character who the brothers had befriended and who shared their hunger for the good life.

CHAPTER TWO

ANGUS STEWART SIBBET was born on 2nd July, 1934, to Mr and Mrs Alfred Sibbet, who lived in Canning Street in the Benwell district of Newcastle. When Angus was eighteen months old, his parents discovered that an attack of polio had left him partially crippled. A prolonged spell of hospital treatment followed and, while he grew up to be broad shouldered and six-foot tall, he always walked with a slight limp.

Leaving school at sixteen, Angus began his working life as a shoe salesman in a shop on the corner of Grainger Street in Newcastle, but what he really wanted was to be a soldier like his father and uncles in World War II. When he was called up for National Service in 1952, the military initially turned him down because of his limp. Undeterred, he wrote to the army medical board demanding a more thorough examination, which was eventually granted, and, at the age of eighteen, he was passed fit and became a national serviceman. He wanted to fight with the British army in Korea so, when his National Service was over, he signed up as a regular soldier and served in Korea and Egypt before leaving the armed forces in 1956.

Angus's older brother James, who was a chief petty officer in the Royal Navy, was protective of his younger sibling, whom he loved dearly but feared was not temperamentally suited to gainful employment in peacetime life. Angus was fun and full of ideas but his appetite for adventure wasn't always matched by a comparable commitment to hard work. In an attempt to anchor him to a grounded project, James got him a job in a Chinese restaurant he'd opened in Woolwich with two Chinamen that he'd met in the navy. 'It was run by Mr Goh, who was of Singapore Chinese extraction and was a friend of mine,' James explained years later. 'Mr Goh was the manager. I was just a sleeping partner with a third share.' Angus, whose only relevant experience was his time spent as a cook in the army during his National Service, was meant to be learning the business as a trainee with a view to, maybe one day, owning a restaurant of his own. 'Mr Goh and I set up the whole idea,' said James. 'My aim was to provide a career for my younger brother. I'd had a history of trying to look after him . . . not that he always wanted me to.'

Chinese restaurants, many of them run by ex-servicemen and merchant sailors who'd spent time in the Far East, were growing rapidly in the UK in the 1950s and the Peking acquired a loyal following. It should have provided Angus Sibbet with a foundation and springboard for the rest of his working life. But James's fears about his brother's susceptibility to temptation were well founded and, after Vincent and Michael Luvaglio came in one night, sounding out Mr Goh about jointly opening a business supplying furniture and fittings to other restaurants nearby, discussions about gainful employment took on a different hue.

Angus was star-struck by Vincent's chutzpah and equally drawn to his friendly and easy-going younger brother. Vincent had lots of plans and seemed confident that, whatever the fate of his proposed scheme with Mr Goh, his horizons would eventually extend way beyond Woolwich and Chinese restaurants. Michael smiled and nodded supportively and seemed happy to be along for the ride. Under the spell of the Luvaglio charm and with the help of money borrowed from his loving brother, Angus began trying to emulate Vincent's lifestyle. Within a year, he owned a few coffee bars himself and was supplying jukeboxes in towns along the south coast from Margate to Eastbourne. He even started dressing and dining out like an imitation Vincent or Harry Lime and, on the back of the proceeds from his new ventures, proposed marriage to a dark-haired, dark-eyed woman five years older than himself. Brenda Sibbet, who had a Spanish, almost gypsy-like aura, had been a hotel manageress in Brighton and Angus's new friends celebrated the match enthusiastically, with Michael Luvaglio acting as best man at the couple's wedding in 1957.

But then the following year it all went horribly wrong and Sibbet was convicted of receiving stolen goods when items from a TV shop in Mitcham that were part of a Vincent Luvaglio scam, ended up in the back of Angus's car. Vincent escaped prosecution but Angus got two years in Wormwood Scrubs, fulfilling the worst fears of his older brother and his father. 'He was a good lad up until then,' remembered Alfred Sibbet ten years later. 'But I think he fell in with bad company. I went once or twice to see him down there and he was mixed up with some unsavoury characters. He kept saying that everything would be all right and that no one could do anything to him. And look how that turned out.'

Alfred may have had reservations about some of his son's new friends but, around the same time that Angus went to prison, Vincent Luvaglio found himself accused of offending another set of brothers: Londoners like himself, who enforced their own set of rules and punishments. In the first few years after his National Service, Vincent had confined his empire building to his home territory south of the Thames. But by 1958, he'd branched out into the East End and had started minding a few illegal betting shops and 'drinkers' not far from the Repton Club in Bethnal Green. Jack Spot and Billy Hill, the old gang leaders who had run the pre- and post-war London underworld, had retired or moved on, in Hill's case to a luxury villa in southern Spain. Italian and Maltese families continued to operate the gambling and prostitution rackets in the West End, while other parts of the capital had broken up into small, parochial manors run by strictly local figures. But in Hackney, Mile End and Bethnal Green, where Vincent Luvaglio had become a presence, things were about to change.

Ronald and Reginald Kray, born within an hour of each other on 14th October, 1937, had also boxed at the Repton Club Gym as teenagers and been called up for National Service. But unlike the Luvaglios, they displayed their indifference to military discipline by continually absconding from their army postings and doing time in the cells in the Tower of London and Shepton Mallet prison. Not more than five-foot-ten inches tall but strong, tough and fiercely loyal to their mother Rose and to one another, the Kray twins returned to civilian life with an appetite for fighting and total contempt for the law.

In 1956, the twins established an HQ in an old cinema-cum-billiard hall in Eric Street in Hackney, where they surrounded themselves with an entourage of young acolytes. To Ronnie, psychotic and fantastical, the billiard hall was to be the command centre for violent Chicago-style raids on rival mobsters. To Reggie – calmer, more measured and more interested in making money – it was the fledgeling base for what would become known as the Firm: a commercial enterprise of sorts wherein the Krays afforded protection to assorted neighbourhood businesses – pubs, shops, illegal drinking dens – who were compelled to pay them a monthly tribute in return for being allowed to trade.

In November 1956, Ronnie Kray began a three-year jail sentence for grievous bodily harm, having been convicted of shooting a Stepney docker in the leg. In the absence of his dangerously volatile brother, Reggie, who had all the makings of a conventional club owner and 'businessman', started running his eye over the Firm's territory with a view to maximising profits. When he discovered, in July 1958, that the upstart Vincent Luvaglio from SW11 was not just minding one of their gambling rackets less than two miles away but taking a cut without the Firm's knowledge or permission, he was very angry. He sought out Vincent, who was now making frequent forays into east London, and subjected him to a humiliating beating. Reggie specialised in what he called his Cigarette Punch, where he offered someone a cigarette amicably with one hand and then, as the victim opened his mouth to take it, punched him in the jaw with the other. Vincent, no match for Reggie Kray despite his boxing training, was knocked down and hurt and warned of possibly fatal consequences if he ever offended again. His very presence in London, it was made clear, would be regarded as an insult to the Firm.

Vince was genuinely terrified and fearful, not just for his own safety but for the lives and well-being of his family.

He was married now too, like Angus Sibbet: his wife Gwen Sinclair from Edinburgh was a petite and fair-haired former model. The couple already had two small children and, when Gwen received an unscheduled visit at home from two unknown men – one of them leering at her on the doorstep and playing with a cut-throat razor – Vincent decided that it was time to get out, even though it meant leaving behind his old life in Mitcham and Morden and his coffee bar business and the jukeboxes, not to mention his anxious parents Frank and Maud and his brother Michael, who could always follow on later. But where they could go to, asked Gwen?

Vincent had an idea about that. Before he went to jail on the receiving charge in 1957, Angus Sibbet had often talked to the Luvaglio brothers about his native Tyneside and the money-making opportunities that awaited them up there if they were prepared to take a chance. Angus had kept in touch with useful friends and contacts who would help them to get a start and painted a picture of potentially limitless growth in a slumbering leisure market that would eclipse anything they'd achieve so far in the capital.

Vincent Luvaglio's mind was made up and, within twenty-four hours of the Firm's men calling at their door, Vincent, Gwen and their two boys had packed their bags, loaded up their car and headed for the Great North Road. Their destination? North … north by north-east.

CHAPTER THREE

IN OCTOBER 1959, the Conservative Party, led by Prime Minister Harold Macmillan, won their third consecutive general election, securing a thumping 100-seat majority over their Labour and Liberal opponents. The PM, who was photographed by Anthony Armstrong-Jones sitting with a cigar in his hand and watching the returns on television in a quiet room at Number 10 Downing Street, declared that 'the nation has made its choice', adding that he and his colleagues were 'deeply grateful for the confidence that has been shown in us.'

At the outset of the campaign, opinion polls had predicted a Labour win. A front-page article in the *Daily Mail* on 10th October acclaimed Macmillan's unexpected gains in marginal seats in the Midlands and North – not unlike Boris Johnson's Red Wall triumphs in 2019 – and attributed the result to voters' fears of Labour's tax plans, which, it said, had 'proved that the class war was obsolete.'

Macmillan had prepared the ground for his victory at least

two years before in his July 1957 speech in which he claimed that, thanks to the boom in the post-war global economy, most of the population had 'never had it so good'. Aspiration, whether to break down old class barriers or just to acquire the latest materialistic delights, be they cars, carpets or a pair of Kayser Bondor luxury nylons ('Give her sheer flattery this Christmas' purred the advert), was one of the keynotes of the age and everywhere there were obliging hire-purchase companies generously offering their services to assist buyers to secure their prize.

Macmillan's Britain may still have been associated with reactionary cultural baggage, typified by the sight of customs officials at Dover seizing copies of *Lady Chatterley's Lover*, and *Tropic of Cancer* by Henry Miller, but young British 'kitchen sink' novelists and playwrights were dramatizing life in industrial towns and cities that were far removed from the drawing-room settings of Terence Rattigan and Noel Coward. John Braine's novel *Room at the Top*, which was published in 1957, told the story of Joe Lampton, a young trainee accountant returning to a Yorkshire mill town after World War II. Joe is working class but he has no interest in socialism or trade unions. He's determined to better himself socially and financially and, in the process, he falls in love with an older woman he meets in the local amateur-dramatics society. But then he jilts her when his other girlfriend, the daughter of a rich businessman, becomes pregnant and her father offers him money, a house and an executive job if he marries her. In 1959, the book was turned into a highly successful film starring Laurence Harvey in the title role, which won the BAFTA for Best Picture and Oscars for Best Actress, for Simone Signoret, and for Best Adapted Screenplay.

When Vincent Luvaglio arrived in the north-east in the

autumn of 1959, he was already happily married to Gwen Sinclair, with whom he would eventually have five children. But in terms of ambition and aspiration, he was every bit as ruthlessly focused as Joe Lampton, while starting off from an even lower economic base. The Luvaglios' first home in the region was a council house in Horden, a Durham mining village on the North Sea coast, twelve miles from Sunderland. In the 1950s and 1960s, the local colliery still employed over 400 men and produced 1.5 million tonnes of coal a year. The village boasted three pubs, three cinemas and a cricket, rugby and football pitch. The mine shut down in 1987 and Horden today has a depressed and visibly run-down air, with high unemployment and above-average health problems. On a fine summer morning in June 2021, an elderly man whistled encouragement to a homing pigeon as it soared majestically above the allotments, prefabs and caravans-cum-sheds down by the railway line. But up the hill behind him, there were boarded-up shops and amenities with many of the old nineteenth-century miners' cottages, streets numbered row by row, either empty or barely habitable.

Lucky enough to move to the north-east before the decline set in, Vincent Luvaglio and his family saw the region towards the end of its industrial prime and it was a very different world to the one he'd grown up in. At the time, an estimated thirty-four per cent of male jobs in the region still depended on traditional heavy industries such as coal, steel and shipbuilding, compared with twelve per cent in Britain as a whole. Between 1959 and 1963, nearly 33,000 male jobs would be lost in those industries. The great shipbuilding yards like Swan Hunter at Wallsend, which had built historic vessels such as the *Mauretania*, the RMS *Carpathia* and the 5th *Ark Royal*, were already holed beneath the waterline and, by 1965, Japan would have usurped the UK as the world's leading ship manufacturer. But as Luvaglio set out to get the measure of his new surroundings, the shipyards and mines still underpinned life and were the backbone of a predominantly male, working-class culture that valued strength – and hard drinking – along with courage, loyalty and skill.

As well as pubs, the community's other great social resource was its extensive network of miners' welfare committees and workingmen's clubs. All told there were about 2,000 members of the CIU or Working Men's Club and Institute Union in 1959 and hundreds of them were situated on Tyne and Wear in Northumberland and County Durham. The roll call on Vince's doorstep included the Sunniside Social Club, the Old Hall Social Club, the Washington Miners' Welfare Club with its proud NUM banner, Pennywell Social Club, Hepworth and Grandage Social Club, Felling Social Club, Consett's Grove and Moorside Social Club and many more.

The clubs' tobacco-filled interiors may have been friendly and companionable but the comforts were basic and the décor drab. They were places for men to smoke and drink beer and play dominoes or darts and billiards, but only a few of them permitted women to have full membership. The pubs in Newcastle and along the Tyne in Wallsend, Jarrow and North Shields were equally macho, percolated in the scent of stale beer and cigarette smoke; refreshments confined to packets of crisps and pickled eggs. The city had its illegal drinking dens that kept their own hours, some of them run by local hard men like Kenny 'Panda' Anderson and Mario Cunningham, and numerous illegal betting shops, often close to the pitheads and shipyard gates, but there were no proper night clubs in the city in 1959 and no out-of-town cabaret performers from London and the US. Vincent Luvaglio would help to change all that.

Vincent's initial progress in the north-east came courtesy of his and his brother Michael's imprisoned friend Angus Sibbet. The Geordie had kept up with influential figures with access to local councillors and housing committees and they helped the Luvaglios find a home. But Vincent's key assistant in those early days was a pitman called Ray Thubron, another old friend of Angus Sibbet's, who lived in a council house in Silksworth near Sunderland and was well connected in clubland. Thubron was a punter – he and Vincent enjoyed forays together to Newcastle and Sedgefield races and nights at Sunderland dogs – and it was with Thubron's help that the Londoner succeeded in selling his first slot machine in the north-east to the Acre Rigg Social Club in Horden. The introduction was made by Ronnie Cuthbertson, a member of the Smith Brothers, a singing act who went around the clubs performing ballads like 'Hear My Song' and 'I'll Take You Home Again, Kathleen', which had been popularised in the 1950s by the Irish tenor Josef Locke. With Thubron and Cuthbertson vouching for him, Vincent was able to charm the club stewards and soon began to realise that he was at the centre of a vast parish of working men's clubs and that many others could be won over with his seductive vision of the future.

Gaming machines were not yet officially legal in Britain in 1959, but big changes to the gambling laws were on the way and Vincent and Michael Luvaglio – and Angus Sibbet – had already sold a few reconditioned machines to amusement arcades in Brighton and Margate. Now as the new decade began, they were anticipating the impact of the prospective legislation on the north-east. It may have been the land of coal and steel and heavy engineering but very soon there would be a new kind of seam to mine: one that replaced hard manual labour with pulling a lever and spinning a reel in the pursuit of bounteous treasure.

According to Dennis Vosper MP, joint Under-Secretary of State at the Home Office in Harold Macmillan's government, the object of the 1960 Betting and Gaming Act was 'not to encourage an increase in gambling' but 'to revise laws which have fallen into disrepute, which are not understood by the public and which consume a great amount of police manpower to enforce them.' The chief component of the act was the legalisation of off-course betting shops, which had existed illegally in large numbers for years, providing lucrative profits for the bookmakers who ran them and employment for the legions of bookies runners who could be seen in pubs and barber shops, on street corners and outside factories, mines and assembly lines in every corner of the country. From now on, off-course betting, previously the preserve of punters prosperous enough to open a deposit account and bet by telephone or telegram, was to be officially permitted and its practitioners licensed and taxed, much to the satisfaction of the Treasury, which had long desired to get a share of the proceeds from the British public's infatuation with a gamble.

The act also sanctioned commercial Bingo parlours, many of them destined to open in converted fleapit cinemas, and what was expected to be small-scale gambling in casinos and members clubs provided the participants applied for membership twenty-four hours in advance and the club was regulated by the UK Gambling Commission. The Marlborough and Cambridge-educated Vosper, who had no personal experience of gambling, was blithely confident that the act would not encourage large-scale commercial enterprises and that 'no private promoter would find it worthwhile' to establish a casino under the bill, despite the lack of any meaningful measures to guard against corrupt ownership, manipulation and protection rackets. As far as 'amusements with prizes' were concerned, the responsibility for their installation, he said, would rest with 'the relevant local authority'.

The willingness of a Conservative administration to back what were called 'Butler's Betting Shops' – named after the Home Secretary, RA Butler – is sometimes presented as proof of a consensus that liberalisation was welcome, in keeping with the spirit of the age and the yearning for a more indulgent and hedonistic lifestyle. But at the bill's third reading in May 1960, there were many vociferous critics of the new measures, including the future Labour Home Secretary, Sir Frank Soskice, who warned, presciently, that the provisions concerning gaming were 'likely to lead to the wholesale introduction of gaming clubs and casinos on a continental scale.' A prospect that similarly alarmed Labour's Eric Fletcher who felt it would be 'quite inappropriate and objectionable in this country.'

The Conservative backbencher AV Hilton (Norfolk SW) was happy with the idea of being allowed to play cards for money in members clubs and private houses but seemed confused by the new procedures regarding off-course betting, and was said to have treated the House to an excruciating impersonation of a cockney accent as he pictured himself enquiring of his milkman (why the milkman?), 'Where's the nearest betting office, Charlie?'

Labour's Dr Horace King, a future Speaker, was more concerned with the morality, or lack of it, of the new law. 'We are trying at present to get by on a philosophy that one can get something for nothing and that it is right to do so,' he warned.

'Britain will certainly not get by in the critical years ahead on such a philosophy . . . the whole of present society is built on a gamble.'

But despite the misgivings of Soskice, King and others, the bill had its cross-party supporters too. Men such as Labour's George Wigg, a future chairman of the Horserace Betting Levy Board, who, like Nucky Thompson in *Boardwalk Empire*, calmly advised his colleagues to 'accept human frailty for what it is.' A position endorsed enthusiastically by the QC and Conservative member William 'Billy' Rees-Davies, who had numerous run-ins with the law during an extremely colourful career. 'Although "nice people" may not talk about it, two-thirds of the population have a bet one way or another most days of their lives,' he said. 'It's a gigantic business and about time Parliament tried to put it, with all its complexities, in order.'

Rees-Davies was the MP for the Isle of Thanet, which included seaside towns like Ramsgate and Broadstairs, and he was careful to put in a good word about the impending influx of 'amusement machines', predicting that their popularity would prove a huge benefit to the economy. 'Machines have to be made,' he reasoned, 'and up to now we have had to buy machines from America because the whole business has been held in such contempt and because its legality depended on the decision of chief constables in different areas whether or not they decided to prosecute.' In Margate and Ramsgate, he went on, there had been no prosecutions but, in Blackpool and Scarborough, there were, leaving 'those concerned with this industry in the gravest difficulty. They could not invent new machines or have them made in this country to be exported to other countries because they didn't know if police permission would be given. Consequently, they have had to buy their machines from America.' Indeed, they had, from suppliers with an expert knowledge of the gaming business and a keen eye on developments in Britain with a view to determining whether it could be the next big market for them to invest in.

The distinction of being the first man to open a casino under the new legislation was claimed by a Welshman, George Alfred James, who opened a club above a shop in the industrial steel town of Port Talbot. It included a 400-seater restaurant and an illuminated dance floor, as well as games of roulette, poker and chemin de fer, and was an instant success. So much so that James branched out in partnership with the comedian Charlie Chester – who was inexplicably popular at the time – and opened Charlie Chester's club in Archer Street in Soho. The two men also owned the Golden Horseshoe casino across the road and croupiers criss-crossed back and forth, dovetailing shifts in the two clubs throughout the night. Chris Miles, who worked as a croupier at Chester's in the 1960s and 1970s, remembers it as 'a hot, noisy, low-life environment' far removed from the hushed tone and sleek ambience he'd experienced at Crockford's, the traditional gentlemen's club in St James's Place.

There was a rather more refined atmosphere in Brighton's Metropole hotel, a favourite haunt of the gangster Mr Colleoni in Graham Greene's *Brighton Rock*, which opened a casino in the hotel's Clarence Room and imported an experienced French maître d' and head croupier, Jean-Marie Cruciani, from the Côte d'Azur.

By the end of 1960, Customs and Excise reckoned that there were at least 100 new gambling clubs operating in London alone, and they were just the registered ones. Numerous private-members clubs, already licensed to offer late-night drinking, installed a few gaming tables and described themselves as casinos.

BANDIT COUNTRY

The rules around the provision of roulette, blackjack and dice games like craps, were shrouded in confusion but not so chemin de fer, which had been the big craze of the 1950s and the mainstay of John Aspinall's previously illegal 'Chemmy' parties in private houses in Knightsbridge and Belgravia. Some clubs only had a few tables but the game was always profitable due to the frequency of hands played per shoe, or session, and the club owner didn't have to provide the bank as the participants took it in turn to be the bank themselves.

The unworldly architects of the new bill, who had supposed their work would merely 'tolerate' private gaming, rather than encourage it, were taken aback by the rapid upsurge and the extent and variety of gambling that was suddenly available. Moral unease continued to characterise debates and questions in the House and of particular concern were the new electronic gaming machines, or 'one-armed bandits'. The act specified that no more than two machines could be made available at a given time in any club or pub premises. But as the Mafia had discovered in Cuba and the US – and as Vincent Luvaglio was about to find in the north-east – the 'bandits' were the proverbial licence to print money. Even if the stakes involved in Britain were no more than a sixpenny bit, the turnover on a busy night in a popular well-attended venue might be huge, guaranteeing a wily operator, who was selling or leasing the machines to the clubs and then retaining a major share of the profits: a daily, nightly and weekly risk-free income.

CHAPTER FOUR

IN MAY 1929, Meyer Lansky, the financial mastermind of twentieth-century organised crime, met with Charles 'Lucky' Luciano in Atlantic City. The New Jersey seaside resort was the hometown and headquarters of Enoch 'Nucky' Johnson, thinly disguised as Nucky Thompson in the TV series *Boardwalk Empire*, and around forty-four per cent of the illicit alcohol brought into the Eastern Seaboard during Prohibition had been landed on the New Jersey shore.

At the time of the Atlantic City conference, the Volstead Act, which had been the source of Lansky's, Luciano's and Johnson's fortunes, was in its tenth year, ever more ignored and ever more unpopular. Rightly expecting the act to be repealed after the next Presidential Election in 1932, Lansky and Luciano began discussing how to divert the profits from bootlegging into gambling instead. Their old friend and confederate Benjamin 'Bugsy' Siegel had similar ideas and assured them that the future lay in the luxurious new gambling resort he was going to develop in Las Vegas in the

Nevada desert. But Ben Siegel's cherished Flamingo hotel project kept getting more and more expensive, requiring continual loans from his partners. Eventually, their patience ran out and, in June 1947, Siegel was shot dead at his home in Los Angeles.

In the meantime, Lansky and Luciano had set up the Crime Commission to resolve disputes between New York's 'Five Families' and laid the ground for a partnership between themselves and the Cuban dictator Fulgencia Batista, who opened the island to Mafia-run gambling in return for thirty per cent of the proceeds. As well as taking over the Hotel Nacional, the most famous watering hole in Havana, the gangsters opened a string of lavishly appointed new hotels like the Riviera, the Deauville and the Sans Souci, all offering high-stakes gaming and top-of-the-range entertainment, with food and drink in luxurious surroundings until the early hours. American tourists and gambling junkets flocked to Havana and Lansky and his partners grew richer by the year. But then, in December 1959, Batista's government was overthrown and the dictator forced into exile by Fidel Castro's Communist revolution. Within months, the Mafia bosses saw millions of dollars' worth of investments wiped out as the new regime first closed their hotels and then, in 1961, nationalised all private businesses.

A lot of the gambling foot soldiers – hotel managers, pit bosses, croupiers – moved to Las Vegas, which had gradually evolved into everything Ben Siegel had always promised it would be. But the search for new financial jurisdictions to locate to would also take Lansky to the Bahamas and the Caribbean and then to Britain where, in the mid-1960s, the Mafia attempted to turn part of London's West End into a mini-Las Vegas with a deceptive sheen of good taste, designed to elevate it above the rest.

There was never anything overtly romantic or sentimental

about Meyer Lansky's view of the gaming business and the people who frequented it. 'There is no such thing as an unlucky gambler,' he once said. 'The winners are those who control the game. The rest are all suckers.' The Lansky model, complete with exotic settings and cabaret acts, was all about enticing the high rollers to stay and keep spending as long as possible until they lost. But it wasn't just about roulette or poker or craps. He also understood that the money-winning bedrock of any future successful gambling enterprise was going to be the slot machines. That is why, in Cuba, he had installed 10,000 of them.

The first rudimentary slots were invented in 1891 by Sittman and Pitt, a manufacturing company operating out of Brooklyn, New York. The coin-operated machines, which were rented to saloons, clubs and cigar stores for a percentage of the revenue, were based around five-card stud and had five reels that spun when activated to deliver an outcome. According to *Jack Harper: King of the Slots* by the American historian William S Reid, the Sittman and Pitt machines were 'rigged from the beginning' and cards were 'strategically removed' from the deck, usually a 10 of Spades and a Jack of Hearts, to reduce the possibility of a Royal Flush.

The machines required a nickel coin to start but couldn't pay out in cash so bartenders would instead offer glasses of beer or cigars to the winners. The games were a hit, despite the technical drawbacks, and, according to Reid, one 'would have been hard pressed to find a bar in New York City in the 1890s that didn't have at least one machine beside the counter.'

Within a few years, a competitor had emerged in the shape of Charles Fey, a Bavarian-born mechanic who lived in San Francisco and invented a much simpler form of automatic machine that he called the Liberty Bell. It, too, drew on the game of poker, with three spinning wheels and five symbols: spades, horseshoes (clubs in the UK), hearts, diamonds and a picture of the cracked Liberty Bell, the symbol of American Independence in Philadelphia. If a spin resulted in three Liberty Bells forming in a row, the spinner would get the largest pay-out: ten nickels, or five cents. San Francisco, the city that the Puritans never reached, had scores of saloons, barber shops, brothels and cigar stores, and Fey's machines were a big hit. So much so that, in 1895, he quit his job as a mechanic to start factory production of his invention, only instead of selling them, he rented them to saloon owners and split the profits with them, fifty-fifty.

In 1898, Charles Fey's Card Bell machine was the first three-reel slot to pay out in cash: others included the Klondyke and the Erie Digger, which was disguised as a children's toy selling candy. Fey refused to either license his proprietary technology or surrender monopoly control and, gradually, other manufacturers, their advances rebuffed, started developing products of their own. The Industrial Novelty Company were making vending machines selling Bell's fruit chewing gum and, in 1907, the Chicago-based Mills Novelty Company, owned by the entrepreneur Herbert T Mills, stole Fey's concept and started producing Bell's fruit slot machines, in which the symbols were bars, apples, oranges, melons and cherries. In the changed moral climate following the San Francisco earthquake in 1906, gambling was officially banned in California so, to get around the law, the Mills machines paid out in fruit-based chewing gum, rather than coins.

Herbert Mills had started using mass marketing and assembly-line techniques in his factories and became known as 'the Henry Ford of the slots'. All the Mills machines were easy to play with no rules to be learned first. You inserted a coin, which unlocked the handle on the side, and then pulled the handle, which started the reels spinning with their series of symbols until they stopped in a sequence. Perforations in plates inside the spinning wheels corresponded with the symbols and, when the wheels stopped on a winning combination, the perforations lined up in a manner that triggered a coin slide from the dispenser paying the winning amount.

During the Prohibition years between 1919 and 1933, the likes of Meyer Lansky, Nucky Johnson and Al Capone insured that there were Mills Bell slot machines in all their speakeasies, with cash prizes and bootleg alcohol available to buy with the winnings. New designs proliferated in the 1920s and 1930s, including the Baker's 'Races and Paces' machines, which had a horse-racing theme and were some of the first to be powered electronically.

In New York City, the slots were the personal demesne of Frank Costello, who had been in the bootlegging business with Lansky, Luciano and Siegel and then followed their lead and turned to gambling. The Mills Novelty Company supplied machines to Costello on an exclusive basis and no other manufacturer's products were permitted. Gambling was officially illegal in New York state but – in a template the Luvaglio brothers would emulate in Newcastle and the north-east – police and politicians were paid off, the right people looked after and an army of salesmen, engineers, collectors and security operatives recruited to track down any machines that went missing or were stolen.

Costello and his partner, 'Dandy' Phil Kastel, illicitly trucked machines into New York City from Chicago just like they used to transport liquor and placed them in bars, drug stores, gas stations and railroad and bus stations and, to evade the law, they rigged some of them to dispense mints under the aegis of the 'Triangle Mint Company'.

In 1933, the Republican Fiorello La Guardia became Mayor of New York on an anti-corruption platform and racketeering and the slots were a prime target. La Guardia armed himself with a sledgehammer and smashed machines in person for the cameras. Costello simply moved his operation to Louisiana where – much like Batista in Cuba – the infamous Governor, Huey 'Kingfisher' Long, was happy to have the slots in his state in return for a 'commission' of $20,000 a month. The machines found their way into even the deepest backwoods bayous, like in Tim Gautreaux's novel *The Clearing*, set in a logging camp in a cypress swamp in the 1920s. The camp's on-site saloon, run by Sicilians from New Orleans, has eight slot machines, as well as bootleg liquor, and gambling and drinking are a constant problem for the camp's owners. When the saloon burns down at the end of the story, the melted hulks of the slots are described as looking like one-armed torsos.

The machines became the catalyst and foundation for other Mob-related activities from casinos to narcotics and bookmaking wire services (like the fake betting shop in the 1973 Paul Newman and Robert Redford film *The Sting*) and, with control over both production and distribution, it was easy for Costello's engineers to rig the pay-outs to their employer's advantage. 'Slot machines built during the 1930s usually had a pay-back of about fifty per cent when they weren't buzzed,' said John Scarne, a New Yorker who worked in the business. 'When half the money you feed in is retained, it doesn't take long before the machine has it all. And when the bug was used, you lost even faster. It was this type of machine that was called the "One-Armed Bandit."'

JAMIE REID

In 1931, gambling was legalised in the state of Nevada and the first slot machines in Las Vegas were in Bugsy Siegel's Flamingo hotel. In the 1940s, 1950s and early 1960s, when you pulled down the lever on a machine, it set the reels in motion and stretched a spring inside, which gradually stopped the reels from spinning, giving the players the illusion of being in control. But from 1964 onwards, the slots were all operated electronically, although they retained a lever to get started. The 1960s machines, which Vincent and Michael Luvaglio would install on Tyne and Wear, had a coin hopper, a coin tray, a coin diverter and a drop box or bucket. The hopper was a container in which the coins available for pay-outs were held. A mechanical device automatically rotated coins into the tray when a player accumulated credits by pressing a 'cash out' button and, when a certain pre-set capacity was reached, the diverter redirected or dropped excess coins into the drop box or bucket, which was a container in the slot machine's base.

A drop bucket was used for low-denomination coins and a drop box for higher-denomination machines. They both had a hinged lid with one or more locks and the contents of the buckets and boxes were collected and counted by the club or casino on a regular basis. The machines were all programmed to pay out a percentage of the money taken over a set period and, as John Scarne testified, in a speakeasy in the Prohibition era, that could be as little as fifty per cent every twenty-four hours. Nowadays, the pay-back in a Las Vegas casino is more like seventy-five to ninety-five per cent and the big casinos on the Strip make an estimated $12m a day from gaming, of which the slots account for roughly sixty per cent of their earnings, seven days a week.

By the 1960s, the dominant slot-machine supplier was Bally, which had begun life as the Lion Manufacturing Company, making punchboards in Chicago during the Depression. Its president, Ray Moloney, had worked in the oil business in Texas and a steel mill in Cleveland before manufacturing pinball machines with Lion. In December 1931, the background to one of his games featured on the cover of the satirical magazine *Ballyhoo* and, the following year, Moloney set up the new Bally Manufacturing Company and diversified into slots, as well as vending machines and pinball.

When Moloney died in 1958, Gerardo Caetano, a member of the Genovese crime family from northern New Jersey, took over the business and his daughter Zola married Mickey Wichinsky, Bally's distributor in southern Nevada and a partner in the Sands Hotel. Five years later, another group of 'investors' led by WT O'Donnell from Cleveland, bought the company for $1.2m, the money supposedly a loan from the Teamsters Union arranged by Jackie Presser, the Mob-related Teamsters vice president and later FBI informant. Questions about the buy-out and the new source of the company's wealth continued to dog Bally for years but had little impact on sales and, by the mid-1960s, they controlled over eighty per cent of the US slot-machine trade.

Bally's best-selling product was the Bally Money-Honey, which launched in 1963 and was an electro-magnetic machine with more reels than its predecessors. It allowed players to bet in higher denominations and insert more coins, resulting in bigger jackpots and automatic pay-outs to the winners, accompanied by sound effects and flashing lights. The side levers became redundant but Bally retained them anyway because the punters loved them and they weren't considered proper one-armed bandits without them.

Bally's products were increasingly in demand in Britain too.

On 4th July, Independence Day, 1960, the US trade magazine *Billboard* ran a big article on the expected boom in gambling in the UK now that restrictions were being lifted. Describing clubs in the UK as a cross between 'smart Soho bistros' and 'working men's clubs in the London slum areas and in the industrial cities up north', it reported that British operators were 'frantically scurrying around to get their hands on all the fruit machine equipment on the market' and that Americans, in the form 'of US coin men who are being set up as distributors', were playing an important role. It specifically named David 'Gabe' Forman, who had been a New York distributor for many years and whose wares, it said, were selling 'about as fast as the machines are being sent over'.

Dennis Vosper and his colleagues in the Home Office may not have heard of him but Gabe Forman was not just any old gaming-machine distributor. His previous job description was 'Executive Vice President of the Suffolk-Nassau Amusement Company' in Freeport, Long Island, and his current employer was Tony 'Ducks' Corallo, a Lucchese crime family boss in New York City. The opera-loving Tony Ducks was looking to target Britain with a surplus of used slot machines that had previously been installed by the Mob in Maryland and New Jersey, and the flamboyant Gabe Forman had been entrusted with selling them.

Forman arrived in London in April 1960, his security guaranteed by Albert Dimes, the Anglo-Italian Godfather and successor to Billy Hill, who grew up in Clerkenwell in the 1920s. 'Italian Albert', as he was known, had a bookmaking office in Soho and his crew included a number of other Italian-related gangsters, like Tommy and Billy Falco and Billy Stayton, whose mother ran a café opposite the Phonographic Equipment Company's offices in Ladbroke Grove. Lennie Martin, who went on to manage the boxer

John Conteh, was involved too, along with the notorious hard man 'Mad' Frankie Fraser, who delivered machines for Las Vegas Coin after Dimes asked Gabe Forman to give him a job. Fraser was simultaneously working for another slot-machine company called Atlantic Machines, which was run by Eddie Richardson, brother of the south-London racketeer Charlie Richardson, and had an office in Great Windmill Street.

Lawyers initially told Foreman that it would take several months for him to get a company set up under complicated British laws. The American achieved it in three days, simply buying up a local business, renaming it Las Vegas Coin and moving into expansive first-floor offices in Poland Street in the heart of the West End. Slot-machine distribution routes were organised in London and the south-east, the west of England, the Midlands, Scotland and the north, where Vincent Luvaglio became one of the company's biggest customers. Foreman also set up a subsidiary company called Las Vegas Parts and Services to maintain the imported machines in much the same way as they maintained and repaired American jukeboxes. Britain's different electrical voltage required transformers and Edward Kemp, a Mills mechanic from Reno, Nevada, was brought over for an 'instructional visit' with the firm's British employees.

Forman reported back to Tony Ducks that he felt the British, unlike their US counterparts, had 'a fairly liberal attitude towards gambling' but, in March 1961, the sleepy functionaries at the Home Office belatedly woke up to his Mafia connections, thanks to information supplied by Robert Kennedy's Justice Department in Washington. They also got wise to the fact that Albert Dimes had shares in Foreman's business and, although the British connection was left untouched, Gabe Foreman was ordered to leave the country. Not that his deportation did much to halt the arrival of Mob-related slot machines into the UK.

The final stages of the Betting and Gaming Act were completed in the summer of 1960. It received its Royal Assent on 30th July and officially reached the statute book at the end of the parliamentary session in October. Long before then, Vincent Luvaglio – who had now changed his name to Vince Landa, partly to disguise what he thought might be his off-putting Italian background and partly to put further distance between himself and the Kray twins – had been actively canvassing north-eastern working men's clubs and taking orders for the new American machines. With the help of his local sidekick, Ray Thubron, he found the club officials and committee men easily beguiled by his charm and London sales talk, and almost begging to be seduced.

CHAPTER FIVE

BY NOW THERE were several new additions to Vince's entourage. The enthusiastic punter on horses and dogs had decided to gamble his future on an unregulated cash business and realised he needed people around him he could trust absolutely. Especially in the role of collectors, whose job was to go around the clubs, counting the take and dividing up the share between the committees and the company. Dennis Richman had worked for Vince in London and the south, once thwarting a police raid on some unlicensed machines they had installed on Brighton Pier by throwing them into the sea. He was joined in 1962 by William 'Buster' Thompson, who had made over £17,000 from a slot-machine business in Kent and whose official job description with Social Club Services was 'admin and promotion'. Other new employees included George Wilson, who was meant to look after 'security, vehicles and PR' and William Edgar, whose responsibility was sales.

Also on the company's books was Angus Sibbet, who had been released from prison two-thirds of the way through his sentence, having kept in touch with the Luvaglio Brothers while he was inside. In late 1959, Sibbet's father, Alfred, was taken ill and Vince offered to have Angus driven up to Newcastle to be by his mother's side. When Alfred Sibbet recovered, his son didn't go back to London, preferring to settle back into his old familiar environment. He had been the prime mover behind Vince's emigration to the north and, when his friend first set up his company, Social Club Services, in 1962, Angus was allotted forty-nine per cent of the shares. His job was to be a collector, going round the venues and counting the take from the machines, which would then be split sixty per cent to SCS, twenty per cent to the clubs and the rest left behind as pay-outs to the punters. It was a larcenous arrangement but not illegal. Angus was also meant to keep scouting out possibilities and recommending new clubs to approach. It was a job that he embarked on with relish and one that, in time, would come to define his life.

Equally fateful was Vince's success in persuading his brother Michael and his parents, Frank and Maud Luvaglio, to move north too. Frank agreed to take on a part-time accountant's role, auditing the company's books and helping with the financial angle, and Frank, Maud and Michael all moved into a house together in Beatrice Road in Newcastle. The task allotted to Michael Luvaglio, who, unlike his sibling, never changed his surname, was to make deals with clubs, not just for gaming machines but also to upgrade their décor and fittings. As well as installing bandits, Vince was planning to sell them everything from new carpets and curtains to dart boards, billiard tables and beer mats. He assured the club committees that, if their facilities were a touch smarter and more comfortable, membership would increase and, with it, use of the slot machines. With their share of the revenue, the clubs could then afford a higher standard of entertainment, which Vincent and Michael would be happy to book for them. If everything went according to plan, Vince promised, the clubs would soon be able to install close-circuit television (CCTV), which his younger brother, the old TV-converter specialist, would oversee, allowing drinkers in the bar to keep an eye on the amateur ventriloquist or singing postman performing in the room next door. And why stop there? Eventually, Vince boasted, they'd be able to book proper professional entertainers instead of part-timers and amateurs.

Doreen Hall, one of two striking and sprightly young sisters from Gateshead, became Vince's secretary, working from the company's offices above a barber's shop in Olive Street in Sunderland. In September 1961, she and Vince were listed as the only two directors of a company called Universal Machines, which had taken over some of the stock formerly held by Las Vegas Coin following Gabe Forman's deportation.

The biggest British slot-machine distributor in the early 1960s was the Phonographic Equipment Company, which was based in a former refrigeration-company showroom in Ladbroke Grove in west London. The business was run by Cyril Shack and Gordon Marks and Shack's older brother, Max Fine, was the chairman. In the run-up to the Betting and Gaming Act in 1960, Phonographic Equipment had already become the largest distributor of coin-operated machines in Europe, selling Williams pinball machines and French-made Jupiter jukeboxes. Throughout the 1960s, they partnered with leading UK coin-machine manufacturers but they were also buying used slot machines from dealers in the US and they acquired a large number of Bally's Bingo machines from Myron Sugerman of the Runyon Sales Company of New Jersey, another Mafia front.

In 1962, Phonographic became the exclusive UK distributor for Bally's games, which were making more money for British operators than any other manufacturer's products. Such was the public's enthusiasm for them and the rapidity with which the slot-machine craze was taking off that Shack and Fine were soon able to boast that there was a Bally Treble Chance in almost every UK club and a Bally's Bingo in every transport café in the land and, when Bally brought out their new range in 1964, the impact on the market was phenomenal. The Bally Gold Award swiftly become the number-one selling slot machine in every club and arcade in the country and Phonographic, now Bally's largest distributor worldwide, were airlifting machines in from the US four or five times a week to meet the demand.

The company had moved to larger premises in Exmoor Street near Ladbroke Grove Station and operators' delivery vans lined up outside each morning waiting for the next consignment to arrive. One-armed bandits were novel, colourful and sexy and, in the working-men's clubs in the north-east, punters were queuing up every night with their sixpenny bits and having to have their time on the machines rationed by club stewards to allow every potential player to have a spin. In that era, famously described by Philip Larkin as *Lady Chatterley* working people were yearning for a shot of adrenaline and excitement – and the possibility of making a small profit – to redeem and liven up long days and weeks of drudgery. And up in County Durham and on Tyneside and Teeside, club committees – made up of otherwise tough, practical, sensible men – were spellbound by the glitter of Vince Landa's products and the salesman's tantalising blend of London and Las Vegas.

What the club officials didn't realise was that the American slots SCS were selling or renting out – purportedly brand new and retailing for £1,250 a time – were actually reconditioned machines worth £375 at best. But if the price seemed too steep, Vince was happy to steer the club committee into the arms of Derwent Finance, another Vince Landa company run by Vincent and his father Frank, which could provide the clubs with a deposit to help them buy their gaming machines or, alternatively, just rent them. He also encouraged them to consider entering into an HP agreement with a firm called North-West Securities and guaranteed that Social Club Services would make the first deposit into the relevant HP accounts.

It was sharp, it was unscrupulous, but it was not against the law and, in those early Wild West years, there were plenty of satisfied customers, like Edward Foster, secretary of the Windy Nook and Carrhill Workingmen's Club in Felling, who said later that he dealt happily with Vince in all their transactions. 'He offered to redecorate the club at less than cost (£7,000 was the total) and did a very good job, making it a showpiece he could bring officials of other clubs to in an attempt to persuade them to also give him work.' Ray Thubron was often at Vince's side when the deals were done and was unstinting in his praise. 'He was a fabulous man. A genius. He could charm the birds out of the trees. I had the contacts in clubland, and Vince had the business brain.'

In 1961/62, Social Club Services had just over fifty working-men's clubs on their books. Between 1963 and 1965, that figured soared to 12,000 machines in 2,500 clubs from Tyneside down to Yorkshire and up to Scotland and back again. When Michael Luvaglio joined the company, Angus Sibbet's forty-nine per cent shareholding was split in two, with Michael given half. And, with Social Club Services' paper worth rapidly approaching the £2m mark, everyone was getting rich, and Vince and his men and women all began to display the visible symbols of their success. Whether they were having lunch with a planning officer or a politician in Newcastle or Sunderland, or driving out to a working-men's club in Jarrow or a mining village in County Durham, the Luvaglio brothers went everywhere in a suit worn with a crisp white shirt and a thin tie. Vincent's wife Gwen and Doreen Hall had immaculately coiffured beehive hair and lipstick and eyeshadow by Revlon and Estée Lauder and, when Doreen came to work in the SCS offices in Olive Street, she wore fitted dresses with nipped waists and pencil skirts as if she was in Madison Avenue, rather than downtown Sunderland.

Angus Sibbet outdid them all with his gold cufflinks and wardrobes full of handmade suits, shirts and ties and, in November 1963, he and his wife Brenda paid £6,500 to buy a show home in Mountview Gardens in Dunston overlooking the Tyne Valley. It seemed the epitome of post-war suburban luxury, with pile carpets, ruched curtains, an en-suite bathroom and a downstairs bar for entertaining. Angus owned a £3,500 Fiat and a Ford Corsair, the first of many cars given to him by the company, and started to employ a driver, Albert Ginley, to convey him round the region.

The year 1963 was also when Vince Landa made good on his promise to Gwen that their children would grow up far away from the terraced streets, chimney smoke and bomb damage that he and Michael had known as boys in south-west London. In September 1963, he paid £50,000 to acquire Dyderdale Hall, a Victorian Gothic house in the middle of a 135-acre country estate. Remote and hidden from prying eyes, the house was forty miles south of Newcastle in the beautiful hill country on the edges of Hamsterley Forest in the upper reaches of the Wear Valley. The approach was on an undulating minor road from Hamsterley village, running downhill across Bedburn Beck and then uphill and down again past a tumbledown estate fence to the lodge gates. A winding drive led 300 yards up past rhododendron bushes and pine trees before opening out into parkland dotted with mature trees with pheasants strutting around in the grounds and scuttling away into the thick woods at the back and sides of the house.

Dryderdale was built in 1872 and designed by Alfred Waterhouse, who also designed the Natural History Museum in South Kensington. It was originally intended to be a shooting lodge for the banker Alfred Backhouse and his family and there had been a local shoot there ever since. A pale sandstone building with a slate roof and an octagonal three-storey tower at one end, the garden side of the house had a first-floor canted oriel, or bay, window supported on a buttress. It faced out over a lawn that sloped down to a lake with woods beyond. When Vince and Gwen and their children moved in, there were six bedrooms, a snooker room and study, an electric lift up to the tower and numerous cellars and outbuildings. In short order, Vince added crystal chandeliers and CCTV cameras operated from a control centre in the study.

Vince Landa may have soon had good reasons to jealously guard his new home and protect their privacy but, to begin with, he and Gwen were happy to throw open their doors both to friends and to influential contacts who might be able to further assist the growth of Social Club Services. And if business could be combined with a conspicuous charitable gesture, generously supportive of the wider community, then so much the better.

In 1963, Vince's friend and colleague Dennis Richman was diagnosed with kidney disease, only to discover that there was no kidney dialysis machine in Newcastle's Royal Victoria Infirmary or anywhere in the north and that to get the treatment he needed he would have to travel to the Royal Free Hospital in London. When Vince Landa heard about it, he got in touch with Newcastle's *Evening Chronicle* newspaper and launched a kidney research fund with Social Club Services contributing an initial £650 (over £10,000 in 2022 money). The target they were trying to raise was £2,000 and donations, published in the paper, came from many of the working-men's clubs that SCS had sold slot machines to. Horden British Legion chipped in with £60, the Farringdon Social Club Charity Show raised £41, the Town End Farm Workingmen's Club put in £35 and there were many more.

On the night of Saturday, 4th December, 1963, having been at Newcastle races with Ray Thubron earlier in the day, Vince hosted a Charity Gala Night at the Rink Ballroom in Sunderland. Guests had been asked to try to guess the gate for Sunderland FC's home game against Southampton on 30th November and the prize for the closest answer was a new £575 Mini. The second prize was a holiday in Barcelona and the third prize was a woman's mink coat.

The Rink had seen its share of big nights. It started out as a roller-skating arena before being converted into a ballroom in the 1950s, when Al Flush and his orchestra were the regular band and there were huge crowds for the Beat The Clock Palais Nights at weekends. On 14th May, 1963, The Beatles had played there and fans had queued ten deep to get in, the line stretching right back into the city centre. It was the beginning of Beatlemania and barricades had to be erected in front of the audience to stop girls from throwing themselves onto the stage. In the years that followed, The Who, Cream, Status Quo and a young David Bowie would appear at the same venue. But that December night, it was the setting for Vince Landa's first big step into the public eye, his and his company's fund-raising efforts praised in local newspapers and on TV across the region.

A kidney dialysis machine was duly installed in the Royal Victoria Infirmary in 1964 and, while Vince's concern for the health of Dennis Richman was genuine, adopting a public face as a charitable 'personality' (albeit one born down south) was a calculated move. Just as the one-armed bandits were transforming the leisure industry, the traditional face of the north-eastern landscape was beginning to change too, bearing the imprint of ambitious politicians that an aspiring gambling magnate would be wise to know.

CHAPTER SIX

THE CLASS WAR may or may not have been over in 1959 but, three years later, with another general election on the horizon, the Conservative government were worried about their marginal seats in the north-east, where manufacturing jobs were in decline. They were also alarmed by the emergence of an increasingly conspicuous working-class figure who was busy accumulating power and intent on change.

Thomas Daniel Smith was born in 1915 in the downstairs front room of a terraced flat in Wallsend. His collier father drank and gambled. His mother worked long hours as a cleaner. Their son attended Weston boys' school, leaving at the age of fourteen to become a printer's apprentice. Eight years later, he founded his own business, painting cinema exteriors across Tyneside. Thomas Dan – or T Dan, as he would forever be known – was intelligent, articulate and determined to make history, rather than be a passive observer. His parents were communists and T Dan's early politics were on the far left. He led a shipyard-workers strike during

World War II and, in 1945, he joined the Labour Party. Five years later, he was elected to Newcastle City Council as the member for Walker and, when Labour took control of the council in 1953, the thirty-eight-year-old became the chairman of the Labour group.

Smith was passionate about slum clearance and redevelopment and, in 1958, his clarion call for action helped him to get appointed chairman of the housing committee. The next year, he was elected leader of the city council and immediately set up a Special Planning department, which would become the engine room for the dramatic changes that followed.

Smith had humour, a booming voice and a physical presence that few could match. The nickname helped. He later explained that it originated when he was about to board a plane in Newcastle one day and had to point out to an airline official that the name on his ticket was T Dan not some other Smith. In office he rapidly acquired an aura and mystique like no other politician in the country: half socialist visionary and half party boss and Citizen Kane figure, unashamedly indulging in a personality cult and driving around Tyneside in a white Jaguar with the number plate DAN68.

T Dan never lacked ideas. He was a big supporter of the expansion of Newcastle Airport and an equally enthusiastic champion of the arts and education, seeing through the upgrade of Newcastle Technical College to polytechnic status, which would eventually be upgraded again to Northumbria University. He said he wanted to transform Newcastle into 'the Athens or Brasilia of the north' but not everyone was sure whether he was a prophet or a charlatan. The project he would most famously be associated with was his embrace of 'concrete utopianism', as it was called in Sweden, which resulted in a rash of brutalist new construction projects from office blocks and council flats to multi-storey carparks, flyovers and a central motorway running directly through the city. Smith and his planners argued that, in an age of rising car ownership, with new models getting cheaper all the time and more and more lorries deserting the railways for the roads, the motorway was essential to avoid gridlock and enable commerce to proceed without a hitch. But in the service of this plan, much of Newcastle's exquisite eighteenth-century architecture was flattened, including John Dobson's Royal Arcade, which was taken down brick by brick with the intention, Smith claimed, of reassembling it elsewhere – but that promise was never fulfilled.

T Dan was equally bullish about the blocks of new high-rise flats he gave the go-ahead to, like Cruddas Park in Scotswood on the western side of the city. They were intended to replace the old rows of terraced houses, still without indoor plumbing, that had been built in the nineteenth century for workers in the Vickers-Armstrong factories that used to make armaments and tanks. Construction at Cruddas Park began in 1961 and, the following year, Smith staged an open day for the public to see how things were progressing, with the Labour Party leader, Hugh Gaitskell, the guest of honour.

Increasingly sensitive about Smith's influence and the collapse of Conservative support in the region, Harold Macmillan sent his party chairman, Quintin Hogg, Lord Hailsham, up to Newcastle in February 1962 with instructions to 'warm things up a bit' and assure voters that the government hadn't forgotten about them. Hogg, a QC, ex-Eton and Oxford, turned up in a pin-striped suit and a flat cap, claiming that he'd left his bowler hat in his car in London and that it was so cold in Newcastle that he'd had to buy a cloth cap to replace the tweed one he'd been going shooting in for the past twenty-five years.

Suitably attired, so he believed, to converse with the working classes, he began a week-long tour of shipyards, coal mines, steel mills and council offices. He didn't think much of south Durham, suggesting that Crook, Eldon and Bishop Auckland could all be pulled down without anyone missing them. Before he returned to Westminster, he said he had 'plans as long as a washing line' and mentioned airports, seaports, motorways, motels and possibly a regional council and some sort of 'big playland holiday area' overlooking the North Sea. But nothing came of it. His report, entitled 'The Northeast: A Programme for Change', didn't come out until March 1963 and mostly focused on the contraction of coal mining in Durham and declining employment in the railway manufacturing towns of Darlington and Shildon, warning that the region's long-standing but outdated industries would be 'unable to sustain the sort of economic regeneration necessary for it to be able to compete effectively' in the future. The way forward, the report suggested, lay in a combination of new towns, like the Peterlee and Aycliffe Corporation, and an expanding service economy, which might eventually replace declining manufacturing jobs.

T Dan Smith was already heavily involved with the Peterlee and Aycliffe Corporation and equally keen on growing the service economy. He was also alive to the potential for profit from the post-war house-building boom that was sweeping across the country, including great swathes of the north and north-east. By the early 1960s, he'd set up a series of public-relations companies, both to promote his own schemes and, less conspicuously, to work on behalf of building-industry clients eager to secure his services. One of his patrons was a Musselburgh-based firm called Crudens, who were the British agents for the Swedish company Ohlsson-Skarne SB, who had devised a concrete, flatpack-house-building system that could be assembled on site.

T Dan got Crudens/Ohlsson-Skarne the Cruddas Park contract, along with similar commissions in Long Benton and Killingworth, while the Yorkshire architect John Poulson, who had been advised to approach Smith by the managing director of Bovis in 1962, was awarded seven accounts with the Peterlee and Aycliffe New Town Corporation, by whom T Dan was employed and paid annually to promote their interests.

As of February 1962 – the same month that Lord Hailsham arrived in Newcastle – Smith was a consultant to Poulson's company and many of his local-authority contacts were recruited to work on behalf of Poulson's interests.

A strangely dull and uncharismatic man given the extent of his avarice and ambition, John Poulson also got in with Alderman Andrew Cunningham, one of T Dan's leading cohorts and another major power broker in the north-east. The father of the future Labour MP and cabinet minister Jack Cunningham, the alderman was head of the northern region of the General and Municipal Workers Union (GMWU), which had more than 100,000 members, and it was said that almost every member of Parliament north of the Trent owed their seat to his influence. Cunningham was also secretary of the Labour Party's Finance Committee, which was chaired by the future Chancellor of the Exchequer and Prime Minister James Callaghan. The alderman's local nickname was 'Handy Andy', which gradually morphed into 'Backhandy Andy' as he worked to ensure Poulson got the contract to design and build a new police station in Sunderland, as well as the Crowhall Tower block of high-rise flats in Felling near

Gateshead, which was Cunningham's hometown. The proceeds of civic corruption enabled 'Handy Andy' – who was chauffeur driven everywhere in a 3.8-litre white Jaguar provided by the GMWU – to take up to nine holidays a year, the cost picked up by Poulson, and obtain a sinecure for his wife, who was nominally employed as an interior designer in one of Smith's companies.

In retrospect, other politicians and commentators would look back with disbelief at the region's corruption in that era and wonder why it wasn't exposed sooner? Part of the answer lay with the forceful personality of T Dan Smith, who was said to rule council committee rooms with 'a rod of iron' but also 'made the lives' of grateful young-cub reporters like the *Newcastle Chronicle*'s Lewis Chester, who could always rely on 'Mr Newcastle' for a good comment or quip.

Doubts had, in fact, been expressed about Smith's integrity as early as 1960 when it was revealed that his decorating business received more than half the external painting contracts awarded by Newcastle City Council and, in 1962, it was noted that he defended the awarding of contracts to Crudens and John Poulson on the grounds of efficiency and cost without disclosing his financial interest. But the political winds kept blowing T Dan's way, especially after the new Labour leader, Harold Wilson, made a speech to his party conference in October 1963 where he referred to the 'white heat' of the technological revolution that was sweeping the country and that would, by implication, fatally expose the amateurish and class-conscious state of the Conservative Party.

It was brilliant politics, placing Labour on the side of science, white coats and the future and leaving the Conservatives struggling to rid themselves of their tweeds and grouse-moors image. A perspective that was hardly improved when Harold Macmillan resigned as Prime Minister on 14th October, citing ill-health, and was replaced not by the Home Secretary 'Rab' Butler or the Chancellor of the Exchequer Reginald Maudling but by the 14th Earl of Home, henceforth to be known as Sir Alec Douglas-Home, who 'emerged' from the magic circle that passed as a Conservative Party leadership election.

In anticipation of the next general election, which happened in October 1964, one of T Dan Smith's PR companies was asked to assist Labour in the north-eastern marginals and, after Harold Wilson had squeezed into 10 Downing Street with a majority of six, Smith was fully expecting to be offered a cabinet post. But the phone call never came, possibly an indication that the wily new Prime Minister was not unaware of the concerns about T Dan's speculative activities. The next year, though, George Brown, the Minister for Economic Affairs, made Smith the head of the new Northern Economic Development Council, handing even more sweeping influence to him and his cronies Poulson and Cunningham, who boasted that more power changed hands in the dining room of Newcastle's Royal Station Hotel than anywhere in London.

It was the era later satirised in *Brassneck*, the richly atmospheric 1973 play by David Hare and Howard Brenton, which featured politicians, property developers and freemasons and dramatized post-war local-government sleaze and corruption with Hollywood-style relish. And it was the era when the north-east's reputation as the 'Big Easy' of urban Britain was cemented, making it the ideal place for other chancers, gangsters and 'bandit men' – like Vince Landa – to do business.

CHAPTER SEVEN

WHEN T DAN Smith talked about the nascent leisure industry as a potential growth area for service-economy jobs, he probably wasn't thinking about gambling and slot machines. But as Social Club Services set sail on a rising tide of excitement and prosperity, other smart men in Newcastle and the north-east were also placing their bets on the public's enthusiasm for a wager.

Traditional industries may have been in decline but, as improving service sector wages and permissive legislation overlapped, a new gloss was sprayed on the entertainment business. The 1960 Betting and Gaming Act had opened the door to night clubs in Britain offering gambling, as well as top quality food, drink and entertainment. Like the Mafia-owned hotels in Las Vegas, the more money the punters lost on the slots or playing blackjack or roulette, the more the clubs would be able to spend on the talent and, in turn, the better the entertainment became, the more popular the club would be and the longer the punters would stick around and spend their money. For as long as the law didn't change, it was a formula that couldn't fail and one that would transform Newcastle into the Las Vegas of the north.

The bar was set high in February 1963 when Marcus Levy, an ambitious young entrepreneur from Wallsend, opened the Dolce Vita on Low Friar Street in Grainger Town. The historic neighbourhood, designed by John Dobson and built by Richard Grainger in the mid-nineteenth century, was synonymous with the magnificent neo-classical architecture of Grey Street and the Theatre Royal. Now the narrow streets on the western edge of Grainger Town were about to become the focus of nightlife in the city on a hitherto unprecedented scale.

Levy, who was in partnership with his two brothers, Norman and David, was just twenty-six years old but, after the end of the Betting and Gaming Act in 1960, he'd had the foresight to travel to the US and sample first-hand the night club and casino ambience in New York and Las Vegas. The Dolce, which was in the warren of narrow streets that made up Newcastle's Chinatown, was a conversion of an old nineteenth-century, four-storey building. It had 6,000 feet of floor space, an illuminated glass dance floor, a cabaret lounge, food and drink for up to 500 people a night and, crucially, one-armed bandits and tables for playing roulette and chemin de fer. It was a luxurious package that proved irresistible to a public hungry for entertainment and a magnet that helped to turn the proud, industrial city into the party capital that it remains to this day.

The opening-night gala featured the Kaye Sisters followed by Michael Holliday, Dickie Valentine and Alma Cogan, all playing to packed audiences 'in their glad rags', as the *Newcastle Journal* gleefully reported. In the months that followed, dozens more showbusiness stars appeared at the club, including Tommy Cooper, Bob Monkhouse, Helen Shapiro, Cilla Black and even a young David Frost, who was heckled by unimpressed Geordies during his stand-up act.

In October 1965, the top of the bill was the hottest new recording star in the country, Thomas Woodward from South Wales, alias Tom Jones, who played the midnight slot and sang 'It's Not Unusual' and 'What's New Pussycat' to an ecstatic crowd. 'The Voice' returned to the Dolce numerous times over the next few years and one of his biggest fans was Vince Landa's partner, Angus Sibbet. The slot-machine collector had become a regular fixture at the club, surrounded by friends and guests night after night and always sitting at the same front-row table. Angus had a minder, an Irishman and ex-boxing trainer called Thomas 'Paddy' Hallett, who also looked after Tom Jones when he was up in the north-east and, on one trip to Newcastle, the Voice came to dinner with Angus and his wife Brenda at their house in Dunston, along with Paddy Hallett and another of Angus's good friends, Michael Luvaglio.

Wally Birch, a Londoner who ran a similar 1960s club, Winston's, in Clifford Street, was adamant that businesses like the Dolce would have been financially impossible without the gambling. 'It gave it that Riviera touch offering customers a touch of glamour when they were just beginning to shake off more than fifteen years of austerity. Don't forget that many people were very poor in the 1940s and 1950s. We never had a bathroom where I grew up. We used to go to the local baths ("more hot in number four") and you had no TV then and your fridge was a fucking windowsill. So, when you went into these joints, you were fucking walking on air.'

On the back of the booming gambling revenues, the Levys were able to book some of the top American acts too, like Billy Eckstein, Ella Fitzgerald and Billy Daniels. A new breed of entertainment entrepreneur had emerged, some of them with links to organised crime, and a lot of the leading US performers were represented by an Englishman from the north-east: Charles Mather from Whitley Bay. The expatriate Mather had led a remarkable life, beginning as a wartime bellboy at the Savoy hotel in London, before joining the army and travelling the world and somehow ending up in Las Vegas in the 1950s, where he started his own talent agency, International Artists Management. He lived in a six-bedroom house overlooking the Las Vegas Country Club and played golf with Moe Dalitz, the former bootlegger who owned the Desert Inn hotel and casino, which he subsequently sold to Howard Hughes for $6.2m in cash and $7m in loans. When Mather sent his signings over to the UK, they usually did a week at the Talk of the Town in Leicester Square and then a week at the Dolce Vita, which he described as 'a wonderful place and the best club outside London.'

Mather, who was elected a member of the Knights of Columbus, was never a Mafiosi but he got on well with the 'wise guys' who were watching developments in Britain with interest as they proceeded with plans to turn London's West End into another mini-Las Vegas, only with what Meyer Lansky called 'a class above the rest'. In 1965, the Colony Club in Berkeley Square was up for sale and Cyril Shack, MD of the Phonographic Equipment Company, was asked if he and his colleagues would like to buy it and turn it into a luxurious gaming club. The approach was made by an American 'investor' called Dino Cellini, who Shack later said he thought was 'above board', even though he knew that Cellini had recently been kicked out of the Bahamas for illegal gaming. Shack, Max Fine and Gordon Marks put up £50,000 for the purchase of the Colony, with Shack and Fine buying two million shares at £1 each. The club was nominally to be run by Alfred Salkind, an English professional gambler, with the old Hollywood star and mobster associate George Raft as the official host and MD.

A few years later, Shack and Fine embarked on a libel case against the *Daily Mail*, accusing the paper of printing lies about their supposed Mafia-related wealth and of 'spiking' their attempted takeover of Butlins. In court, Shack agreed that, in the run-up to the Colony Club deal, he may have had conversations 'with gentlemen with colourful Italian names' and Dino Cellini, Angelo Bruno and Jimmy 'Blue Eyes' Alo were mentioned along with Meyer Lansky, but Shack professed ignorance of George Raft's underworld connections. Cross-examined by Sir Elwyn Jones, QC, he accepted that the Betting and Gaming Act had given a green light to many Americans to enter the UK and that, in 1960, his company, Phonographic, had purchased 'a few machines' from Las Vegas Coin Ltd. He also admitted that, by 1964, they enjoyed a 'special relationship' with Bally, who were dependent on him for 'information on what kind of coin-operated machines would be acceptable in Britain.'

The *Mail* would have settled the action out of court and Fine was in favour but Shack insisted on pressing on and, in the process, further glimpses emerged of Phonographic's dealings with the Mob. The court heard that, in October 1964, Albert Dimes paid £17,000 to an American lawyer called Herbert Itkin – who, unbeknown to Dimes, was an FBI informant – which was intended for Gabe Forman's boss, Tony 'Ducks' Corallo. The money was not to settle a gambling debt, as Fine claimed, but the sum Phonographic owed Forman for a stock of machines he'd sold them that had not been paid for at the time he was deported from the UK. Phonographic lost the libel action and their rivals, Scientific Games Ltd, picked up a lot of their slot-machine business.

The truth about Phonographic and the Colony Club set-up is that it was a front to disguise the fact that it was a Mafia-run business with Lansky and the Philadelphia mob boss Angelo Bruno as co-investors. Its success, though short lived, was a testament to the presiding genius of the silver-haired Dino Cellini, regarded by Meyer Lansky as the pre-eminent casino manager of his day. Cellini was the son of an Italian immigrant barber, and he grew up in Steubenville, Ohio, a tough factory town on the Ohio river adjoining the West Virginia state line. The local Mob chieftain was Jimmy Tripodi, who looked after things there for the Cleveland Mafia from the end of Prohibition until his retirement in the late 1970s.

Other than Cellini, Steubenville's most famous resident was Dino Crocetti, who grew up to become Dean Martin and who, as a teenager, worked as a card dealer and 'stick man' in Tripodi's and his partner Cosmo Quattrone's backdoor casino, run out of the Rex cigar shop. Cellini worked in Rex's too as, a craps-and-dice dealer and croupier and acquired a reputation as an 'ace mechanic' who could break a customer's winning streak and hustle a rich punter.

Cellini's biggest job to date had been running Lansky's Riviera hotel and casino in Havana up until the Cuban revolution in 1959, and it was said of him by fellow gambler and wise guy Johnny Roselli that he combined 'mathematical genius with self-discipline, class, style and charisma'. He spared no expense at the Colony Club, bringing 'all his own people and tables' over from the States, including a huge New York-style double-end craps table, and setting up a special croupiers' school in Hanover Square run by the Lebanese brothers Bobby and Freddy Ayub.

The Colony, which intended to target Greek and Middle Eastern high rollers, as well as aristocratic refugees from John Aspinall's Clermont Club, also in Berkeley Square, wouldn't open until March 1966. But almost a full year before George Raft first spun the roulette wheel at the Colony, another similarly designed venue opened on Tyneside as the ever more prosperous Vince Landa and his brother Michael dazzled Newcastle with a night club of their own.

By 1964, Social Club Services was allegedly making Vince at least a million a year, the earnings spread between fifteen different companies and, following the success of the Dolce Vita, the 'Bandit King' was in the mood to expand. In July 1964, he sold a share in SCS for £100,000 and spent £52,000 to buy an empty three-storey brick building in Bath Lane, which was no more than a five-minute walk away from the Dolce on the western edge of Grainger Town. A further £65,000 was spent on the conversion of the property into the deluxe Piccadilly Club, which opened in April 1965 amidst a blaze of publicity with copious amounts of free champagne handed out to the first-night customers. The new club had three bars, dining facilities serving Indian and Chinese food, a dance floor, a cabaret lounge with curved walls and a casino called The Nevada Room where, as well as roulette, blackjack, poker and the ubiquitous slot machines, they unveiled a new racing game called Horsearama along with a table for craps, which Geordies remembered being played in the city by American Air Force men stationed nearby in World War II. The club's license, negotiated with the help of T Dan Smith-appointed councillors and officials eager to help in return for a kickback and free membership, allowed it to stay open until dawn.

Waiting to greet their guests in the lavish reception area that first spring evening were the three directors of Victoria Enterprises Ltd, as the club's registered ownership was termed. There was William 'Buster' Thompson, Albert Barron – who was the official licence holder – and Michael Luvaglio, grinning happily at becoming a big player in his own right and out from under his brother's shadow at last. Less than five years had passed since they'd moved up to the north-east but there they were – the cocky, confident boys from London in their slimline Italian suits, Chelsea boots and shirts from Aquascutum, flash cars parked outside – welcoming tough, hard-headed men from Tyneside and their bouffant, made up and ready-to-roll girl-friends and wives.

It was a formula that bowled people over, as recalled by Stan Henry, co-owner of the Bailey Group, who opened the Cavendish Club at the bottom of Grey Street in Newcastle later that year:

Up until the Londoners arrived, there had been pubs in Newcastle and the working-men's clubs, but they were just for drinking in and then you went to a chippy and, if you ever went to a proper restaurant, it was in a hotel and the menu would be in French. We gave Geordies real night clubs and a touch of glamour they'd not seen before: thick carpets, sexy lighting and swooning music, and they went overboard. Wages and living standards were going up in jobs outside the old heavy industries and we built up a regular trade, locals who came two or three nights a week, and it wasn't just a youth thing linked to the Beatles or Carnaby Street. We had lots of married couples too.

Whereas many of the working-men's clubs still excluded women or accorded them second-class status at best, night clubs like the Dolce Vita, the Piccadilly and the Cavendish not only employed them as waitresses, croupiers and receptionists but welcomed parties of unattached working women out for a good night, who came to play the tables with their own money and tried to outsmart the men.

It was the industrial north as it had never been seen before with the city of Newcastle in the prime of its life and, for a brief time, as the Swinging Sixties hit top gear, it seemed as if Vincent Landa only ever backed winners. He had taken to driving around in a white Jaguar just like T Dan Smith and was also importing cars from the US, and his personal collection, sometimes housed at Dryderdale Hall, sometimes at the Wheatsheaf Garage in Sunderland, included a Pontiac Grand Prix, a Cadillac and an Arcadian limousine. 'We went daft,' remembers Ray Thubron. 'We all had flash American cars and I used to park mine outside my council house in Silksworth. We had parties, wild nights out at clubs and trips to London and the continent. Vince was big, all right, and getting bigger all the time.'

In a surprise move in September 1965, Buster Thompson resigned as a director of Victoria Enterprises – reputedly with a fat pay-off from Vince and a stack of slot machines – and was replaced on the board by Landa, who also moved his brother aside and appointed himself as the Piccadilly Club's new managing director. If the ever loyal and acquiescent Michael felt hurt or badly treated, he didn't show it. His official salary at the time was just £30 a week (£552 in 2022 money), but he enjoyed his job going round Northumberland and Durham supplying clubs with furniture, fittings and CCTV, and his nights out in Newcastle too, and nobody had a bad word to say about him.

Alan Sibbet – Angus Sibbet's nephew and the son of James – never forgot how exciting it was visiting the Piccadilly with his father when he was a boy. 'My dad used to service the fruit machines in a lot of these clubs for my uncle in the 1960s. I was only five or six but my other "uncle", Michael, who owned the places, used to give me Coca-Cola from the bar. He seemed like a god to me. Then I'd listen to the bands and be dazzled by the girls. Sadly, it all changed and went bad but those were interesting times, all right.'

In January 1966, Michael moved out of his parents' house in Beatrice Road and moved into a bigger Edwardian house he'd bought half a mile away in Chelsea Grove. He'd started a relationship with Pat Burgess, a receptionist at the Piccadilly, and the two of them set up home there together. Michael's closest friend and male companion continued to be Angus Sibbet. They met up during the week to discuss potential new deals to be struck and Michael often dropped into Angus's house in Dunston on Sunday afternoons, sometimes staying for dinner, like the night when Tom Jones was a guest. At other times, Michael and Pat might join Angus's party at the Dolce Vita, sitting at his usual table in front of the cabaret floor, and they all of them kept late-night hours, often not going to bed until 2 or 3am.

Angus's role at Social Club Services was still that of a collector but, in the night clubs and out and about on his rounds, he was beginning to give people the impression that he was one of the heads of the company. His driver, Albert Ginley, said that he 'generally put on quite an act of being a very important man, indeed.' He had helped Ginley purchase a Ford Corsair like his own and trusted him to chauffeur him around everywhere and be discreet about his many extra-marital relationships.

Angus Sibbet, bespectacled and bearded at a time when beards were not commonplace in the north-east, was far from being monogamous. In fact, he was serially unfaithful to his wife Brenda, who appears to have put up with it up to a point in return for a comfortable house and a high standard of living. The couple had a daughter, Karen, born in 1959 and enrolled in a local private school, and, while neighbours in Dunston didn't see them very often, they had the impression of a happy family unit. But outside of the marriage, Angus was having an affair with Vince's secretary, Doreen Hall, and simultaneously sleeping with her sister Joyce but without Doreen's knowledge.

Such complex arrangements needed careful management and the complicity, willingly given, of friends like Michael Luvaglio, as well as the inscrutable Albert Ginley. The twenty-six-year-old Joyce Hall had a flat in St Edmund's Road in Gateshead, while Doreen lived on the other side of the Tyne in St George's Terrace in Jesmond, a smarter, more affluent neighbourhood with rows of three- and four-storey nineteenth-century houses. Albert Ginley, who rented an attic room there, said that Angus usually spent half the week overnight at Doreen's and that he was in the habit of phoning one sister and telling her he'd been held up by work and would be late for their appointment when he was actually on his way to see the other one. But Ginley added that the bearded Casanova never rang either of the sisters from the Dolce Vita, as there was always too much background noise, preferring to go outside onto Low Friar Street and use a payphone.

Angus may no longer have held the forty-nine per cent of Social Club Services he'd been given at the outset, his share having been split with Michael, but he was still describing himself to strangers as 'a gaming company executive'. But it was unclear, even to his friends, exactly how much money he was really earning? Was he the indispensable figure in the company's affairs that he appeared to be? Or was he perhaps getting ideas above his station? There was meant to be a collection from every 'bandit' once a fortnight, with sixty per cent of the takings still going back to Vince, Michael and Social Club Services, twenty per cent to the club committee and the remaining twenty per cent left in the machines to pay out winnings. But there were rumours that Angus had started making extra collections on his own account, taking up to £50 a time several nights a week and splitting it with the club stewards. He had a key to unlock all the machines but had also discovered how to prise the back off the older machines with a screwdriver, enabling him to tamper with the jackpot, keep some of the cash and report a false return.

Vince Landa – the man who'd brought Angus into his orbit back in 1957 – was rumoured to be not unaware of his collector's activities and to tolerate them as long as he also continued to grease the palms of club committees. In the meantime, Vince was busy buying influence on his own account. Dryderdale Hall may have seemed to some like a secretive hideaway deep in the forest but it was often the venue for long, late-night parties with dinner, drinking and card games, as Vince and Gwen entertained not only fellow club owners and gaming executives but politicians, businessmen and all manner of powerful figures right up to T Dan Smith and Alderman Andrew Cunningham. The hospitality was generous and the air tinged with expensive scent and a mixture of champagne, scotch, rum and coke and Rothmans and Benson & Hedges' cigarette smoke, every big night at the Hall further impressing guests with the scale of their host's wealth and accomplishments.

Vince, Gwen and their children were taking ever more exotic holidays to faraway places and their sitting room was crammed with trophies and treasures from all over the world, including masks from Mexico, wooden gods from the Pacific, bongo drums from Africa, model elephants from India and sheaths, daggers and bullfighting banderillas from Spain. When T Dan Smith was asked to arrange a relaxing Mediterranean holiday for Foreign Secretary George Brown, it was Vince Landa who stepped in to recommend a hotel he knew in Majorca, where he just happened to own a 'luxury villa' in the grounds along with several holiday apartments.

Visitors from the south began to notice a change in Vince's style and manner as he went from being the enthusiastic Londoner trying to gain a foothold in the north-east to the gambling kingpin who wore dark glasses in daytime – even in winter – and drove around everywhere in one of his big, imported American cars. Strangers who only knew him by sight almost appeared to bow at the knee in his presence, as Michael Green, the sales director at Phonographic Equipment, discovered on a trip to the Social Club Services HQ. 'I was with Vince Landa one day in his flashy American Buick in Sunderland. He couldn't find anywhere to park, so he called over a policeman and asked him to look after his car for a while. "It will be my honour, Mr Landa," replied the cop.'

Michael Green saw a man deservedly enjoying the fruits of his enterprise and substantially boosting Phonographic's profits in the process. Ten years later, the Glaswegian-born playwright Cecil Taylor would take a very different view in a play he wrote for the Royal Shakespeare Company called *Bandits*, in which a gambling magnate loosely based on Landa would be depicted as 'tunnelling into a heart of darkness' and 'exploiting people who were already exploited and recruiting new people to exploit them in different ways.' But as Nucky Johnson had observed in Atlantic City in 1929, the public didn't have to be dragged in off the street. They were willing participants in their seduction, and their enthusiasm for the 'bandits' seemed undiminished by the many spins of the reels that failed to bring up that elusive jackpot.

At the more upmarket end of the gambling and entertainment scale, the growing demand for the kind of night out promised at the Dolce Vita and the Piccadilly encouraged other local players to open night clubs in Newcastle too. The most memorable was Club 69 on the Westgate Road, which was owned by the property developer and racehorse owner Joe Lisle. His customers were waited on by Bunny Girls as they ate Chinese food in the club's restaurant, drank Bacardi and coke in the bar, listened to Engelbert Humperdinck and gambled on roulette and chemin de fer. The silver-haired Lisle, who was one of the north-east's leading boxing promoters, owned racehorses too, trained by Denys Smith near Bishop Auckland. The best of them were King Cutler, a winner at the Cheltenham Festival, and Sixty-Nine, named after the club and victorious in the Great Yorkshire Chase at Doncaster in 1969 but, whenever Joe had a winner, it was champagne on the house.

Other rivals to the Piccadilly, the Dolce and the Cavendish included the Birdcage, a converted banana warehouse in Stowell

Street, and Billy Botto's in Byker, which was owned by a local bookmaker who had betting shops in Jarrow and Gosforth and pitches at Newcastle races and Sunderland dogs. Further out there was La Strada in South Shields, the Blue Parrot in Sunniside, where Mandy Rice-Davies of the Profumo affair fame became a regular attraction, and the Rex Hotel, the Pickwick and the Crescendo in Whitley Bay, where the gambling was run by a shrewd operator called Ray Grehan. But as well as the night clubs with their tuxedos, high heels and crooning entertainers, Newcastle and the north-east was about to rock to another kind of music every bit as exciting as the Bill Haley sound in the previous decade.

The most influential figure in the R&B revolution on Tyneside was Mike Jeffery, a Londoner like Vince Landa and Michael Luvaglio, who had served in the regular army in the 1950s before heading north and enrolling as a mature student at King's College, Newcastle (which became Newcastle University in 1963). The moustachioed Jeffery founded the University Jazz Club and then opened the Downbeat Club in Carliol Square in the city and a coffee bar on High Bridge Street called the Marimba with another music club, El Toro, on the first floor.

On the night of Monday, 13th November, 1961, the two clubs – which were empty at the time – were gutted by fire, prompting speculation that they had been deliberately set ablaze to claim the insurance money. Arson or not, the insurers paid up and Jeffrey, now in partnership with the Whitley Bay club owner Ray Grehan, ploughed the money into buying a site above the Handyside Arcade in Percy Street. The duo promised Geordies 'dancing in the Latin Quarter' with music provided by 'some of England's prime jazz bands'. The A'Gogo, as it was called, opened on 6th July, 1962, dimly lit with lime green chairs and black walls posted with pictures of American jazz greats like Earl Hines. But within a short time, the A'Gogo evolved from beards, berets and polo-necked jerseys into a definitive ground-breaking setting for the new rhythm and blues, with The Animals, Newcastle's home-grown sensation, the club's first house band. In July 1964, the Walker-born Eric Burdon's titanic voice propelled their version of the old standard 'House of the Rising Sun' to the top of the hit parade and, in September of that year, it topped the charts in the US too.

As well as the music, the A'Gogo had a restaurant serving hamburgers and steaks, a gaming room where Ray Grehan set up his roulette and blackjack tables and one-armed bandits, and a pair of terrifying bouncers in the shape of local hard men Tommy Findlay and his brother Dave, victors of the so-called 'Battle of Percy Street' in 1963. And always there in the background was the slightly sinister figure of Mike Jeffrey, the eminence grise who wore tailor-made dark suits and dark glasses at all times but – unlike Vince Landa – insisted they were necessary to combat his short sight.

Throughout 1964, 1965 and 1966, countless other chart-topping performers appeared on the A'Gogo stage, from The Who, Wilson Pickett, Chuck Berry and Alan Price – who left the Animals in May 1965 and set up on his own – to Cream and the Spencer Davis Group. Over the same period, Newcastle was graced by Bob Dylan, Roy Orbison and the Walker Brothers at the Odeon and The Beatles, Little Richard and Dusty Springfield at the City Hall.

Simultaneously, Tom Jones was making recurring visits to the Dolce Vita, sometimes alongside the popular north-eastern comedian Bobby Pattinson, the two of them doing an 8pm show at the Flamingo in Darlington and then jumping into Pattinson's car and racing back up to Newcastle in time for the midnight slot at the Dolce. The Gateshead-born Pattinson, who only retired from stand-up aged eighty-one in 2015, used to say how enamoured Jones was of his dark-green Jaguar Mark X. 'I remember Tom saying to me, "When I get my first car, it's going to be one of these,"' he recalled in 2015.

The Dolce Vita regular Angus Sibbet and his friend Michael Luvaglio were big fans of the Jaguar Mark X too and, in 1966, Michael gave an identical one to Angus as a present. From now on, the sleek green Jag, usually driven by Adam Ginley, would convey the collector on his rounds of the working-men's clubs instead of the Ford Corsair they had travelled in before. Starting in March 1966, there was a new address that Angus sometimes had to call at: a former furniture showroom in Low Row, Sunderland, that Vince Landa had bought and turned into the company's new sales and maintenance HQ. Angus Sibbet's brother James, who had left the Royal Navy in 1964, worked there repairing and maintaining the hundreds of machines that were now being supplied by Social Club Services and its sister company Coinamatics Amusements Ltd, which was also run by Vince and his brother Michael. The Low Row headquarters contained filing cabinets full of company papers, a teak desk and a cocktail cabinet for the boss and his clients and guests. Vince's secretary – and Angus's mistress – Doreen Hall, was assigned to work part of the week in the Olive Street office and part of the week in Low Row, where meetings would sometimes take place between Vince, Michael and Angus Sibbet.

At the end of the winter of 1966, business booming and the economy heating up, Vince, Michael and their parents, partners, families and associates seemed to be rich, inviolable and to have almost everything they could possibly want. But then, in the first week of March, 300 miles away in London, there was an outbreak of violence, involving murder and lurid headlines that would feed into the vital organs of the club scene in the north-east and threaten the Luvaglio brothers and everything that they'd achieved.

CHAPTER EIGHT

ON THE EVENING of Monday, 7th March, 1966, Eddie Richardson and Frank Fraser paid a visit to a night club in south London called Mr Smith and the Witch Doctor. It was situated on the first floor of the old Savoy Opera House in Rushey Green in Catford. Richardson and Fraser had already been there earlier in the day, discussing the terms under which they would provide the club with protection inside and on the door, in return for having their one-armed bandits installed as the club's only gaming machines. The club's owners, Dougie Flood and an ex-wrestler called Bill Benny, were Mancunians who owned similar businesses in the north-west. Everyone agreed that Mr Smith's was an enjoyable and well-run club with good food and drink, entertainment supplied by Bertie Green, who ran the Astor Club in Berkeley Square, and nightly games of roulette, blackjack and chemin de fer. It might not have been Mayfair but it was extremely popular with the south-London demi-monde and should have been a sound investment for everybody involved. But there was a problem.

Flood and Benny were worried that they might lose their licence due to the anti-social behaviour of a small group of locals who reckoned they were the club's protectors and that they were entitled to drink and gamble there as often and as late as they liked. Richardson and Fraser, first-division gangsters by comparison and members of the infamous firm led by Eddie's brother Charlie, were there to persuade them otherwise. The two men, smartly dressed in suits and ties but unarmed, were expecting it to be a relatively simple and straightforward task.

The weather in south London that night was dry and mild and, as Richardson and Fraser got out of their car, couples were strolling up and down and going in and out of the pubs on Rushey Green while families in the adjoining terraced houses were settling down to watch television: *The White Heather Club* and Hugh Lloyd and Terry Scott on the BBC, with *Double Your Money* on ITV.

When Eddie Richardson walked up the stairs and into Mr Smith's he saw that the 24-year-old Billy Hayward, a barge-worker from Abbey Wood, was already there, along with his friends Peter Hennessy, Billy Gardiner, Henry Botton and the thirty-year-old Richard Hart, a minor associate of the Kray twins who had recently been released from prison. They were all sitting at a table up on the balcony, drinking and making a bit of a noise and, when they saw the new arrivals, they joked and exchanged a few words but seemed cheerful enough.

Richardson and Fraser settled down on the other side of the room, drinks and food ferried to their table, and, as the evening wore on, they were joined by the other Richardson gang members, Harry Rawlins and Ronnie Jeffreys. When the hitman Jimmy Moody came in too, around 10pm, the Hayward-Hennessy faction began to fear that the whole Richardson crew was descending on the club, armed and ready for action. Fraser said that Billy Hayward was especially jumpy as he had been having an affair with the wife of Roy Porritt, a mechanic at Eddie Richardson's company, Atlantic Machines, and Hayward convinced himself that Richardson and Fraser had come to punish him for it.

As the clock passed midnight, Hayward and Hennessy covertly sent out for weapons, including a sawn-off double-barrelled shotgun and a .45-calibre pistol. The club's licence ran until 3am but, with Hayward's group showing no signs of drinking up and leaving, the management asked Eddie Richardson to 'have a word with them' and tell them it was time to go home. And that's when it all kicked off. The Gunfight at the O.K. Corral reimagined as what became known as The Battle of Mr Smith's Club.

Any other lingering guests had fortunately been ushered out of the door by the waitresses and, as Richardson got up and approached Hayward, the remaining croupiers and bar staff hit the floor. It started with Peter Hennessy shouting at Richardson and challenging him to a fight. The two of them went at it on the dance floor and Richardson fell backwards, a beer glass shattering on a table. Then Dickie Hart pulled out the .45 pistol and shot Harry Rawlins in the arm, blood spurting everywhere, and, all of a sudden, men were hiding behind chairs and tables and ducking for cover. Jeffreys was shot in the groin and stomach and Eddie Richardson sprayed with shotgun pellets in his buttocks and right leg. As he described it in his autobiography, *No Handcuffs*, Frankie Fraser had jumped on Hart to try to disarm him and had taken a bullet in the thigh. As he attempted to drag Hart outside, the pair tumbled down the stairs together and, at some point, Hart was shot dead with his own gun. Fraser managed to get out of the club and back onto the street, where he collapsed in a next-door garden. The whole area, previously quiet and sleeping, was woken by the sound of gunfire and approaching sirens, the club management having called 999.

Jimmy Moody managed to get Richardson and Harry Rawlins into his car and drove them to East Dulwich hospital and left them there. When the police arrived at Mr Smith's, they found Richard Hart's dead body at the bottom of the stairs, but Frankie Fraser was still alive and he and Jeffreys were taken by ambulance to a hospital in Lewisham. All the other surviving combatants were arrested and taken into custody.

Eddie Richardson has always maintained that he and Fraser were the victims of an assault, rather than the instigators, but the Battle of Mr Smith's Club was to prove disastrous for business with long-term consequences both for the Richardsons and their enemies. Two nights later, on 9th March, 1966, Ronnie Kray, envious of the Hollywood-style gunplay in south London and desperate to emulate it and avenge the death of Dickie Hart, was tipped off that the Richardson-gang hard man George Cornell, who had missed the shootout at Mr Smith's, was drinking with a friend in the Blind Beggar on Whitechapel Road. The pair had gone to visit Jimmy Andrews, another Richardson gang member who had been injured in Catford and who was in the Royal Whitechapel hospital across the road from the pub.

Cornell and Kray detested one another, Cornell having called Ronnie a 'fat poof' when bumping into the twins in the Astor Club the previous December. Seeing his chance, Ronnie walked into the Blind Beggar on 9th March, accompanied by his minder 'Scotch' Ian Barrie. It was shortly after 8pm and 'The Sun Ain't Gonna Shine Anymore' by the Walker Brothers was playing on the jukebox. 'Well, look what the dog's brought in,' Cornell is alleged to have said, at which point Ronnie Kray pulled out a Luger and shot him through the forehead.

The killing may have thrilled Ronnie with its sense of power and invincibility but, as Eddie Richardson wrote years later, Kray had picked a moment 'when he knew I was in hospital, the gang had been arrested and Charlie was out of the country (in South Africa)' so perhaps it was not quite as fearless as it seemed. Kray would not be arrested until March 1968 but the newspaper coverage at the time was full of headlines about GUN MURDER AT THE BLIND BEGGAR and the carnage a few nights before at Mr Smith's. Ronnie Kray loved it, his Al Capone-like fantasies running at full stretch. But one group of businessmen were anything but impressed, knowing that gang fights and brazen killings in public places would result in a demand for crackdowns by the law, which could potentially affect the profitable running of their concerns.

The new Colony Club in Berkeley Square had opened for business in the very same month as the Blind Beggar and Mr Smith's shootings. The American owners had spent millions on the renovation and were determined to do everything in style. Gaming was available from 1:30pm each day 'until the last customer leaves around five or six am,' said Dino Cellini, who glided around discreetly from table to bar, to restaurant and back again. Alfred Salkind, the nominal owner, and George Raft, the public face of the club, were there every night too. Raft, clad in a blend of the best Beverley Hills and Saville Row tailoring, playing himself as he laughed and chatted with the gamblers, lighting cigarettes and buying drinks.

Maintaining an assured and affable image was all important to Dino Cellini and his masters in the US. In February, the new

Labour Home Secretary, Roy Jenkins, had made a speech in Parliament that suggested that Harold Wilson's government was a lot more alert to the consequences of the bonanza unleashed by the 1960 Betting and Gaming Act than their Conservative predecessors. Britain had unintentionally 'become a gamblers' paradise, wider open in this respect than almost any other country,' said Jenkins. The new betting shops required permits but gambling clubs did not and there must be 'licensing of all clubs to stamp out the gangster menace.'

At the Colony, which recruited 2,500 members, including the visiting film director John Huston and the stars Lee Marvin and Yul Brynner within the first few months of opening, the Mafia did everything they could to discourage the local gangster menace. According to the venerable underworld figure Freddie Foreman, whose territory was south London and who had a gaming club in Balham called the 211, there were monthly pay-outs from the Colony to himself, the Nash family from Islington in north London and the Kray twins. 'That was how it worked like in New York. You had to look after all the firms that got a bit out of anything.' Foreman, who like Vincent Luvaglio had been one of Gabe Forman's best customers and purchasers of machines when he came over in 1961, said that the Americans regarded the Krays as little more than 'neighbourhood thugs'. Nicknaming them 'The Brothers Grimm', they were prepared to pay them a regular pension on condition they stayed away from the Colony and its smartly dressed clientele. But the twins were 'the worst trouble', according to Foreman, because they kept turning up with 'fucking ugly-looking people with scars down their faces. They fucked up everything that they touched. They were in their own fucking world that they couldn't see out of.'

East End toughs certainly weren't the kind of clients Cellini and Raft wanted to see walking in off Berkeley Square. Two former Scotland Yard detectives were employed to mind the door and maintain security and they were under orders to avoid any kind of confrontation in plain sight. The Mob's way, as they had demonstrated in Las Vegas, was never to do anything on their doorstep that would embarrass the local sheriff. What might happen out in the desert was another matter. Ignoring the public furore about London gangland, which was stoked further by the arrest of Charlie Richardson on 30th July – the day of the England-West Germany World Cup final at Wembley – Cellini and his partners busied themselves promoting the Colony's involvement with popular social and sporting events. They started screening big boxing matches for members and George Raft, who had boxed himself as a boy in the US, provided inter-round commentaries on Muhammed Ali's successful world heavyweight title defences against the British contenders Henry Cooper at Highbury on 21st May (stopped in round six) and Brian London at Earl's Court in August (Ali knocked him out in round three). They also sponsored a valuable motor race – the Colony Sporting Club Trophy at Silverstone – and Raft was there to greet the winners at Ascot and Sandown races too.

Outside the worlds of the casino and the sportsbook, earnest discussions were continuing about the morality, or otherwise, of legalised gambling. In an attempt to show polite society there was nothing to be afraid of, Raft agreed to participate in a *Tatler* article in which the Bishop of Southwark, Mervyn Stockwood, was his guest at the Colony for a day. The bishop, who had appeared several times on television, was regarded as something of a liberal within the Church of England and was subject to snide comments about his 'south-bank religion' – a codename for homosexuality – by more reactionary elements. He did advocate homosexual law reform but was only tolerant up to a point and, ten years later, in a televised debate about Monty Python's *Life of Brian*, he told John Cleese and Michael Palin that their film was 'blasphemy' for which they'd get their 'thirty pieces of silver'.

Stockwood arrived at the Colony after church on a Sunday morning, attired in a three-piece tweed suit and sensible brown shoes. After what he admitted was 'a very good lunch', he exchanged a five-pound note for a handful of coins to try his luck on the one-armed bandits. Given a tour of the gaming tables, he was unable to discover visible signs of debauchery and ruin and, thanking Raft for his hospitality, concluded that gambling should be nationalised 'within a socially useful context' and the wages of sin used to address public spending needs. His host was too polite to comment.

The *Tatler* article appeared on 26th September, burnishing rather than tarnishing the Colony's image and, regardless of the Bishop's recommendations, the club continued to hoover up money for its investors. But up on Tyneside that summer, Vince Landa, Michael Luvaglio and their fellow night club owners and gaming executives had been forced into playing reluctant hosts to less benign guests than a tweed-suited C of E cleric. The Kray twins, who were not welcome in the Colony and had sold their interest in their Wilton Place club, Esmeralda's Barn (now the site of the Berkeley Hotel) in 1963, paid brief visits to Newcastle but only once together. The twins were supposedly looking to expand the Firm's activities outside the capital but, for all their threatening image, they were always East End boys lost outside

London and their attempts to muscle in on night club businesses in the north of England were short lived.

Ronnie and Reggie's visit in June 1966 seemed to be more about pleasure than advancement. They arrived off the train from King's Cross with a group of minders and boys, along with the American former heavyweight boxing champion Joe Louis, who had been employed as a greeter at Caesar's Palace in Las Vegas by fellow boxer Sonny Liston's bookmaker, Ash Resnick.

'The Brown Bomber', as Louis was known, won twenty-five consecutive title fights between 1937 and 1949 and was one of the first African Americans to achieve the status of a national hero. He was one of the Krays, heroes too and Ronnie was trying to promote the idea of Louis doing a tour of northern night clubs and performing a stand-up routine, a bit like Jake La Motta at the end of *Raging Bull*. But away from the ring, the boxer's timing was terrible and, after a few inglorious attempts, it was swiftly apparent that he had no singing abilities either. But the old champ was the guest of honour that night as he and Ronnie and Reggie's party descended on the Dolce Vita. The astute owner, Morris Levy, had been given advance warning that they were coming and sent a limousine to greet them at Newcastle Central Station.

The top of the bill at the Dolce that night was the American singer Billy Eckstein, famous for his 1950 recording of 'That Old Black Magic Called Love'. He was another one of Ronnie Kray's heroes and Levy insured that the Londoners had the best table in the room and proceeded to smother them with love. 'They were starstruck,' he said. 'We gave them a whole lot of whisky, gin and vodka on the house and never charged them for anything. I think that's what kept them quiet.'

The Dolce Vita's regular photographer, Tommy Oxley, who was a part-time court usher, took a great picture of Ronnie Kray, Joe Louis and their companions sitting up at the front by the stage. He also sneaked another one of Ronnie 'with a bloke sitting on his knee' but he kept that one to himself until long after the twins had gone to jail.

Ronnie was always appreciative of Levy's hospitality, especially when the Geordie donated £5,000 to the twins' defence fund when they were on trial for murder at the Old Bailey three years later. By then, Morris Levy had sold the Dolce Vita to Stan Henry and the Bailey Group but Ronnie Kray never forgot the unsolicited contribution to his legal expenses, describing the Levys as 'true friends when they were in short supply'.

Reggie Kray's solo visit to Newcastle, which came a month later, was less convivial and more intimidating. Ray Grehan, who had been Mike Jeffrey's co-director at the A'Gogo and the Downbeat, was his chosen guide. Grehan had pulled out of his partnership with Jeffrey after acquiring gaming rights in Mecca clubs in a number of cities across England. Speaking in 1992, he said that Reggie came to see him in his Windsor Crescent office in Westerhope on the western side of the city. He had two henchmen with him: 'one with a gun in a shoulder holster and the other one a giant.' Grehan deliberately played down his gambling interests and attempted to divert Kray by buying him dinner at the Imperial Hotel in Jesmond and then conducting him on a night club tour.

They went to Billy Botto's on South Shield's Road, then to the Cavendish and then to the Piccadilly, where Ronnie Pipe, a fellow Londoner who played the piano in the Piccadilly's house band, The Sounds, remembered the general panic at the realisation that 'the Krays were in. Very large chaps they were, with an escort of CID men right behind them. We heard the police even had chairs in the corridor of their hotel to keep an eye on them.' Reggie Kray wasn't particularly interested in the house band. It was the owner of the club he'd come to see. 'Reggie said to the club staff, "Is Vince in?"' said Ray Grehan.

'Ring him up and tell him I want to see him.' I could tell there was some sort of vendetta going on. 'Strictly between you and me,' Reggie told me, 'Landa didn't do me a particular favour when he left London and came up here to hide. I just wanted a word with him.' I thought, Phoof, I know what sort of word you're going to have. Well, Landa didn't appear and there was a rumour he hid in the basement and told the staff to say he was out, so we went on to Club 69, owned by Joe Lisle. But Joe knew all about the Krays' background and no sooner had we sat down than he came over, very brave, and said, 'I don't want you in my club. Get out,' and out we went. It was a well-known fact that the twins didn't like operating outside London. They'd had a go at Manchester too and been very unsuccessful and I think they felt exposed outside their own patch. If it hadn't been for me opening a club in London (the Troubador in Mayfair), I don't think Reggie would have bothered coming up to Newcastle at all.

Reggie Kray may have continued to nurture an antagonism towards Vince Landa but neither of the twins ever set foot on Tyneside again. Not that Vince could have been sure of that in the summer of 1966, by which point his moods and demeanour had become harder, edgier and more changeable, as if there were other threats he had to be aware of, including some much closer to home. Why else would he have hired a self-proclaimed 'fun-loving criminal' with a biography and back story to match?

It's not as if Dennis Stafford was a local man. He was a Londoner, like Vincent and Michael, who had served nearly ten years inside, becoming a major embarrassment to both the police and the prison service. He was a lover of 'flashy suits and E-type Jags'. He was another bandit man . . . heading off up the Great North Road.

CHAPTER NINE

THE TRIAL OF the Kray brothers – Ronnie, Reggie and Charlie – in March 1969 was one of the longest and most dramatic British criminal trials of the twentieth century. But it was not the first time the twins had appeared in the dock at the Old Bailey. In May 1950, they and two accomplices were tried there on charges of causing grievous bodily harm arising from a teenage gang fight outside Barrie's dance hall above a branch of Burton's, the tailors, in Mare Street, Hackney.

From the moment the sixteen-year-old Krays had walked in that night, they and their friends had seemed intent on causing trouble. At the end of the evening, they picked on a local boy called Roy Harvey, who was flamboyantly dressed as an Edwardian 'Ted' and had been talking to a very attractive girl. Harvey was flung to the ground and kicked repeatedly, the attack witnessed by fellow teenagers Dennis Siegenberg and Wally Birch, who were also attacked and, being heavily outnumbered, made a run for it. Harvey had to be taken to hospital in an ambulance and, when the police investigated and brought charges, Siegenberg and Birch were both called on to testify. Under cross-examination, they said they didn't recognise the accused and, as a result, the twins were acquitted for lack of evidence. It was an early example of adherence to the imperative rule of the milieu, that you should never grass someone up, but, despite getting off, Reggie Kray wouldn't forget Dennis Siegenberg and harboured a grudge against him for years afterwards.

Dennis was born within the City of London in 1934 but he did his growing up in Hackney. His father, Joe, was a racecourse bookmaker, rarely seen without his trademark Homburg or bowler hat. He had a little office in the jewellery quarter in Hatton Garden and, as well as laying bets, was renowned as a fixer, or straightener, who, for a price, would act as an intermediary between criminals and the police, discovering how much it might cost for a case to be dropped or a vital bit of evidence mislaid.

Young Dennis had a childhood not dissimilar to the Luvaglio brothers, playing among the rubble and the bomb sites in east London, organising apple-scrumping expeditions – a criminal offence at the time of rationing – and always on the lookout for Artful Dodger-like scams and opportunities. Not long after his appearance at the Old Bailey, his father changed his surname to Stafford at the request of his other son, Lou, who had a job selling cinema advertising with Pearl and Dean. The older boy was marrying into a wealthy English gentile family and had decided that his Jewishness no longer fitted the image he wanted to project. And so it was that Dennis Siegenberg became Dennis Stafford.

By this time, Joe Stafford was also running a pub – the Duke of Wellington near Spitalfields Market – and some of Dennis's first post-school jobs were in the market, working for a company that supplied the hotel trade with fresh fruit and vegetables. Employment was interrupted by National Service, which he did mostly in Korea, becoming familiar with firearms, as well as learning more dodges and dives from enterprising squaddies. The twenty-year-old who returned to civilian life in 1954 was fit and good looking in a slick, cheeky, brilliantined sort of way and he slipped easily into the role of charmer and spiv, attracting and seducing numerous women and financing his wardrobe and late-night entertaining from a variety of harmless fiddles.

But then, in 1956, the irrepressibly confident wide boy moved from petty crime into more serious offending. On 27th July, 1956, the habitually well-dressed Stafford was sentenced to seven years' imprisonment at the London Sessions, having pleaded guilty to two counts of housebreaking in Walton on The Hill and West Byfleet in Surrey. He was also charged with receiving stolen property from a house in Camberley and a stolen car worth £1,040 and of being in possession of an automatic pistol loaded with two rounds of ammunition. Stafford, who asked for a further seven offences to be considered, including five of receiving stolen goods from housebreakings in Surrey and Berkshire and one of cheque fraud, always maintained that the gun – a wartime German Luger – had been planted on him by the police.

'Dennis the Menace', as the papers christened him, was locked up in Wormwood Scrubs but not for long. In November 1956, he and a fellow prisoner called Tony Hawkes, an ex-army officer and upper-class conman, escaped over the wall and made it back to Dennis's mother's flat in Wardour Street, where her son had secreted £200. The pair then headed to King's Cross station and bought first-class tickets to Newcastle, which neither of them had ever been to before but Stafford said was the biggest English city he could think of well away from London.

Within a week – and displaying impressive entrepreneurial skills – the escaped convicts had transformed themselves into a Mr Lewis and a Mr Whelby, running a fictional textile-and-garment business called Onalbourne. The aim of the enterprise was to open assorted bank accounts, order large amounts of fabric on credit and then sell it and make off with the cash. They opened an office in Pink Lane, not far from Newcastle Central Station, moved into a flat in Osborne Road and did a lot of socialising with women who came to their showroom to inspect and try on their stock. It was all great fun and a howling success until one of their clients, unconvinced by their knowledge of the fashion business, became suspicious and informed the police. Hawkes, ever the con-artist, promptly ran off with their profits, leaving Stafford dangerously exposed.

With the local police closing in, he hopped on a train back to London and, despite being a wanted man, spent many happy hours and nights in his friend Wally Birch's club, Winston's, in Clifford Street near Savile Row, where the Duke of Kent was a regular and where Dennis met and started a relationship with a dancer called Maxine Lee, who was also known as Eileen Cook. Simultaneously, he was frequenting the gay club the Londoner, next door to the theatrical costumier Bermans in Irving Street, just off Leicester Square. The Londoner, run by George Baron and Paul Clay, was popular with both homosexual and heterosexual couples who appreciated its discreet atmosphere and style.

To publicly identify as a gay man in Britain in the 1950s was to court danger, humiliation and arrest. Sir David Maxwell-Fyfe, Conservative Home Secretary between 1951 and 1954, had pursued a vindictive campaign against what he termed 'exhibitionists and proselytisers' engaged in 'a disgusting male vice' and 'plague' and thousands of men were entrapped and charged with gross obscenity and sodomy. Ironically, it was Maxwell-Fyfe who commissioned the Wolfenden Report, which would recommend that homosexual acts between consenting adults in private should be decriminalised, but he was no longer in office when it delivered its findings. It is highly unlikely he would have acted on them, and his successors were equally reluctant, the law not being changed for another ten years.

In the meantime, gay men still went in fear of persecution and blackmail but there were places where they could get away from victimisation, and the sheltered and sophisticated ambience of the Londoner was one of them.

Dennis Stafford – a highly sexed man with many female lovers – was also attractive to men and never so macho that he felt uncomfortable in gay company. He may not have engaged in gay sexual relationships himself, unlike the Kray twins, but he returned to the Londoner many times when he was in the capital and on the run and, in 1957, the co-owner, Paul Clay, put him in touch with a gay friend of his called Douglas Sargent who lived in Trinidad and was the heir to the Sandeman Port fortune. With Clay's encouragement, Stafford acquired a false passport under the resoundingly camp name of 'Marcel Birch' and took passage on the French Line cruise ship, the SS *Antilles*, from Southampton to Port of Spain, where Sargent was waiting to greet him with rather more of a fanfare than was sensible.

Marcel Birch settled down in a comfortable apartment overlooking the cricket ground at Queen's Park Oval and pretended to be dabbling in import and export for a range of

British companies, including the gay sportswear manufacturer Teddy Tinling, who designed the dresses for the women tennis players at Wimbledon. It was his ex-lover, Maxine Lee, who inadvertently caused Stafford's downfall. She had been talking to his father, Joe, unaware that he was being watched and that his phone was being tapped by the police. When she sent Marcel Birch a telegram saying that she was going to board a BOAC flight to the Caribbean that evening, the GPO referred the details to Scotland Yard. The authorities were alerted in Trinidad and, three hours before Maxine's plane was due to land, Dennis found himself in custody once again.

One of Stafford's fellow cellmates in the Royal Gaol in Port of Spain was the notorious gambler and pirate Boysee Singh, whose gang had allegedly murdered around 400 people while hijacking shipping between Trinidad and Venezuela. The exotic Singh had a fast boat moored at the wharf in Port of Spain and Stafford tried to encourage him to join him in an escape plot. But Singh was under sentence of death and he grassed up Stafford's plans to the prison governor in the hope it would earn him a reprieve. It didn't work and Boysee Singh was hanged on 7th August, 1957, by which time Stafford was already back in Britain. Lawyers retained by Dennis Sargent had spent three months trying to fight his extradition but it was money wasted and, on 10th June, two Scotland Yard detectives accompanied him on the flight back to the UK.

As the plane touched down at London Airport, Princess Margaret's lover Group Captain Peter Townsend was setting off on a round-the-world trip at the beginning of his enforced exile and the last British troops were leaving Egypt at the end of the Suez debacle. But Stafford's return was deemed the more newsworthy story and a large contingent of tabloid journalists and photographers were waiting to greet him. The dapper Dennis didn't disappoint, telling them that it was 'good to be home again' but that he could 'do with the weather being a bit better'. From London, he was taken by train back up to Newcastle and formally charged with eight counts of obtaining goods by false pretences and fraudulently converting money advanced to the fictional Onalbourne company for his own use. In October, he appeared at Newcastle Assizes and was speedily found guilty and sentenced to another eighteen months in prison on top of the seven years he'd been jailed for before escaping from Wormwood Scrubs in 1956.

The Home Office were not fond of escapees, especially cheeky ones that tried to make fools of them and the police, and Stafford's reward for his audacity was to be sent to the grimmest and most inhospitable prison in Britain. HMP Dartmoor was built in the early nineteenth century and originally used to house French prisoners during the Napoleonic Wars. When Stafford was there, the grey, granite walls of his cell used to run with water and, on winter mornings, it would have turned to ice. The food was uneatable, visits rare and the remote moorland setting near Princetown surrounded by dangerous bogs and mires like the 'Great Grimpen Mire' imagined by Sir Arthur Conan Doyle in *The Hound of the Baskervilles*. Yet, despite its fearsome reputation, Dartmoor was not wholly escape proof, as Dennis Stafford and William Day were about to prove.

According to Stafford in his autobiography, the thirty-year-old Day was 'a short guy, about my own age' who came from a Gypsy family and was as intent on breaking out as the crafty Londoner. They were both assigned to work in the tag shop, dismantling wartime gas masks and attaching tags to a range of unwanted objects. It was tedious, mind-numbing work but, as the days and weeks passed, Stafford and Day began to see that the old stone building on the prison's perimeter was a weak link, poorly guarded and in proximity to all sorts of discarded items that might come in useful. Stafford was on 'Special Watch', which meant that he had to wear a uniform with yellow patches on the shoulders and warders were meant to check up on him at regular intervals. But he proved as quick-witted and guileful as the scrounging POWs in Stalag Luft 3 and gradually he and Day managed to construct and hide an improvised ladder from a pole they found behind some old scaffolding.

On the afternoon of 6th January, 1959, the pair climbed over the outer wall. It was raining heavily and a thick mist had descended over the moor, which was exactly what they'd hoped for. But while it may have helped Stafford and Day to escape detection, it also made it extremely difficult for them to find their way. The prison authorities sounded the alarm and rings of foot and motorised police were soon spreading out around the jail up to twenty miles in each direction. The fog got so bad that, in places, a car's headlamps could only penetrate a few yards ahead and even those familiar with the area continually lost their sense of direction.

In *The Hound of the Baskervilles*, Selden, a desperate convict, escapes from Dartmoor prison but falls to his death running away from the ghostly hound. Bill Day's fate was sealed when he scrambled over a fence to avoid being seen by an oncoming car and jumped unintentionally into a reservoir. Day couldn't swim and, although Stafford claimed later that he'd jumped in after him and tried to save him, it was without success. Wet through, cold and exhausted, Stafford continued on foot and eventually found an old Ford in a garage behind a hotel building in Yelverton.

Remembering the tricks he'd learned as a teenager in Hackney, he managed to hot wire it and, riding his luck hour by hour, followed the signposts to Exeter and from there to Bournemouth where he knew an old girlfriend who ran a club in Poole. She took him in, clothed him and looked after him for the next forty-eight hours and then he took a train back to London. The police eventually found the stolen car abandoned in Bere Regis.

The daring escape, his second in three years, may have been gratifying to Stafford's ego, elevating him to celebrity status in the prison population, but he didn't have long to enjoy it. He was recaptured six weeks later, on 20th February, 1959, after being spotted on a London street in the company of his old friend Wally Birch. The hunt for Stafford and Day had been led by Detective Chief Superintendent Herbert Sparkes, who was based at Canon Row police station. Day's body had been fished out of Yelverton reservoir on 16th February and Sparkes, who didn't believe the rumours about Stafford having already slipped out of the country, had told his men to concentrate on the escaped convict's known haunts in the West End.

Around 9pm on the evening of the 20th, the Flying Squad officers Detective Inspector Geoff Candlish, who had met Stafford before, and Detective Sergeant Ivan Reynolds were cruising around in an unmarked car, heading up Whitcomb Street between Trafalgar Square and the Haymarket. Crowds were coming and going from cinemas and theatres and picking their way around the parked cars. Stafford was standing on the pavement outside Constables bookshop and talking to Birch and an unidentified woman friend. As usual, he was wearing an expensive suit and a well-cut overcoat, his disguise limited to a cap and spectacles (more Marcel Birch than Dennis the Menace), and Candlish recognised him immediately. He and Reynolds drove around the block and then back up Whitcomb Street, where they jumped out, ran up behind Stafford and grabbed him by the arms. 'I think you're Dennis Stafford,' said the detective. There was a brief scuffle and a cry of 'help me, Steve' before Birch and the woman ran off and Stafford was overpowered and bundled into the unmarked police car, which took off at speed, its bell ringing loudly like a scene from *The Blue Lamp* or *The Lavender Hill Mob*.

When they got to Cannon Row, Stafford admitted he'd been living mainly in London since the escape and gave his account of how Billy Day had jumped into the reservoir and how he had been unable to save him. Joe Stafford was informed of Dennis's capture and he went to see his son but there could be no fixing or straightening-out of this one and, on the afternoon of the 22nd, the press were out in force again to witness the celebrity jail breaker's return to Dartmoor. Stafford arrived at Waterloo station, handcuffed to a warder and looking almost comically dapper in suede shoes and a smart charcoal-grey suit, worn with a white shirt, silk tie and white top-pocket handkerchief. Friends, fans and supporters had gathered on the platform to wave him goodbye, and they handed him cigarettes, sandwiches and nuts and raisins as he boarded the train. Ahead of him was a three-hour journey to Tavistock, followed by a five-mile drive back to the Moor, where he was put in solitary and on a bread-and-water diet – as was the custom with escapees in the 1950s – until he'd been seen by a magistrate.

There would be no more break-outs but, just to be sure, the Home Office moved Stafford around several times to make sure he didn't get too familiar with his new accommodation. Then in October 1962, he was allowed out of Wakefield Prison for the day to marry Pat Smithson, a twenty-three-year-old ex-model from Gateshead whom he'd met up in Newcastle during the Onalbourne fraud. Smithson had become pregnant and had her baby, named Paula, while Stafford was on the run in Trinidad. She still knew him as Paul Lewis and only discovered his real identity in the papers when he was flown back to the UK. Struggling financially and longing for a father for her child, she had contacted Joe Stafford who, in turn, had gone to see his son in jail and told him that he was honour bound to marry her. 'Dennis is determined to forget his past and settle down to a new life when he comes out,' he told the press.

Contrite or not, Dennis served his last few years in Armley Prison in Leeds – another grim Victorian bastion with minimal comforts – and was released from there early on the morning of 10th March, 1964. TV cameras followed him again as he went into a café and enjoyed a cigarette and a cup of tea. For a while, he attempted to make a home with Pat and Paula, first in Newcastle and then in London. He tried changing his name again, to Dennis Fielding, and, with the help of his father, was given a few legitimate jobs. But working as a salesman for £30 a week didn't suit a chancer and thief like Dennis and, after Pat had spilled some of the details of her husband's criminal past, the job openings dried up.

On 7th September, 1964, Stafford got twelve months in jail for car theft and an extra twelve for possessing a firearm within five years of his release from prison. Pat Smithson went back to the north-east, the marriage effectively over, and, when Dennis came out this time, he went straight back to the West End. His friends George Baron and Paul Clay employed him to book acts for them at the Londoner, where he got to know Danny La Rue and the pianist Russ Conway. He enjoyed both straight and gay company and wearing the sharp suits and unrepentant smile of a professional wide boy and villain. And that's how things were when Vince Landa met up with him in the Londoner one night in 1965.

Vince was down south on one of his riotous club outings for Social Club Services employees and, as well as enjoying the nightlife, he was looking for tips and advice on how he could improve things at the Piccadilly. He'd read all about Stafford in the newspapers and heard about his impudent con trick with Onalbourne in Newcastle in 1956. He explained that he wanted somebody who really understood the club and cabaret scene to come and work for him in the north-east. But was it just to book acts? Or was Vince already getting nervous about his personal security and looking to recruit some professional assistance? Someone handy with a gun, for example.

Whatever the wages and the incentives offered, Dennis Stafford was won over. The 'fun-loving criminal', as he entitled his autobiography, had a new lover, Salena Jones, the black American jazz singer, who was herself eager to explore the north-eastern club scene, having been assured there were no racial barriers there to booking black performers. Vince said he could find Dennis and Salena a house in Peterlee, courtesy of the Peterlee and Aycliffe New Town Corporation, and that he'd provide them both with a car.

At some level, Stafford must have wondered if he hadn't already used up all his share of luck in the north-east and whether it would be a mistake to go back. But Vince was such a charmer and it sounded like a serious money-making opportunity. So, in the spring of 1966, Dennis Stafford accepted Landa's offer and, with Salena Jones in tow, set off up to Newcastle to join the bandit men.

CHAPTER TEN

THE FURNISHED ACCOMMODATION that Vince Landa had promised Stafford and Salena Jones turned out to be 109 Westmorland Rise in Peterlee. It was one of dozens of identikit cheap houses built by T Dan Smith's clients, Crudens/Ohlson-Skarne, and Landa was able to obtain it on the back of favours he had done for Smith and Alderman Andrew Cunningham.

The new town had been inaugurated in a spirit of socialist idealism back in 1947 and named after the Durham miners' leader and Methodist preacher, Peter Lee. The intention was to move miners and their families out of their pitmen's cottages in the East Durham villages and rehouse them in a comfortable, fully equipped, modern community. Laid out like an imitation of suburban America, there was a grid network of streets, a central shopping area and leisure centre and a bus station overlooked by the local working-men's club, where Social Club Services had installed two of their gaming machines. Sunderland was thirteen miles away and Newcastle, which was more Dennis and Salena's scene, twenty-three, but it could be driven in just under forty minutes. As good as his word, Vince provided Stafford with a SCS company car: a sporty Fiat 2300 Coupe, while Salena was given a white Mercedes.

The new couple – a white man and a black woman, living together but unmarried – were an exotic and unfamiliar sight in County Durham in the 1960s and their lives and backgrounds an immediate source of curiosity. One of the things that Salena had in common with Stafford is that they both had changed their names. She had started out as Joan Shaw from Newport News, Virginia, and her uncle was a vaudeville performer called Bootsie Swan. Her singing career began in black churches and choirs in the south but, frustrated by the endemic racism and limited working opportunities for her in America in the 1950s, she had moved to Europe and remodelled herself as Salena Jones. In London, she had appeared regularly at Ronnie Scott's Club, which was where Stafford first met her, and, in the north-east, she did shows at the Piccadilly, Dolce Vita and the Cavendish, as well as having occasional night-time slots on Tyne Tees Television.

The couple kept late hours, often not arriving home until dawn, and employed a housekeeper and cleaner, Lilian Bunker, to look after the house while they were gone. Stafford was on an official wage of between £25/£35 a week plus commission of £5 to £25. But Vince Landa had also given him a third share of the Piccadilly Club, which was officially owned by Victoria Enterprises Ltd, of which Vince was both a director and the main shareholder, the other one being his brother Michael. Nominally, Stafford's job at the club was to keep an eye on the balance sheet and book the acts. Some of the performers were the winners of amateur talent contests like 'Ah Pong', the Chinese ventriloquist and the Honourable Maureen

Campbell-Torrington, who was a female wrestler from Bayswater. Others were hardened professionals like the comedian Bob Monkhouse, who had hosted quiz shows, written gags for other comics and appeared in a *Carry On* film as well as doing stand-up in London and the north. In his 1994 autobiography, *Crying With Laughter*, Monkhouse said that, as well as managing the Piccadilly, Stafford worked at the Birdcage and at the Dolce Vita too, where Monkhouse once had a rather chilling encounter with him. 'I met him there and found him menacingly intense when he asked me to shorten my 80-minute act. "If I lose gambling time because of you . . . it upsets me," he said.'

Monkhouse took the hint and cut back accordingly. It could have been Ben Siegel or Nucky Johnson speaking and it was a sharp reminder that the real purpose of the entertainment was to attract punters into the clubs and then pass them on to the casino side, where the staff would endeavour to keep them there until they lost whatever money they had arrived with. It was the same business model perfected years before in the US by Siegel, Johnson and Meyer Lansky and the implication was that Dennis Stafford – the 'fun-loving criminal' – was partly brought up to Newcastle to make sure it was adhered to in Vince Landa's clubs.

Bob Monkhouse wasn't the only one to be discomfited by the contrast between Stafford's dapper, smiling appearance and the cold intent in his eyes but Dennis appeared to like it that way. 'No-one quite knew what to make of me,' he wrote in his autobiography years later. 'I was a sort of mystery man who was brought up from London by Landa.' Did that mean that Vince felt that danger was close at hand and, after events at Mr Smith's and the Blind Beggar, he and his family might be at risk?

Stafford had been in Newcastle when Reggie Kray made his

unscheduled visit that summer and claimed to have 'had a word with Reg and advised him against trouble.' But trouble in the city there was, beginning in May 1966 when a fire at the Quay Club caused £8,000 worth of damage. The R&B club, smaller and more intimate than the A'Gogo, was in Side, the narrow street behind the Castle that ran downhill towards the river beneath the shadow of the railway arch and the Tyne bridge. The club, which had opened in December 1965, was owned by George Hoffman and Bob Lewis and managed by Bob Keith, who had been a floor manager at the A'Gogo. Situated opposite the Crown Posada pub, it was aimed primarily at the eighteen–thirty-year-old generation and, in February 1966, the twenty-one-year-old art student Bryan Ferry, from Washington, County Durham, had played there with his band, Gas Board. Other breaking acts to have appeared there included the Pretty Things and the Yardbirds.

One night when Tom Jones was in town, headlining at the Dolce Vita, he'd gone down to the Quay Club after his show to listen to the bands with the rest of the Friday-night crowd. When Eric Burdon of the Animals heard about it, he allegedly raged about the cabaret star's presence as if it was somehow not authentic or compatible with the club's image. He got in a car and drove past the Quay Club and chucked some empty bottles in through the open door as a protest.

There were more than just a few broken bottles after the 18th May fire. Police and firefighters found an empty can of paraffin in the cellar and immediately suspected arson. There was no casino at the Quay Club, though they did have a few gaming machines and they were catering to a very different clientele to places like the Dolce Vita and the Piccadilly. If it were suddenly forced out of business, the most obvious beneficiary would be the A'Gogo owner Mike Jeffrey, whose Marimba and Downbeat clubs had burned down in suspicious circumstances in 1961. There were rumours about links to protection rackets in London but, on Ronnie Kray's visit to Newcastle, he had been more interested in boys, booze and Billy Daniels than extorting payments and his twin brother had been seen off by Joe Lisle. But was that really the end of it? Were there likely to be more fires and incursions from the capital or maybe Glasgow? And was a proper gaming war brewing in the city?

The tension grew throughout the summer months, fuelled by talk of fights being started deliberately in clubs to scare away the customers and owners receiving threatening phone calls and demands for money. Then, on the night of 11th September, 1966, the Pear Tree garage in Gateshead was burned to the ground. The owner, Harry Sibley, also owned the Blue Parrot Country Club in Sunniside. Nicknamed 'Danger Man' because of his resemblance to the actor Patrick McGoohan, star of the popular TV series *The Prisoner*, Sibley was a fixture at the Dolce Vita and a member of Vince Landa's inner circle, sometimes being invited to parties and card games at Dryderdale Hall.

The assumption that Harry Sibley had been targeted because of his closeness to Landa seemed to be confirmed a fortnight later when the Piccadilly Club itself was destroyed by fire. It happened in the middle of a Sunday afternoon when the club was closed to the public. Two eyewitnesses, sitting on a bench at the corner of Stowell Street, saw two men run out of the building just before the blaze started, jump into a car and drive away. They said that both men were wearing boiler suits and that one of them had glasses on and yellow industrial gloves. Over sixty firefighters and half-a-dozen fire engines were called to the scene but all to no avail.

The Piccadilly's luxurious curved cabaret and bar, the Nevada Room casino, the Horsearama game and the Chinese and Indian restaurants that had all opened to such a fanfare eighteen months before were gutted by the blaze.

On the face of it, the fire appeared to be a grievous blow to Vince and Michael Luvaglio. After commitments to breweries and creditors, the club – valued at £50,000 – was reporting a turnover of between £2,000 and £3,000 a week and had only recently paid a £5,000 gaming-tax bill on the casino. On 27th February, Vince gave a statement to assembled reporters from Tyne Tees Television and the local press confirming that several members of the club staff had recently received threatening phone calls and offers to keep order in return for money. 'If Newcastle becomes like London,' he warned, in a nod to the violent Kray-Richardson feuds, 'we might as well emigrate to new pastures.'

Chief Inspector James Dobson of Newcastle CID acknowledged the suspicion that London underworld figures were looking for night clubs in the region, in anticipation of an offshore oil strike in the North Sea (which eventually occurred off the coast of Scotland in December 1969) and subsequent economic boom. Dobson observed that the police were at 'a dreadful disadvantage in matters like this as very few people will come forward to make statements' but he added, pointedly, that he planned to 're-interview the principals concerned' – the principals being Vince, Michael and club manager Dennis Stafford – and that the case would remain open. No action was ever taken against them, or anyone else, regarding the fire but Dobson knew perfectly well that, for all the talk about London gangsters, deliberately torching a business to claim the insurance money was one of the oldest scams in the criminal playbook. In Newcastle, Mike Jeffery was still suspected of burning down the Marimba and the Downbeat and his man, Bill Keith, had been the manager of the Quay Club. Had Jeffery had anything to do with the fire at the Piccadilly? Or had Vince Landa commissioned the burning of his own club?

If Vince was really feeling under pressure from as yet unnamed predators, he gave little indication the next month when he and Gwen opened the doors of Dryderdale Hall to a feature writer and photographer from the *Newcastle Journal*. In the same week that *Alfie*, starring Michael Caine as a cockney Lothario, was playing at the Jesmond Picture House in Newcastle, the article reflected on the mercurial rise off another charismatic south Londoner. 'Each age has offered its own opportunities for people to make a fortune,' it began. 'Vince Landa's was as a result of the gambling revolution and, in particular, working-class gambling. For Mr Landa is essentially a one-armed bandit magnate.'

It was an era when women were meant to provide silent, smiling, unthreatening support to their men but it was the magnate's wife, Gwen, who did most of the talking. Fair haired, brown eyed and pictured with her three daughters, Claire, Susan and Carol, she was adamant that everything Vince had done was 'for the children and the family and to give them a better and different life to his'. Readers were conducted on a tour of Dryderdale's sitting room, with its two great curving sofas, upholstered in gold velvet – where every north-eastern big shot had sat and been entertained, including T Dan Smith and Alderman Cunningham – and then the panelled dining room, in dark tones and with a dining table big enough for a banquet.

Still tanned from a trip to the Caribbean, where they had rented a house and taken the children, Gwen Landa explained that they were planning to go to Australia for some sun after

Christmas too. 'We've been almost everywhere except South America and Russia,' she said. 'We don't feel it's a good policy to save money up until we're older. Better to enjoy it while we're young. But we've made provision for the children.' Gwen, who said that she still did all the cooking when they had guests, talked vividly about the days before they left London when they were living in a small, three-bedroomed house in Mitcham and her husband was 'a television representative and trainee manager in a store. It's been a struggle. But he's worked so hard. I don't see a lot of him but he's always at home at weekends and for things like birthdays and holidays.'

The writer was fascinated by the three telephones and seven television sets, including ones in the kitchen, the study and at the foot of the couple's bed, and the CCTV camera trained on the driveway. 'We use it mostly to keep an eye on the children when they're playing outside,' said Gwen. There was no mention of the armed security men and guard dogs supposedly roaming the grounds. The tour ended with a walk around the lake and the garden and a glimpse of the dazzling collection of cars, including two white American Pontiacs, one each for husband and wife.

For his part, Vince said that, despite the fire at the Piccadilly, he still had plans to expand his night club kingdom. He had his eye on a possible sight in Chester-le-Street and, closer to home, he was thinking of developing Shell House, the shooting lodge on the edge of his estate, into a country club where there would be 'facilities for golf, shooting and swimming' and maybe for overnight stays too. He didn't deny the rumours that he was considering proposals to float Social Club Services on the London Stock Exchange in the new year. He couldn't go into too much detail yet, he said, but he might start off by trading around forty-nine per cent of the shares, rumoured to be worth as much as £8m (or more like £130m in 2022 money).

Roy Jenkins and his advisers at the Home Office may have had gambling clubs in their sights but Vince's undaunted optimism and continued faith in the future of the British gaming industry appeared to be shared by the Americans. SCS, with over 2,000 working-men's clubs on its books, was still buying machines each week from Phonographic Equipment who, in turn, were continuing to boost Bally's sales figures to record levels in Europe and worldwide, further lining the pockets of their owners in the US. On 27th November, six days after Salena Jones appeared on *Nightspot* on Tyne Tees Television, Angelo Bruno (the 'quiet Don' portrayed by Harvey Keitel in *The Irishman*) came over to London with Meyer Lansky on a gambling junket. The pair stayed at the Hilton hotel on Park Lane, met with Albert Dimes and discussed how they would divide up the proceeds from installing more of their gaming machines in London and elsewhere in the UK. Bruno already owned forty-seven per cent of the Victoria Sporting Club where Dimes, wearing his bookmaking hat, had an office at the back, and Bruno and Lansky were the co-owners of The Pair of Shoes run by the Swedish poker player Eric Steiner (and nowadays the site of Robin Birley's ultra-fashionable 5 Hertford Street), as well as the Colony Club.

The Berkeley Square showpiece continued to be the Mob's vanguard operation in Britain, run impeccably by Dino Cellini and his brother Eddie, the models for the characters Dino and Eddie Pennino, who present Hyman Roth (Lansky) with his giant birthday cake in *The Godfather Part II*. The business plan at the Colony and the Pair of Shoes was simple, smooth and utterly ruthless. Mark Sykes, an aristocratic Englishman who worked as a greeter at the Pair of Shoes, remembers bundles of money being raked up each night and padded envelopes stuffed with cash being flown out to New York and Miami twice a week. Lansky and Bruno weren't worried – at least not at the moment – about prospective gambling reform in the UK. Politicians, they believed, could always be bought. What they didn't want was a scandal or more clumsy acts of violence shattering the surface of their carefully contrived world.

The bookmaker Victor Chandler, himself a fearless gambler and whose father owned the Casanova Club in London's Chesterfield Street, used to say that anyone who remained in a casino for longer than half an hour was a fool. Some went much further. CP Taylor, the left-wing playwright and author of *Bandits*, said gambling clubs were 'a seedy temple in which sex and money are the twin pillars' and people 'run around like mad in the pursuit of happiness.' But as the Christmas season approached on Tyneside in December 1966, there were countless Geordies, husbands and wives, men and women, straight, gay, hen parties and stag dos for whom dressing up for a night out amidst the warmth, soft lighting and luxury fittings of the Dolce, the Cavendish or the Birdcage was irresistibly seductive and fun. And among the eager clubbers, gamblers and office parties was the ever more expensively dressed Angus Sibbett, one of the principal seducers and bandit men, according to CP Taylor's view, and, according to his own account, Vince Landa's fellow gaming executive and collector in chief.

What a world the Bandit Men inhabited, people were thinking. Elderly residents of Newcastle who remember them – women like Margaret Scott, who was a manageress at the Dolce Vita in its heyday – contrasted their wardrobes with twenty-first-century scammers and drug dealers in their hoodies and tracksuit trousers.

Angus Sibbet, she said before she died in 2018, would no sooner have turned up at a working-men's club in a hoodie and a pair of trainers than 'he would've walked into the Dolce stark naked.'

By late 1966, Angus was in possession of his expensive new company car, the dark-green Jaguar Mark X saloon – similar to the comic Bobby Pattinson's car – presented to him by his friend Michael Luvaglio. Always clad in a bespoke suit and tie and a smart overcoat and with his personal chauffeur Albert Ginley at the wheel, he cut an ever more imposing figure as he was driven around Tyneside and County Durham greeting customers old and new and collecting the profits from the Social Club Services machines. His official wage was £100 a week plus commission but the word around Tyneside was that he was now spending more like £1,500 a week, much of it in night clubs and on entertaining the sisters Joyce and Doreen Hall, the two mistresses at the heart of his deceitful but energetic love life.

Angus was 'always making friends' according to Albert Ginley and inviting them to his regular table at the Dolce Vita. His relationship with Vince Landa and Michael Luvaglio went back to the early days in London and the Chinese restaurant in Woolwich and, while he no longer saw much of Landa, he and Michael were often in each other's company, willing the slot-machine goose to go on laying the golden egg. Michael knew all about Angus's affairs but was also a loyal friend of his wife Brenda and daughter Karen, as well as one of the guests at the house in Dunston when Tom Jones came to dinner. By comparison, Albert Ginley reckoned that in the eighteen-month period between Dennis Stafford's arrival in the north-east in 1965 and the end of the following year, Sibbet and Stafford 'only met about half-a-dozen times'. After the fire at the Piccadilly Club, the Londoner was officially continuing to book acts for the working-men's clubs but Ginley said his exact role in the firm's activities was 'not clear'.

Angus was excited that Christmas about an impending deal he and Michael were doing with the Newcastle Transport Club, which would involve SCS redecorating the club premises and installing CCTV. There was good money involved but the conclusion of the negotiations would have to wait until the New Year as, on 20th December, Vince, Gwen and their children, along with Frank and Maud Luvaglio and Michael and his girlfriend Pat Burgess, flew out to Majorca to enjoy Christmas in the sunshine at Vince's luxury villa. There was more than enough room for them all as Landa also owned apartments in the grounds and up in the hills behind Palma. It wasn't just a Luvaglio family gathering either. There was no invitation for Angus Sibbet but Dennis Stafford, Vince's new 'mystery man' went along too. He didn't take his wife and daughter with him and he didn't take Salena Jones either because she was working in Newcastle night clubs over the holidays. Instead, the rarely celibate Stafford took along another girlfriend, Julia Burlinson, who had formerly been a receptionist at the Piccadilly Club.

While his employers were away, Angus Sibbet enjoyed more nights with Joyce and Doreen Hall at the Dolce Vita watching Tom Jones, whose latest single 'Green, Green Grass of Home' was the official Christmas number one, and the special *Midnight Show* on Christmas Eve starring Ronnie Carroll, Syd Little and Eddie Large and Lance Percival. The next day, he was at home in Dunston with Brenda and Karen. Snow started falling after lunch as the three of them and their bull mastiff dog, settled down indoors to watch television: *Billy Smart's Circus*, *The Black and White Minstrel Show* and John Wayne in *The Comancheros*. A week later, the New Year, celebrated by the BBC with *Ring in the New*, featuring Andy Stewart, and *The White Heather Club*, broke with the news that Alf Ramsey had been knighted for leading England to victory in the 1966 World Cup and that the triple Cheltenham Gold Cup winner, Arkle, had received dozens of gifts and get-well cards and was behaving like a model patient as he recuperated in his box at Kempton Park after breaking a bone in his hoof in Boxing Day's King George VI Chase.

On Tuesday, 3rd January, all of the Luvaglio party, bar Gwen and the children, flew back to the UK. Vince was staying in London that night as he had an appointment to see his accountant but Michael and the others carried on to Newcastle, where Stanley Robinson, who worked for SCS at the Low Row office, picked them up and drove them into the city. Michael and Pat were dropped off at Chelsea Grove, where Michael's cousin, Brian Ginger, was living on the top floor. He took Frank and Maud home to Benwell and then ferried Dennis Stafford back south of the river to his wife Pat Smithson's house in Low Fell, Gateshead, where he spent the night.

The next day, 4th January, Ginger drove Stafford and Michael Luvaglio back to Stafford's house in Peterlee and then on to Low Row, where they met up with Angus Sibbet. The philandering collector, who had spent the night at Joyce Hall's flat, was frequently late for meetings and generally preferred to schedule appointments in night clubs after dark. But Joyce Hall said that he was so looking forward to seeing Michael and getting back to work again that he had been 'in a jubilant frame of mind' that morning, 'cracking jokes and making fun' as he got up and got dressed. He'd been expecting to see Vince Landa at Low Row too but he was told that Vince had rung up from London to say that he was flying back to Majorca after getting a call from Gwen saying that she was worried about their son, Dean, who might be developing appendicitis.

In Landa's absence, the others discussed the Newcastle Transport Club deal and then, at 1:30pm, Albert Ginley drove them round to the SCS accounts office over the District Bank in John Street in Sunderland. They spent around forty-five minutes there and then went on to the Wheatsheaf garage on the A1346, which was where Vince Landa kept his fleet of cars for services and repairs. Michael and Dennis had a transport problem. Dennis's Fiat was being re-sprayed and was not yet ready, while Salena Jones needed her white Mercedes to get to work. Michael Luvaglio told the garage manager, Arthur Rowley, that they would have to take Vince's new red E-type Jaguar, which had also been left there by Landa for servicing.

Regarded by some as 'the most beautiful car ever made', the red E-type had only come off the production line the previous February. It had caramel leather upholstery and could accelerate from 0 to 60mph in six seconds. Rowley was reluctant to hand it over without Vince's authorisation but Michael assured him it would all be all right and, fortuitously, Dennis Stafford had a key.

Before they parted, Michael said that Angus Sibbet proposed a further meeting between the three of them that night at the Dolce Vita. 'Too noisy,' said Michael. 'Then how about the Birdcage?' said Angus. Michael said he'd ring later to confirm. With Stafford doing the driving, he and Michael then headed back to Low Row, where they were joined by Salena Jones, who had been unwell over Christmas but was seemingly taking Stafford's Majorca liaison with Julia Burlinson in her stride. At around 5pm, Michael said he called Angus Sibbet at his home in Dunston and suggested meeting him at the Birdcage at half past midnight. They were all night owls and it was not unusual for them to meet up so late but Michael added that his brother Vince might be going to call him from Spain at the Chelsea Grove number around midnight, so he'd need to stop off there first.

Dennis Stafford and Salena Jones then went back to Peterlee in the red E-type and Michael took one of the Arcadian limousines and drove up to Denton in Newcastle to pick up Pat Burgess from her parents' house. She was washing her hair, so Michael went round to see his parents in Benwell for a few hours, returning at approximately 10pm to collect Pat and drive back to Peterlee, where she was pleased to see her friend Salena again. But Michael and Dennis Stafford weren't staying. They said they had that appointment with Angus Sibbet at the Birdcage, and Pat Burgess, Salena Jones and the housekeeper, Lilian Bunker, would all testify later that they left Westmorland Rise in the red E-type around 11:30pm.

The temperature was dropping and it was a cold, dark and cheerless night as the two men drove back up through Sunderland towards Newcastle, stopping first at Chelsea Grove and parking the red E-type on the street outside. But the midnight phone call from Vince in Spain never came so they got back into the car and drove the short distance down to the Birdcage in Grainger Town, arriving – said club director John Bowden – between 12:30 and 12:40am, and both looking and acting quite normal. There was no sign of Angus Sibbet, and Doreen Hall said later that, at approximately 1:20am, Michael rang her at her flat in Jesmond and asked if Angus had gone back there? She said no.

Having not eaten any supper that night, Michael and Dennis ordered some food in the club and, not long afterwards, Stafford went outside, so he claimed, to get some duty-free cigarettes that he'd brought back from Majorca and left in the E-type. He said that the car had been shunted about fifteen feet down Stowell Street and that there was some damage to the rear end, as if it had been in an accident. He drew it to the attention of the club doorman, Matthew Dean, who went outside to have a look and admitted that he had heard a loud bang about half an hour beforehand that could have been a collision. It had been snowing since midnight and Stafford and Dean claimed they saw tracks in the snow where another vehicle might have backed away down the narrow street.

There was still no sign of Sibbet by closing time, so Luvaglio and Stafford left the Birdcage and went back to Chelsea Grove, waking up Brian Ginger to make doubly sure Vince hadn't rung from Spain – and he hadn't – and then, with Stafford still at the wheel, they got back in the E-type and drove back to Westmorland Rise in Peterlee. Pat Burgess and Salena Jones said they arrived sometime after 3am and then they all went to bed.

Angus Sibbet had spent the evening of 4th January enjoying himself in the usual manner. At approximately 5:30pm, he'd left his family home in Dunston and Albert Ginley had driven him over to Joyce Hall's flat in Gateshead. St Edmund's Road was in a traditional working-class neighbourhood of back-to-back houses with outside lavatories, coal bunkers and washing lines hanging in the yard. Ginley waited politely downstairs as Angus and Joyce disappeared into the bedroom, re-emerging around 7pm, when Ginley drove Angus back over the Tyne bridge and up the central motorway to Joyce's sister Doreen's flat in more affluent Jesmond. The great seducer washed and changed, splashing on some aftershave and putting on a clean suit and shirt, a smart tie and his favourite short, dark-blue camel-hair coat. Then, making an excuse to Doreen about having an important collection to make, he gave Albert Ginley the rest of the evening off and got into the Jaguar Mark X, which he kept parked in St George's Road, and drove himself back to the flat in Gateshead, where Joyce was dressed up, made up and ready for a good night out.

Alex Spandler, manager of the Dolce Vita, said that Angus came in that evening 'about 9pm with, I think, a party of six – three men and three women – and I said hello to him in the hall.' Mr Sibbet, he added, was 'a great entertainer' who would regularly book tables for eight and was 'well-known among my staff and very popular with all of them'. Angus had a habit, Spandler had noticed, of getting up from the table halfway through the evening and going outside, sometimes returning after a few minutes (no doubt after ringing a mistress on a payphone), sometimes not coming back for more like an hour or more when he was presumed to be away on a job collecting cash from some gaming machines.

That night, Angus's party included his sister Sheila and Joyce's friend, Anne Euington, from Windy Nook, all three of the women bouffant and beehived, chatting, laughing and smoking Player's Number Six. They were sitting, as always, at his favourite table, practically on the cabaret floor, and served by the waitress Edna Anderson, who had known him for two-and-a-half years. The twelve days of Christmas were not quite over yet and the menu still had a festive theme. Angus and Joyce both had the turkey with roast potatoes and brussels sprouts, and Angus drank Bacardi and coke.

The comedian Dave Allen was due to come on stage at 11:30pm. But at around 11pm, Angus got up, as usual, and said he had to go out. 'Where to?' asked his sister. Angus said he had 'to meet Mick at Shiney Row' (a mining village in Houghton-le-

Spring about thirteen miles south of Newcastle). Sheila wasn't sure if he meant he was meeting Michael Luvaglio, whom he usually referred to as 'Mike', or his Irish minder, Paddy Hallett, whose nickname was Mick. 'But you'll miss the cabaret,' she said. 'Can't be helped,' her brother replied, implying he would be back later. He didn't say anything to her about an appointment with Michael and Dennis Stafford at the Birdcage at 12:30am.

On his way out of the club, Angus bumped into the resident photographer, Tommy Oxley, who had taken the pictures of Ronnie Kray and his entourage the previous summer. Angus owed him for a set of prints he'd ordered of photos of himself and his friends with Tom Jones. He paid Oxley in cash and thanked him and then went out into the snow in Low Friar Street, got into his Jaguar Mark X and headed off into the night.

CHAPTER ELEVEN

'A MURDER HUNT was launched in County Durham today,' was how the Newcastle *Evening Chronicle* broke the news in their lunchtime edition on 5th January. Superintendent Harry Lockerbie of Peterlee police reported that 'the body of an unnamed man' had been found in a snow-covered car under a railway bridge in the village of South Hetton. Residents had been woken up before dawn by the sound of police cars arriving to commence a major investigation. Tom Leak, the shot-firer from the local colliery who had made the discovery, had remained at the scene with Leslie Marshall and the other miners as the police photographer began to take pictures of the dead man's car. The dark green Mark X Jaguar saloon appeared to have sustained extensive damage, including a stalled radiator, which had robbed the engine of its water cooler and prevented it from being driven any further.

The pathologist, Dr Jack Ennis, was the man who peeled back the dead man's overcoat to reveal the bullet wounds. The fifty-six-year-old Ennis was a much-liked and respected figure who had done his medical training at Barts in London in the 1930s and then joined the Indian Medical Service. At the onset of World War II, he had been working at the Far East Pathological Laboratory in Singapore and, when the Japanese invaded in 1942, both Ennis and his wife, Elizabeth, were captured and interned but in separate camps. Unlike many of their fellow prisoners, they managed to survive three years of captivity and were reunited after the war ended. They moved back to Britain in the late 1940s and settled in County Durham, where Ennis had officiated at dozens of untimely deaths but rarely a murder.

Controversially, the pathologist only conducted a brief examination at the scene, explaining later that he didn't want to 'disturb the body'. Gunshots in the snow in a Durham mining village in the early hours of a winter's morning sounded like a scene out of a western. What could possibly have happened? The crucial question was going to be the approximate time of death? Had rigor mortis already set in – as Dr Seymour Hunter claimed – before Ennis took his first look? And was the dead man's left leg bent or straight, as Tom Leak said it was when he first saw the body? The answers to those questions would have to wait, as it wasn't until after 11am that Detective Sergeant Frank Morgan from the Major Incident Unit in Aycliffe, was able to organise a tow to take the car, with the dead man still inside it, in a convoy of six police vehicles, to Peterlee police station. The body was undressed and the bullet wounds photographed, and then wrapped up in cellophane and taken in a van to the mortuary in Easington, where it was laid on a lead-covered table.

Finally, at 1:15pm, eight hours after Tom Leak had discovered the dead man (a delay that the esteemed pathologist Francis

Camps would be highly critical of), the autopsy began. The body's temperature, taken with a rectal thermometer, was 64°F. Jack Ennis confirmed that death had been due to bullet wounds of the aorta and heart, that death would have occurred in no more than a minute and that the deceased would have been incapable of any powerful movement. The fatal bullet was the one which had hit the left shoulder and then tracked down the right hip bone, hitting numerous 'vital structures', and Ennis felt the wounds could not have been inflicted while the dead man was sitting in the car. 'I visualise the deceased had opened the car door and was emerging holding the door with his right hand somewhere near his abdomen,' he wrote. 'The first injury he would receive was that which passed through the right lower forearm and the loin tissue. I visualise that he ducked, and in the course of stooping, he received the second wound, probably the one behind the left shoulder, followed very quickly by the one in the lower chest. He would then fall forward on his face and on the front of his body. This falling forward would be responsible for the injuries found on his face.' Ennis added that there were no signs that the dead man had fought back. In conclusion, his verdict, based on the body temperature, was that the murder must have taken place sometime between midnight and 4am but that it was more likely to have been earlier, between midnight and 1am.

No murder weapon had been found at the scene but the bullets removed from the corpse were 7.65-calibre cartridges fired typically from a handgun like a Walther PPK. George Price, the senior experimental officer at the Home Office northern laboratory in Nottingham had been contacted and was travelling to County Durham to examine both the bullets and the car.

The fact that the dead man was six feet tall and weighed over thirteen stone and had been found not on the ground but in the back of the Mark X convinced Detective Superintendent Ronald Kell that the crime must have been committed by more than one person. As Kell, DS Morgan and their team examined the personal effects, valuables and other items found on the dead man's person and in the car, it was also clear that the motive for the killing had not been robbery. The deceased was still wearing a gold Omega wristwatch. His wallet and driving licence were intact and, like a bookie or regular punter, there was a wedge of £150 in his right trouser pocket. They also found a leather collection bag – a bandit man's slot-machine bag – on the dashboard of the Mark X.

The personal items told the police that they were looking at the body of Angus Stewart Sibbet of Mountview Gardens in Dunston – although some of them had already recognised him, as he was a conspicuous character in the region – and, that afternoon, they began to contact his next of kin. His sixty-six-year-old father, Alfred Sibbet, his mother Joan, his sister Sheila and his brother James, who came out to Peterlee to make the official identification, were all devastated but none more so than his loving but ill-used wife Brenda, who had to explain her husband's death to their eight-year-old daughter, Karen. As well as talking to the relatives, the police put out an appeal to the public via the press and TV asking witnesses to come forward and help with their enquiries, and that is when the sisters, Joyce and Doreen Hall, heard the news and tearfully realised that there would be no more afternoon delights and happy nights out with Angus at the Dolce Vita. Then, around 3:30pm on the afternoon of 5th January, DS Kell received a tip-off.

Despite not getting home to bed until 3am the night before,

Dennis Stafford was up early on 5th January and, at 9am, he got in the red E-type and went to Zip Cleaners in Peterlee with some suits and other laundry that he said he'd worn on holiday in Majorca. He then went back to Westmoreland Rise to collect Michael and the two of them drove to the Wheatsheaf garage in Sunderland to show Arthur Rowley the damage to Vince Landa's car. Stafford said it had taken 'a bump and a bang' and needed to be repaired at once as Landa was returning from Spain the following Monday. But there were no panel beaters at the Wheatsheaf, explained Rowley, so the car had to be taken to Roker Car Sprays on East Wickham Road in Sunderland, where they'd be able to fix it.

Dennis and Michael Luvaglio, borrowing another car from Rowley, went on from the Wheatsheaf to the Social Club Services offices in Low Row and it was there, during the afternoon, that they said they first heard the news on the radio of Angus's death. To begin with, it sounded as if he'd been in some sort of accident but, when the pair went back to the Wheatsheaf to watch the six o'clock news on Arthur Rowley's office TV, Sibbet was described as having been shot. Rowley and other witnesses at the garage said that Michael was visibly 'shattered and almost feinted' before Stafford helped him into their car and drove them back to Peterlee, where Pat Burgess and Salena Jones gave Michael some aspirin and put him to bed.

Dennis Stafford was in bed too – very early by his standards – wearing pyjamas but not asleep when the doorbell at Westmoreland Rise rang at 10:20pm that evening. Pausing to put on a silk dressing gown and slippers, Stafford went downstairs and opened the door. It was Detective Superintendent John Collinson of Durham CID and he asked both Dennis and Michael Luvaglio to accompany him to Peterlee police station. Dennis, notably cool under pressure and protesting, 'This is ridiculous,' went upstairs and woke Michael. They both got dressed and then, about ten minutes later, and without saying goodbye to Pat and Salena, came back down, left the house and got in the back of DS Collinson's unmarked police car.

What Stafford and Luvaglio didn't know is that the 'murder room' at Peterlee had received a phone call earlier that afternoon from a local Sunderland PC who had gone to the Wheatsheaf garage with a routine enquiry about a tax disc. While he was there, he was told that a nearly new red E-type Jaguar belonging to Vince Landa had been brought in, damaged, that morning and was now at Roker Car Sprays for repairs. The phone call coincided with a discovery made by Superintendent Arthur Chapman and his men, who had found traces of red paint on the Jaguar Mark X consistent with it having been in a collision with another car.

Frank Morgan had promptly gone over to Roker Car Sprays and taken photographs of the damage to the rear end of the E-type, which was then towed under police escort back to the fire station in Peterlee, where further paint samples were taken. Morgan also talked to Arthur Rowley at the Wheatsheaf and established that Michael Luvaglio and Dennis Stafford had been in possession of the car when it appeared to have been in an accident – possibly near Pesspool bridge – the previous night.

DS Collinson said that Michael was 'in a certain amount of distress' as he went with him to the police station, where he was the first to be interviewed by Ronald Kell between 12:20am and 1:15am. Michael recounted his and Stafford's movements over the previous twenty-four hours, including the intended meeting with Angus Sibbet at the Birdcage that had never taken place, and expressed his shock and sadness at the death of his 'good friend'.

Kell pressed him on exactly what time he and Dennis had left Peterlee to drive to Newcastle and what time they had got there.

Following the pathologist's report, Kell was looking at a theory that the murder may have been committed between 11:15pm and midnight. Two witnesses had already come forward to say that they had seen a red E-type Jaguar and a dark-green Jaguar Mark X saloon travelling together in the vicinity of Pesspool Bridge between those times. Henry Johnson, a miner, was waiting for a bus in South Hetton at 11:45pm when the two cars passed him heading towards Easington village on the A182. His bus arrived four minutes later and was going in the same direction. Joseph Knight, a thirty-one-year-old schoolteacher, was driving home from Houghton le Spring to Thornley when, at the crossroads of the A182 and the B1285, he came up behind a red E-type and a Mark X travelling together in the same direction. The E-type was in front and he said he was surprised that two such powerful cars were going so slowly. He overtook them near the Cosy bingo hall and turned right to go towards Haswell but he couldn't remember the precise time. The Mark X was also seen stationary under the bridge by several other passing motorists between 12:25am and 12:50am, leading Kell to suspect that the shooting had taken place before 12:.25am and before Luvaglio and Stafford drove back to Newcastle to secure an alibi.

The forty-six-year-old Kell, a wartime naval officer who had been a policeman since he was demobbed in 1945, saw Michael as the potential weak link who could help the police incriminate Dennis Stafford – the professional criminal, dual prison escaper and serial flaunter of authority – who the detective superintendent and his colleagues already liked for the killing. He later told Michael's Newcastle solicitor, Henry Mincoff, that the police knew his client hadn't committed the murder and that, if he just said that Stafford had left him for an hour or an hour and a half on the night of the 5th, he would not be charged. But Michael doggedly maintained that he and Stafford had spent most of the daytime of 4th January and all of that night together until they went to bed at 3am. Mincoff warned him that, in alibiing Stafford, he was placing himself in grave jeopardy.

After Michael's interrogation, it was the turn of Dennis, the fun-loving criminal, who was grilled by Kell in the presence of his solicitor, Graham Andrews, beginning at 1:45am. He refused to make a formal statement and would only answer questions about his movements. The interview lasted until 3am and then, even though it was still less than twenty-four hours since Angus Sibbet's body had been found under Pesspool bridge, Stafford and Luvaglio were both cautioned and told that they were being held on suspicion of murder. Kell had no gun and had as yet been unable to ascribe a motive for the killing, but he was working on a supposition that there had been a falling-out among thieves, which is how he regarded the bandit men of Vince Landa's Social Club Services who had come up from London and corrupted the good working people of the north-east, and he suspected that money was at the root of it.

The detective superintendent had also come into the possession of another intriguing piece of circumstantial evidence, handed to him by an emotional Doreen Hall at Peterlee police station at 9:15pm that evening. It was a note written by Angus Sibbet that he had left for her at St George's Terrace the previous night. 'I am meeting Mick at Shiney Row tonight at 11:15,' it said. 'He wants me to spring a back off a machine for him. I am sure I will not be able to do it. But I must try I suppose. I will ring. Just come home for some tools. Love and Love and Love and Love and Love and Love and Love and Love and Love And Kisses xxxxx.' Anyone who knew Angus well, and that most definitely included Doreen Hall, could have told DS Kell that he usually called Michael Luvaglio 'Mick', not 'Mike', although he did sometimes refer to his Irish minder and occasional driver, Thomas 'Paddy' Hallett, as 'Mick'.

The note was never presented in court as it was deemed to be hearsay evidence. But it was in the back of Kell's mind as he and his men recovered two suits and some of the shirts that Dennis Stafford had taken to Zip Cleaners and, along with some items of Michael's clothing, sent them for examination by Norman Lee, the principal scientific officer at the northern forensics laboratory. He was also given the red paint fragments found on the damaged Mark X bumper by Superintendent Chapman, hair, blood and urine samples taken from Stafford and Luvaglio, and a bloodstained page from the telephone directory found in the call box at South Hetton.

As the investigation continued to gather speed, the police heard from two more potentially crucial witnesses who'd been in South Hetton on the night of 5th January. James Golden, a thirty-three-year-old miner, said that he'd finished his shift at the colliery at 11:15pm. He showered, changed and then set off home on his bicycle, going in the direction of Easington. He was on the A182 around 11:40/11:45pm (he said it was more like 11:50pm in his first statement but later changed his mind) when he was passed by two cars – a red E-type Jaguar and a Jaguar Mark X saloon – going about 60mph and travelling together.

The other witness was Nora Burnip, a farmer's wife who lived with her husband, James, at West Moor Farm, 250 yards from the A182 and about a quarter of a mile away from Pesspool bridge.

She was in bed but not asleep that night when she heard two loud cracks around 12:20am. She had got up and looked out of her bedroom window and couldn't see anything but now, having heard about the murder, she wondered if they could have been gunshots. DS Kell was wondering too and, at 9:40pm on the night of 6th January, Dennis Stafford and Michael Luvaglio were officially charged with Angus Sibbet's murder.

The news that the killers had been tracked down already, less than forty-eight hours after the shooting, electrified the local media. DS Kell had a reputation for speedy enquiries but this was unprecedented, even by his standards. He wasn't the only one who was pushing for a swift resolution either. Powerful political figures like T Dan Smith and the Durham Police Authority chairman, Alderman Andrew Cunningham, busy milking the construction boom in the north-east and their connection to John Poulson, didn't want trigger-happy cockney gangsters moving in and turning Newcastle into London or Chicago. Conflict and racketeering was as bad for their business as it was for the Americans running the Colony Club down south. Maybe Luvaglio and Stafford were guilty. Maybe they weren't. But getting somebody convicted – and soon – and shutting the story down was in all their interests.

At 9am on the morning of 7th January, the accused were brought in handcuffs to Peterlee Magistrates Court for a hearing. They were surrounded by fifteen uniformed police officers and a dog handler. Dennis Stafford, trying to maintain his usual sartorial standards, was in a grey suit and waistcoat with a white shirt and a blue striped tie. Michael Luvaglio was in a white open-necked shirt and a blue suit. There were about thirty people in the public gallery, including the distraught Pat Burgess and Salena Jones, and they heard Michael and Dennis described as 'company directors' of Victoria Enterprises Ltd, former owners of the Piccadilly Club, while Angus Sibbet, awarded in death the status he'd always craved in his lifetime, was referred to as 'a gaming chief'. The proceedings lasted little more than twenty minutes and ended with both men being remanded in custody to Durham prison. The press – local and national – were out in force and, in their copy that day and the next morning, there was feverish talk of gambling wars beginning in the north-east and possible attempts to free Stafford and Luvaglio by force. As far as some of the journalists were concerned, Michael's Italian surname was the only clue they needed. The Mafia were in Newcastle.

A large consignment of police officers spent the rest of that day, January 7th and the days that followed on their hands and knees conducting a minute search of the A182 in the vicinity of West Moor Farm. Beneath grey skies and in icy winds, they scoured the road and the verge between the entrance to the farm and the right turn, fifty yards on, into Pesspool Lane, which ran across open country towards Haswell. Late on the afternoon of the 7th, they found red and amber Perspex fragments and other debris in the lane. On the 9th, they found clear glass and more amber and Perspex and a mirror-type reflector on the A182 about a quarter of a mile from South Hetton. Then, on 10th January, they found a pair of spectacles, more glass, flakes of red and green paint and the Mark X's front number plate, leaving little doubt that the two cars had collided thereabouts. They still had no luck in finding the murder weapon but, on the afternoon of the 10th, they discovered seven spent cartridge cases: two on the left-hand side of the road going towards Easington, one on the kerb, one beside it on the path and three others on the other side of the road, one of them in the gutter, eighteen feet away from the rest.

On 16th January, the pathologist, Dr Jack Ennis, testified at the official coroner's inquest into Angus Sibbet's death, affirming that his estimated time of death was between midnight and 4am – a much bigger window than the one Kell and the police were focusing on.

Two days later, Angus's funeral took place at St Nicholas's Cemetery in Newcastle. The cortege set out from the house in Mountside Gardens he had bought with Brenda and included his sister Sheila and his elder brother James, who had been dismissed by Social Club Services the previous year. There were over 150 mourners, many of them Angus's night club friends, including Morris Levy, Alex Spandler, Edna Anderson, Tommy Oxley, the band leader George Ricco and other staff from the Dolce Vita, where he'd spent his last night. Plain-clothes police officers mingled with the crowd and, despite the wintry weather, the doors of the sandstone chapel were left open so that all of those who had to stand on the forecourt outside could hear the service. Angus and Brenda's six-year-old daughter, Karen, was not at the funeral but a special bouquet from her lay with her mother's red roses on top of the coffin.

There were many other bouquets, some of them extravagant tributes that would have done justice to a Chicago gangster's funeral in the days of Al Capone. One of them had a simple card attached, which said it had been 'sent by Mr Vincent Landa', who had returned to Britain from Majorca on 9th January as expected but, whether he missed his old friend and one time partner or not, he wasn't present at the cemetery.

CHAPTER TWELVE

ON WEDNESDAY, 15TH February, Dennis Stafford and Michael Luvaglio were back in Peterlee Magistrates Court for the committal hearing, which was like a dress rehearsal for the trial proper and an opportunity to test witnesses and get evidence on the record. Undeterred by showers of rain and sleet, crowds queued outside from 8am. Those who succeeded in getting in heard a statement from Stafford's solicitor, Graham Andrews, complaining about the conditions in which his client was being held in Durham prison, where he was only allowed to eat food with a spoon. The Home Office had said these measures were necessary to 'maintain good discipline' and deny the prisoner the kind of escape opportunities he had seized in the past in Dartmoor and Wormwood Scrubs. Andrews alleged Dennis was being 'treated like an animal' and, with a literary flourish, compared his experience to that of the falsely accused Edmund Dantes in *The Count of Monte Cristo*. It wasn't clear if Joe Stafford's son was familiar with the Alexandre Dumas novel but he liked the nickname.

The court was treated to a brief summary of the evidence collected so far by Norman Lee of the northern forensic laboratory, who said that the red-paint debris recovered from Michael Luvaglio's jacket and Dennis Stafford's suit was identical to the paint on the red E-type. He believed that most of the blood from the deceased's clothing would not have been present until sometime after his death so anyone handling the body straight after the shooting would have been unlikely to acquire much on their person. But having examined Michael Luvaglio's trousers, he had found a small bloodstain on the inside of the waistband. The blood belonged to Group A – the same as Angus Sibbet's – although he didn't say that A was the second largest blood group in the country, accounting for roughly a third of all NHS patients. Lee admitted that he had also found bloodstains on the transmission tunnel of the Jaguar Mark X. They were 'relatively fresh' but belonged to a different blood group to Angus Sibbet and to Michael Luvaglio and Dennis Stafford. He declined to estimate precisely how long the blood had been there – 'probably no more than three or four days' was all he'd say – but the disclosure was invaluable to the lawyers preparing Stafford's and Luvaglio's defence. It opened up the possibility that either Angus had had a passenger in his car that night or that someone other than Michael and Dennis Stafford had been involved in the shooting.

Was it also entirely coincidental that on the night of 16th February, halfway through the committal hearing, there was another violent incident in Newcastle that may have had a direct bearing on the case? It concerned Angus Sibbet's former minder and occasional driver, Paddy Hallett, who had also acted as a bodyguard for Tom Jones when he was on Tyneside. The thirty-three-year-old Hallett was leaving the Birdcage Club at 2am after having a drink with the singer Vince Hill and his wife. He was walking along Cross Street and heading towards his car when he heard an engine revving loudly behind him and turned round to see a grey Jaguar saloon driving straight at him at speed. At the wheel was Robert Snowdon, a former doorman at the Piccadilly Club, and there were three other men in the car with him: Malcolm Tully, Kenneth McKenna and George Stewart, who yelled out of the open window, 'This is for you, you fucking grass.'

Hallett, who had no doubt they meant to kill or seriously wound him, jumped out of the car's path and started running back the way he'd come, turning left into Friar's Alley, which led to the Dolce Vita car park. He was pursued by Stewart, who was brandishing a knife and shouting, 'I'm going to make sure you don't talk.' The two men started fighting just as Constable James Herron, who had been on foot patrol in Westgate Street and heard the sound of screeching tyres, appeared at the top of the alley. Stewart turned and ran back the way he'd come, and Hallett and the PC chased after him. PC Robert Pattinson, Heron's fellow beat-patrol officer, saw Stewart and the other three men dash into Bower's late-night restaurant in Pink Lane and, when Hallett and the two PCs followed them, they saw Tully point at the Irishman and say, 'Let me at him. I'll murder him.'

Stewart, Tully, Snowdon and McKenna were all arrested and charged with GBH and attempted wounding. Refusing to give fingerprints, they were remanded in custody until 24th February leaving open important questions that begged an explanation. Was Hallett expected to give evidence at the Peterlee hearing the next day? Evidence for the defence or the prosecution? Might someone have been anxious to make sure that he didn't mention that meeting with 'Mick' that Angus Sibbet was supposed to have had in Shiney Row at 11pm on 4th January? Might they also have been afraid that Paddy Hallett would reveal who had set him and Michael Luvaglio up as bait to lure Angus to his death?

Whoever was behind it, the attack on Hallett was another instance of the kind of lurid publicity that gaming-club figures, politicians and city bosses like T Dan Smith (who was meeting the PM Harold Wilson at Newcastle Airport on 17th February) were desperate to avoid. From the point of view of Michael Luvaglio and Dennis Stafford, it was also the worst kind of background to their forthcoming trial, which was due to begin at Newcastle Assizes on 6th March. Public opinion, aggravated by dramatic headlines ever since the Battle of Mr Smith's Club the previous year, was in a state of heightened anxiety about organised crime and increasingly suspicious of 'gaming executives' with Italian names. The Home Office, sensing the prevailing wind, could feel a backlash against the libertarian atmosphere created by the 1960 Betting and Gaming Act and Roy Jenkins, in possession of fresh intelligence acquired by the FBI, decided – none too soon, some would say – that it was time to crack down on the Americans in London.

The impetus came from Herb Itkin, the labour lawyer and FBI informer who had infiltrated Mafia families on the Eastern Seaboard. The evidence Itkin supplied to the US Justice Department helped convict Tony 'Ducks' Corallo, the Lucchese family crime boss who had sent Gabe Forman to London in 1961 to set up Las Vegas Coin and start selling American gaming machines in the UK. Itkin's testimony laid bare the extent of Mob involvement in gambling in London, especially at the Colony Club and, on 25th February, the club's seventy-one-year-old frontman, George Raft, who was 'on holiday in the US at the time', was refused permission to return to Britain. His exclusion was announced by the Home Office in a letter to his solicitor, Joel Tarlo. The decision that the old movie star's 'continued presence in the UK would not be conducive to the public good' had been taken by the Home Secretary personally and there was no right of appeal.

Raft, who was at home in Beverley Hills, put on a good performance as always, claiming to be 'at a loss to understand' why he'd been barred. 'I regard London as my second home,' he said. 'I pay taxes there and here too. I have no idea what it's all about.' He'd been planning to fly back to Heathrow on Sunday, 26th February but 'now I don't know what to do. I'd hate to land there and just be an embarrassment.' Alfred Salkind, the straw man and puppet owner of the Colony, decried the Home Office action as 'completely unjustified', adding that there had 'never been any suggestion of trouble' at the club (which was true), while the Miss World promoter, Eric Morley, chairman of the 400-strong British Gaming Association, chipped in helpfully too, saying that he'd had 'no complaints' about the Colony, which was 'a bona fide member organisation'.

The smooth running and absence of trouble at the Colony and at the Pair of Shoes in Hertford Street was down to the skilful management of Dino Cellini. The fifty-one-year-old, who held 9 of the 220 shares in the Colony, had originally been admitted to Britain for 12 months under the 1953 Aliens Act, which stated that a person may be allowed in providing he or she 'is in a position to support themselves', and now he was applying for an extension. But the public mood was not favourable. Roy Jenkins had spoken further in Parliament about gambling clubs providing outlets for swapping hot money for gaming chips and then cashing the chips in for clean cash. He'd also warned of the risks of credit betting encouraging gamblers to play for stakes they couldn't afford. As gambling debts were not enforceable by law in the UK at the time, it was an incentive to gangsters to use strong-arm tactics to recover the money and stage brawls in clubs to alarm the clientele and compel the owners to pay them for protection. The police, he said, were confronted by a boom in protection rackets with Scotland Yard in the midst of their 'biggest ever gang-busting operation'. Did that mean that professional villains – British or American – were looking to move out of the capital and set up elsewhere? In Newcastle, the Las Vegas of the north, for example?

In the public mind, the whole gambling firmament, welcomed as an end to post-war parsimony in 1960, now seemed to be under suspicion and associated with corruption, with little distinction between high rollers playing roulette and chemin de fer in Mayfair – or Catford or Newcastle – and the bandit men supplying gaming machines to working-men's clubs.

It was against this backdrop that Durham CID continued to try to hone their case against Michael Luvaglio and Dennis Stafford. Timing – and a very tight schedule – was at the heart of their case. On the night of Saturday, 4th March, two days before the trial was due to begin, Detective Superintendent Arthur Chapman and DS Frank Morgan drove an E-type Jaguar from Pesspool Lane in South Hetton to the Birdcage Club in Newcastle. The car was similar to the one Luvaglio and Stafford had been driving on the night of 5th January. With Morgan at the wheel, the detectives set out at 11:44pm and arrived at the club at 12:31 am, including three stops of a total of nine minutes and stops at traffic lights totalling one minute. On the way, they said they obeyed all speed restrictions and never went above 70mph. The police contention was that the murder had taken place between 11:50 and 11:54am and the test drive was designed to prove that Luvaglio and Stafford could have committed it and still got to the Birdcage, and their alibi, by half past midnight.

The police theory was that Michael and Dennis had left Westmoreland Rise in Peterlee at more like 11pm than 11:30 and driven up the A182 and then on to the B1284 north of South Hetton, where they had intercepted Angus Sibbet, who was coming down the A182 from Newcastle. Both cars stopped, reckoned DS Kell, and one of Luvaglio or Stafford got out and got in beside Sibbet in the Mark X and then the E-type turned around and the cars headed back down the A182 towards South Hetton, possibly under the pretext of continuing on towards Stafford's house in Peterlee.

About half a mile past South Hetton, the E-type came to an abrupt halt and the Mark X collided with the back of it. Either Dennis Stafford or Michael Luvaglio then got out and shot Angus Sibbet at close range and the two men manhandled the body into the back of the Mark X, getting Sibbet's coat jammed in the door. Then, with one of them driving the Mark X and the other the E-type, they drove on – which was when James Golden saw them – before turning right into Pesspool Lane, which was as dark as it was narrow, where they hastily attempted to clean the Mark X and wipe away the evidence. They then continued up Pesspool Lane to Haswell, where they turned right again on to the B1280 before re-joining the A182 west of South Hetton, going in the direction of Easington and most probably intending to dispose of the body in the North Sea. But close to Pesspool bridge, the Mark X had stalled due to overheating from the damaged radiator so they abandoned it, leaving the heater and the windscreen wipers on, and drove at speed – on icy roads in

January – back to Newcastle, where they were seen arriving at the Birdcage Club between 12:20 and 12:30am.

There was a lot of speculation involved and the forensic evidence was far from conclusive but the forensic-science expert, Norman Lee, had said that, in his opinion, there could be no doubt that the two cars had been in a collision on the A182, not just due to the cross transference of paint but also because they had found a tiny bit of aluminium, which was obviously the tip of the U on the Mark X's MUP number plate, and because a circular mark on the M had been caused by the exhaust pipes of the E-type. Lee also said that five cartridge cases from a .32-calibre pistol found scattered beside the A182 exactly fitted the bullets lodged in the woodwork of the Mark X and in Angus Sibbet's body.

All they had to do now was prove their case in court.

CHAPTER THIRTEEN

ONE OF THE most ironic moments in the 'One-Armed Bandit Murder Trial', as it became known, came when one of the barristers solemnly told the court that the defendants were 'not on trial for their lifestyle', whereas both the prosecution and the judge, Mr Justice Patrick McCarthy O'Connor, made continual tart references not only to Luvaglio's and Stafford's involvement with clubland and gambling but also to their domestic arrangements and the fact that they lived with women who were not their wives. The inference to the jury was unmistakeable: the accused were part of a low-life culture that ordinary, decent, working people would be repelled by, making them all the more likely to find the men guilty of murder.

Unfortunately for Michael and Dennis, the news agenda that fortnight seemed to be dominated by stories of crime and criminals, be they real or fictitious versions. In the US, Jimmy Hoffa – the President and 'Grand Caliph' of the Teamsters Union and unofficial banker to the Mob – had been ordered to surrender to US Marshals on 8th March. After years of evading justice, Hoffa had finally been convicted of jury tampering, attempted bribery and fraud, and was facing a thirteen-year stretch in Lewisburg federal penitentiary. (President Richard Nixon commuted his sentence in 1971 in return for Hoffa's guarantee that the Teamsters Union would support Nixon's re-election campaign the following year).

In Britain, Frankie Fraser's sister, Mrs Evelyn Brindle, and Charlie Richardson's secretary were charged with jury tampering and attempts to pervert the cause of justice ahead of the Richardson gang 'torture trial', which would shock the nation when it began in April. At the same time, the 'Great Train Robber', Ronald 'Buster' Edwards, who had been captured in June 1966 and depicted as a more traditional and less threatening villain than the Richardsons and Krays, announced that he was dropping his appeal against his twenty-five-year prison sentence. His decision proved handy publicity for the new film *Robbery*, which started location shooting in London on 6th March. Starring Stanley Baker, who was a friend of Albert Dimes and other underworld faces, and directed by Peter Yates, who went on to make *Bullit* with Steve McQueen, it was loosely based on the Great Train Robbery. Filming began in an abandoned secondary school in Notting Hill, which had been transformed into the Aylesbury court room where the real train robbers' trial had taken place in 1963. Ironically, George Raft had been due to play a supporting role but his untimely exclusion by the Home Office meant that Baker and his co-producer, Michael Deeley, had to look elsewhere.

Baker had hoped that *Robbery* would have an edgy and hard-boiled feel, unlike the cliché-ridden cosiness of traditional British gangster films like *The Blue Lamp*. He and Yates weren't quite able to pull it off and British cinema would have to wait another four years for the definitive example of the genre. But even as the cameras were rolling in west London, Lord Ted Willis, creator of the archetypal cosy and avuncular police TV drama *Dixon of Dock Green*, was warning the House of Lords that London had become 'a dirty city' awash with vice and gambling and that, as long as there was 'easy money' to be made, the mobsters and racketeers would continue to 'flow in like rats'.

Strong words and as likely to have lodged in the minds of the jury in Newcastle as the words to Engelbert Humperdinck's first chart-topping single, 'Please Release Me, Let Me Go', which was the official number one in the week beginning 6th March. The singer, whose real name was Arnold Dorsey, was already a regular performer at the Dolce Vita in Newcastle and was due to appear on *Top of the Pops* on Thursday, 9th March. That same evening, the BBC began a repeat of series two of *The Likely Lads*, the comedy about two young, working-class men from Tyneside starring James Bolam and Rodney Bewes and written by Dick Clement and the Northumberland-born Ian la Fresnais. The interplay between the two leads, one of them streetwise and cynical, the other aspiring to middle-class respectability, was witty and sharp, often resulting in unintended trouble and embarrassment.

The two likely lads on trial for the One-Armed Bandit Murder were Londoners, not Geordies: men who'd come north to make their fortune. But they, too, had contrasting personalities and aspirations. Michael, a devout 'young Catholic gentleman', as they were called at his school in the 1950s, unmarried and close to his mother and father, had only ever wanted to build a profitable and respected business in the gaming industry, whereas Dennis, the Jewish East End wide boy with the rampant sex drive and the tailor-made suits, liked to parade his rule-breaking flair like an animal marking his territory with his distinctive scent.

Michael Luvaglio had never been in a court room before in his life. Dennis Stafford had been in several, from London to Newcastle to Port of Spain, but, despite his innate self-confidence, neither Dennis nor Michael could fail to have been intimidated by the Grade 1-listed building that was the setting for their trial. Designed by John Stokoe in the Greek Revival style and built in 1811, Moot Hall feels like an overwhelming statement of authority and power. Steep steps lead up to the double doors at the front, flanked by four giant columns reminiscent of a federal building in Washington DC. The cells where prisoners are confined when the court is not in session are down in the basement and have their own separate entrance at the back.

The building opposite the courthouse used to be the headquarters of Northumberland County Council. Constructed in 1910, it's now the Vermont Hotel, its chunky exterior and darkly lit interiors and bar feeling more American than British: a steel town maybe, like Cleveland or Pittsburgh. The view beyond the hotel is of traffic flowing over the iconic Tyne bridge and trains clattering over the railway arch. On one side of Moot Hall, a steep and narrow stairway drops fifty feet down to the Quayside and the river and, in 1967, with redevelopment only just beginning, the terraced streets and back-to-back houses of Gateshead climbed uninterrupted up the hill on the opposite side.

It's less than a ten-minute walk from Moot Hall to Newcastle Central Station and Dennis Stafford had let it be known that he'd ordered champagne to be put on ice in the Royal Station Hotel, confidently expecting that both he and Michael would get off. It was the job of Mr Henry Scott, QC, leading counsel for the prosecution, and his number two, Richard Castle, to make sure that they didn't.

Press and public interest was at fever pitch and the court was packed each day of the five-and-a-half-day trial. Michael's parents, Maud and Frank Luvaglio, and Pat Burgess and Salena Jones were present every day in the public gallery. The presiding judge was a Catholic like Michael but from a very different background. O'Connor had been educated at Downside and Merton College, Oxford, and was a future chairman of the Downside Old Boys Association. The fifty-two-year-old, who had only been appointed a High Court judge in 1966, listened impassively that Monday morning as Mr Scott made his opening statement.

'This is predominantly a case, ghastly and hideous as this murder was,' Scott began, 'which is not without a certain grim fascination in the part, you the jury, can play in assessing the evidence and the reconstructions which have been made.' He described the body found in the back seat of the Jaguar Mark X under Pesspool bridge in South Hetton, the car that had seized up due to damage to the radiator and the bullet wounds found on the body of Angus Sibbet, who had been 'killed in a most wicked and atrocious manner'. The Crown's contention was that Luvaglio and Stafford, who were described again as 'company directors', had murdered Sibbet near where the car was found, most probably because he was suspected of 'skimming', or stealing money, from their business behind their backs, and then hurried back to Newcastle to try to give themselves an alibi.

The prosecution would show, said Scott, that Angus Sibbet's Jaguar and a red E-type Jaguar belonging to Michael Luvaglio's brother had been in a collision near South Hetton. Evidence that the police had recovered nearby included cartridge cases, plastic and other fragments, spectacles and paint samples that matched the two vehicles. Despite there being no eyewitnesses to the crime, the prosecution were relying on what he called 'the eloquent testimony of the two cars involved'. He implied that the defendants had intended to drive Sibbet's body away in the Mark X after the killing and dump it, perhaps in the sea, which was less than ten miles away, but that the car seized up and had to be abandoned.

To the surprise of many, Tom Leak, the shot-firer who had first discovered Angus's body under the bridge at 5:15am on 5th January, was not called as a witness. But his friend and colleague, Leslie Marshall, who had tried and failed to find a pulse, was. The court also heard from Nora Burnip about the loud cracks she heard at 12:20am on the night of 4th/5th January and from James Golden, who repeated his story about cycling home at around 11:45am and being passed by the two cars, going about 60mph and 'travelling so close together'. Questioned by the owlish Rudolph Lyons, QC, appearing for Dennis Stafford, Golden admitted that he heard no subsequent shots or squealing of brakes.

Henry Johnson described how he'd been at the bus stop in South Hetton at approximately 11:46pm when he was passed by the two Jaguars heading in the direction of Easington and saw one person in the E-type and two in the saloon. Then the prosecution called George Wells, a retired miner who lived opposite Stafford and Salena Jones in Peterlee and who said he saw the red E-type leave Westmoreland Rise at approximately 11pm on the night of 5th January, but then seemed in some doubt about the precise time when challenged by the defence.

There was lengthy testimony from Stanley Denton, the Senior Experimental Officer at the Gosforth Forensic Laboratory and an expert on cases involving firearms, explosives and road-traffic accidents. Renowned for assiduous analysis and reporting, the Yorkshire-born Denton explained how and where he believed the collision between the two cars had taken place on the A182, with the Mark X first overtaking the E-type and then the E-type overtaking in turn and coming to a halt, which was when the other car ran into the back of it.The evidence about the two cars was crucial to the prosecution case. But what the press were waiting for were details of Angus's 'colourful love life', as it was referred to, and his former driver, Albert Ginley, went into some detail about it as he was questioned about Angus's movements on the day and night before his death. Explaining that he'd worked for him for about eighteen months, he admitted that, as well as his wife, Mr Sibbet had had 'two lady friends', one 'disposed in Gateshead and the other in the Newcastle area'. Ginley confirmed that, on 4th January, he'd driven Sibbet to a meeting with Luvaglio and Stafford in Sunderland then taken him back to his marital home in Dunston before conveying him first to Joyce Hall's flat in Gateshead and then on to her sister Doreen Hall's house in St George's Terrace in Jesmond, where he himself rented a room. He left Angus there and went off to see his own girlfriend, returning to St George's Terrace later that night, where he heard the phone ring around 1:20am and Doreen answer it, but he never saw Angus Sibbet again.

Asked to describe Angus's job, Ginley used the fateful phrase about him 'collecting the harvest' from the bandit machines. Angus was always 'lavish with money', he said and, when they turned up at one of the working-men's clubs, he would 'put on an act of being a big man and one of the heads of the company.' The company in question being Social Club Services, Mr Scott reminded the jury, which was owned by Michael Luvaglio and his brother Vincent.

Under cross examination by Raymond Dean, QC, for Michael, and his junior, Peter Taylor (who would go on to be a High Court judge presiding over the Jeremy Thorpe trial in 1979 and the Hillsborough Inquiry ten years later, eventually becoming Lord Chief Justice), the thirty-year-old Ginley feigned ignorance of Angus's minder, 'Paddy' Hallett. But he added pointedly that Angus had been a good friend of Michael Luvaglio, who was a friend of Dennis Stafford, whereas Sibbet and Stafford had rarely met, perhaps no more than half-a-dozen times in eighteen months.

Matthew Dean, the doorman at the Birdcage Club, testified that Dennis Stafford had called him outside into Stowell Street at around 1:20am on 5th January to look at the back of the red E-type, which appeared to have sustained some damage. Then Angus's lovers, Doreen and Joyce Hall, were called – the two sisters looking remarkably similar to the actress Mary Ure, who was married to Robert Shaw and had played Jimmy Porter's wife, Alison, opposite Richard Burton in the film version of *Look Back in Anger*. Pale, pretty and soft spoken, they corroborated Albert Ginley's account of Angus's movements on that final day and night up to the moment when he'd left Joyce, James and the others at their table in the Dolce Vita. The note that Doreen had found telling her that he was going to meet 'Mick' at Shiney Row at 11pm that night was never presented: you'd have to pass through the village of Shiney Row if you were on your way from Newcastle to South Hetton but the prosecution agreed with the police that the note would be struck out as hearsay.

On Wednesday, 10th March, the pathologist, Dr Jack Ennis, took the stand and testified as to the nature of Angus's bullet wounds and his estimated time of death. He admitted that he hadn't known that the local GP, Dr Seymour Hunter, had detected rigor mortis when he'd looked at the body before Ennis arrived at Pesspool bridge on the morning of 5th January. He was subjected to a lengthy cross examination by Rudolph Lyons for Stafford, who repeatedly asked why he hadn't taken the body temperature earlier and why he had changed his original estimate of the time of death from midnight to 4am to between midnight and 1am, which fitted the police and prosecution case more conveniently. Ennis repeated what he'd said before at the magistrate's hearing in Peterlee. He would have 'disturbed the body', he said, if he had examined it in the car and had no choice other than to wait until the afternoon when it was in the mortuary. He also re-affirmed his view that none of Sibbet's wounds happened in the car. If he had been shot by someone sitting behind him, as Mr Lyons suggested, he would have fallen out on his side, not on the front. 'It is possible to fall with the chest upwards,' said Lyons but Ennis was adamant. 'I don't see any soiling at the back, which I would have expected in that case.' He reiterated his belief that two of the shots were inflicted while Sibbet was in a semi-crouching position facing the line of fire and that death was due to 'a haemorrhage caused by the bullet wounds to the aorta and heart.'

George Price, the ballistics expert from the Home Office laboratory in Nottingham, was called and produced a 7.65mm Walther automatic pistol for the jury to see. He said he thought this was the type that had been used to kill Angus Sibbet. He'd examined the Mark X Jaguar and found a bullet hole in the woodwork at the top back of the driver's seat. He'd later examined three 7.65 bullets found in Angus Sibbet's body and concluded that they were capable of being fired from a self-loading Walther.

He pointed to bullet holes in the dead man's overcoat and said that some of them were surrounded by an intense area of blackening and powdering, which suggested that the pistol was very close to, or actually touching, the overcoat when it was fired.

Raymond Dean, QC, for Michael Luvaglio, pressed Price to explain why there was no residue found on either Michael's or Dennis Stafford's clothing, surely impossible if one of them had actually fired the gun. Price countered by saying that, when a pistol of this type was discharged under certain circumstances, there may be a residue on the firer's hand – which he assumed the accused had hastily cleaned up after the killing – but he would not expect residues on the firer's clothing, providing the gun was fired 'in the orthodox manner'.

The testimony of Denton, Ennis and Price was perceived as vital to the success or failure of the prosecution case. What came next was more in the realm of circumstantial evidence.

Mary Crammen, the manageress of Zip Cleaners in Peterlee, confirmed that Stafford had come in early on the morning of 5th January with a consignment of suits and shirts. But questioned by Rudolph Lyons for the defence, she added that Dennis was a regular customer and that it was not unusual for him to bring in several suits a week.

Crammen was followed into the witness box by James Sibbet, who said that the last time he saw Angus alive was around 9:45pm on the night of 4th January and then described the harrowing experience of going to formally identify his brother's corpse in Easington mortuary the next day. He said that Angus often carried hundreds of pounds' worth of slot-machine takings around with him, a detail that Mr Scott offered to the jury as perhaps another contributory factor behind the murder. Was Angus's bounty legitimate profit or cash he'd been stealing from Vincent and Michael Luvaglio?

What Scott didn't say was that Angus always carried the money in his leather collection bag, which was clearly visible on the dashboard of the Mark X in the police photographs taken in Peterlee on 5th January. Yet neither the bag nor any of the 'harvest' it might have contained was ever seen again. The photographs had also shown an open packet of Bahama cigars on the car dashboard. Angus's friends and lovers could have told the court that he never smoked cigars. So how did they get there? Were they ever checked for fingerprints? And had there been a cigar-smoking passenger – or a murderer biding his time – travelling with Angus in the car? These were only some of the mysteries that the trial never satisfactorily addressed.

Instead, the prosecution kept returning to their focus on the narrow timescale during which they claimed the murder had taken place on the night of 4th/5th January. Clifford Miller, a van driver from West Hartlepool, said he was driving along the A182 in the direction of Easington around 12:45am and saw the Jaguar Mark X parked under Pesspool bridge with its sidelights on and the driver's window open. And then, finally, Reuben Conroy, a lorry driver and livestock transporter, said he was heading in the opposite direction and passing under the bridge at approximately 12:50am when he, too, saw the car parked awkwardly with its sidelights on and the windscreen wipers working.

On Friday, 10th March, the defence began to present their case, attempting to chip away at the timings postulated by the prosecution. All eyes were on Salena Jones as she entered the witness box wearing a crisp, white, two-piece suit and a blue hat. As a successful and conspicuous black woman, she was still very much a novelty in the north-east in 1967. Jones testified that Dennis Stafford and Michael Luvaglio had left the house in Peterlee between 11:30 and 11:40pm on 4th January, not at 11pm as first claimed by their neighbour, George Wells. They returned, she said, between 2:30 and 2:50am. She and Pat Burgess were still up, playing Scrabble (Pat confirmed the story), but she admitted that Stafford 'must have left fairly early' the next morning as she was still asleep in bed when he went out. She said she didn't speak to him until later that day, when he rang her and asked if she'd read the papers. 'He said someone had got killed and that his name was Angus. I had only met him once.' Salena added that, when Dennis and Michael Luvaglio arrived back between 6 and 6:30pm, Michael was visibly 'in a state of shock' and she gave him tea and a tranquiliser. She said that he had not been in that state at all when the pair had come home the night before.

Pat Burgess and the cleaner, Lillian Bunker, both confirmed Salena's account that Dennis and Michael had left Peterlee around 11:30 or 11:45pm on 4th January. Pat – who said she had been living for about a year with Michael Luvaglio at Chelsea Grove – said that, when Michael and Dennis Stafford arrived at the Peterlee house at approximately 6pm on 5th January, they had 'seemed a bit shocked, especially Michael'. She and Salena had given him a cup of tea and he had gone to bed around 7pm and, at the time, she thought this was 'because his friend Angus had been killed in a motor accident'.

Lillian Bunker, who lived at Hetton-le-Hole, not far from Pesspool bridge, confirmed to Henry Scott that, early on the morning of 5th January, she had seen Dennis Stafford leaving the house carrying suits and shirts he said he was taking to the dry cleaners in Peterlee.

Thomas Feather – a bus driver on his way home and passing under Pesspool bridge at approximately 12:45am – said he saw a Mark X Jaguar parked under the bridge with its sidelights on and that he also saw an arm come out of the side window and wave him on.

Thomas Purvis, who, like Tom Leak, was a shot-firer at South Hetton Colliery, said that he passed the Jaguar under the bridge at 2:25am and saw no damage.

John Bowden, the manager of the Birdcage Club, and Allen and McGarry, who had been doing the cabaret there on the night of 4th January, said that they saw Stafford and Luvaglio at the club between 12:30 and 12:40am, looking clean, tidy and unflustered.

It was all helpful testimony up to a point but the jury, the press and the public gallery understood that Purvis and Bowden were mere supporting acts. One of the two dramatic high points of the trial came when Michael Luvaglio spent eighty-two minutes in the witness box at the end of that morning. White-faced and clutching the rail, he broke down in tears when his counsel, Raymond Dean, asked him, 'Did you shoot Angus Sibbet?' 'No sir,' he replied. 'He was a friend of mine. There was no bad blood between us.' He said that there were a number of business organisations in the area dealing with gaming machines and that competition was very keen. Newcastle Transport Club would have been a good sale. He and Angus had ideas about redecorating the whole club and installing CCTV and a disco and it would have been worth around £8,000 but they didn't get the contract. Michael had been to one committee meeting at the club before Christmas and he should have gone to another one but there was no time. On 21st December, he was leaving for

London on the night train, as he and Dennis Stafford had an early plane to catch to Majorca the next day.

While he was away, Michael told the court, he had left some financial transactions relative to the Transport Club deal in Angus Sibbet's hands and had also given him £200 of the company's money just before Christmas hoping for more sales. Questioned carefully by Raymond Dean, he said that Dennis Stafford didn't actually work for Social Club Services but that, after the fire at the Piccadilly Club, he'd been acting as a booking agent for artists at the other working-men's clubs where SCS had an agreement.

Questioned about his movements on 4th January, Michael said that, at 5pm that day, he had telephoned Angus Sibbet and asked if he would meet him at the Birdcage as arranged at 12:30am. He assured Dean and the jury that he didn't leave Peterlee for Newcastle until approximately 11:30pm in his brother's red E-type Jaguar and that the journey on icy roads via Sunderland took about thirty to forty minutes. He said that he spent fifteen minutes at his house at Chelsea Grove, waiting for a phone call from Vince that never came, and then went on to the Birdcage, arriving just before 12:30am. At around 1:20am that night, he had rung Doreen Hall in Jesmond to see if Angus was with her, but she said no.

Cross-examined by Henry Scott for the prosecution, Michael accepted that the red E-type and the Mark X Jaguar seemed to have collided, though he felt the damage to the E-type in the police photographs looked bigger than the damage he had seen outside the Birdcage Club when he and Dennis Stafford had got into the car to drive back to Peterlee. He said that they'd had to borrow his brother's car because Salena Jones might have needed her white Mercedes to go to work and there was no other option. He understood that Dennis Stafford had taken the E-type back to the Wheatsheaf on the morning of the 5th to be sure it would be repaired before Vince was due to return on 9th January.

Scott asked if Vincent Luvaglio had rung up at all on 4th January or on the 5th once the death of Angus Sibbet became known. 'I can't say for sure,' replied Michael. 'I never spoke to him . . . so not as far as I know.'

After Michael's testimony, the defence called Gladys Hill and Robert Anderson, neighbours of Michael's and Pat Burgess in Chelsea Grove, who said that they had seen a red E-type parked outside the house at midnight on the 4th. They were followed by Dorothy Brady of Spring Garden Lane, Newcastle, who worked for Vince Landa and who said she went to the Birdcage Club on the night of 4th/5th January, arriving at 12:35am, and saw Michael and Vincent Luvaglio's car, the red E-type, parked outside there but that, when she left about 1:30am, the car had gone.

When the court rose at the end of that Friday afternoon, not to resume until Monday, Michael and Dennis were driven back to Durham prison. Meanwhile, the city of Newcastle prepared to enjoy the weekend. Some of the Fleet Street reporters covering the trial had gone back to London to their offices and their families. Others stayed on to sample Tyneside hospitality in the city's pubs and clubs. Cat Stevens and the comedian Frank Carson were appearing at the Dolce Vita and the Barron Knights at the Cavendish. But the young and the curious packed into Mike Jeffrey's Club A'Gogo in Percy Street, where a twenty-four-year-old American, co-managed by Jeffrey and the Newcastle-born Chas Chandler, the former bass player of The Animals, was due to play two sets on 13th March: one at 8pm for the 'under eighteens' and the other at 2am in the Jazz Lounge.

Among the spectators that night was Gordon Sumner,

a fifteen-year-old grammar-school boy from Wallsend, who'd heard amazing things about the young guitarist who had arrived in the UK in December 1966 and had already played at Darlington Football Club, South Shields and the Kirklevington Country Club. Sumner had bought his first single, 'Hey Joe', which had reached number six in the charts, and, the following week, Jimi Hendrix would release his second big hit, 'Purple Haze', as he continued his brief but dazzling trajectory towards fame and immortality. That night in the A'Gogo, he stunned Sumner and the rest of the audience with his 'breath-taking virtuosity', leaving the teenager, who would grow up to become Sting, sleepless in bed, 'my world view significantly altered'.

There would only be another two-and-a-half years in which Sumner and other aspiring musicians, and the legion of Hendrix fans, could enjoy the unforgettable power of his live performances. When the audience attending the very different but equally compelling performance in Moot Hall re-assembled again on Monday, 16th March, the top of the bill was the self-styled 'gentleman gangster' Dennis Stafford, making his eagerly awaited appearance in the witness box.

CHAPTER FOURTEEN

IMMACULATELY TURNED OUT for the occasion, despite the deprivations he said he'd been suffering in prison, Dennis Stafford was an old hand when it came to answering questions under oath. Unlike Michael Luvaglio, whose testimony felt natural and unrehearsed, Dennis was economical and chose his words with great care.

'Did you kill Angus Sibbet?' asked his QC, Rudolph Lyons.

'No, sir,' replied Stafford.

'Were you a party to the killing?'

'No, sir,' again.

With Lyons prompting him, Stafford described how he had come up to Newcastle in 1966 at Vince Landa's behest to manage the Piccadilly Club, which was owned by Victoria Enterprises Ltd, of which Landa was the main shareholder and a director. After the Piccadilly burned down, he said, he was put in charge of booking artists for other clubs run by Vince's companies, even though he had no prior experience (which, given his involvement with George Baron and Paul Cley at the Londoner, was not strictly true). He admitted that he lived with Salena Jones, who was not his wife, and recounted the arrangement whereby Vincent Landa had promised to arrange a furnished house for him in Peterlee and a car for each of them. He said his pay was about £25/35 a week with commission on top, out of which he gave £10 a week to his estranged wife, Karen, who lived in Low Fell with their child, and he admitted owning 'about eleven' suits and having paid up to £25 each for them in London.

Like Michael had done the previous week, Stafford recounted his movements on 4th January and said that it was his fellow defendant who had invited Angus Sibbet to a meeting at the Birdcage at 12:30am that night, Sibbet's suggestion of the Dolce Vita having been discarded as too noisy. Michael had called Vincent Luvaglio in Spain earlier that day to get permission to use his brother's E-type – for which Stafford had a key – and they had left Peterlee at 11pm and stopped off at Chelsea Grove before going on to the Birdcage, where Stafford had left the car outside in the street, unlocked. Sibbet 'didn't turn up' and so Dennis went out to get some cigarettes from the car and that's when he saw the damage to the E-type and that the covers on the rear lights had been knocked off. He said that he and Michael left the Birdcage at about 2:15am, returning via Chelsea Grove, and got back to Peterlee at approximately 3am and went to bed. The next morning, he took three suits and nine shirts to the cleaners. He also said that, when Michael heard the news of Angus Sibbet's death on the television later that day, 'he almost passed out'.

Henry Scott for the prosecution paused theatrically before standing up and looking Stafford in the eye. Then he began his cross-examination. 'Was it just a coincidence?' he wondered, that at 11:15pm on 4th January, Dennis and Michael had set off from Peterlee in a red E-type Jaguar five miles away from South Hetton where the collision occurred? Stafford shrugged and kept silent. An E-type was not a common sight on these roads, was it, asked the barrister? Stafford repeated Michael's explanation that earlier that day they had phoned Vince Landa in Majorca and asked for permission to use the car. A red E-type and a Jaguar Mark X were seen going under Pesspool bridge at 11:45pm, said Scott, and later, six-tenths of a mile away from where the Mark X had been abandoned, paint and reflectors from a damaged E-type were found on the A182.

'So I have heard,' said Stafford.

'And more debris was found under the bridge,' added Scott.

'So I have heard,' said Stafford again.

'That paint is identical to the paint on your E-type Jaguar,' continued Scott.

'Apparently so,' said Stafford.

The broken glass was from the Mark X and cartridge cases from the bullets fired were found on the same stretch of road, said Scott.

'So I understand,' said Stafford.

'They fitted the bullets that killed Angus Sibbet,' said Scott.

'I don't know if they were fired from the same gun,' replied Stafford.

The prosecutor paused once again and then looked at Judge O'Connor. 'No more questions, my Lord,' he said and sat down.

With no eyewitnesses, no murder weapon and only an implied motive, the trial moved on to the concluding stages and, on the afternoon of 13th March, Henry Scott began his closing statement. Once more, he paused, as if in reflection, before commencing his address. While expressing regret for the deceased's death in passing, he depicted an immoral, licentious and high-rolling lifestyle; a London lifestyle foreign to the north-east that, by implication, applied to all the 'bandit men' and could leave no doubts about the guilt of the accused. 'Angus Sibbet was a very curious man,' he said, who had a wife and two mistresses and, on the day of his death, he had been with both of them. He 'collected the harvest' from the fruit machines, he continued, echoing Albert Ginley's words, and had been given the use of 'a very luxurious, expensive and powerful car.' It was a world in which 'the servants of Vincent Luvaglio, the brother of the accused, were well equipped with worldly goods and with money, thinking it impossible ever to travel by bus or train.'

Having completed that bit of character assassination, Scott moved on to the fateful collision that had provided the prosecution with their one indisputable and gilt-edged argument. Stafford and Luvaglio, he said, had claimed that the car accident had happened outside the Birdcage Club but, as well as the paint debris, a vital piece of evidence, forensically analysed by Stanley Denton, was a small piece of lettering from the number plate on Angus Sibbet's car, which was found by the police near the murder spot. 'If that accident happened on the A182,' said Scott, then 'these two men committed that murder. There is no other way out of it.' They were lying when they said they were in Newcastle at midnight and lying about a collision outside the club. Did the jury really believe that 'some painstaking person' would have collected the little fragments of reflector glass and Angus Sibbet's spectacles from outside the Birdcage, taken them to Pesspool Lane and dropped them there? Or collected the cartridge cases and scattered them about too?

If someone else took the car from outside the club, said Scott, they must have had a set of keys that fitted it and known they could take it, have the collision and bring the car back to the Birdcage without it being missed. Dennis Stafford had the keys all night. His excuse for going outside on 'that cold, wretched, snowy evening' was that he wanted some cigarettes from his box of duty free but 'surely it was only to draw the attention of the doorman to the damage.'

Scott finished by declaring, scornfully, that it was 'extraordinary' that Dennis should have gone to the cleaners the very next morning with a shirt that, even after cleaning, had a tiny bit of red Perspex on it . . . the same as from the lens of the red E-type.

It was then the turn of Rudolph Lyons, representing Stafford, to not only cast doubt on the prosecution's arguments but to offer a possible alternative explanation as to who or what lay behind Sibbet's murder. He suggested that 'the real killers' may have used a second red E-type deliberately in order to throw suspicion on Vince Landa, who had 'built up a very substantial business empire'. Hinting at the possibility of a gaming or gangland war, which chimed with public fears of racketeering and was the tabloids favourite theory, he suggested that, if Landa was got rid of, others would be happy to step into his shoes and get their hands on the rich pickings. 'It has fallen to your lot,' he told the jury, 'to wander through a labyrinth of contradictory and confusing evidence.' What the prosecution must prove, he went on, is that 'these two accused men shot Angus Sibbet . . . that is the vital issue . . . and the prosecution have utterly failed to prove it.'

To back up his argument, Lyons went through key points of the prosecution case, disparaging them one by one. Bloodstains had been found in Angus Sibbet's car that were not from the same group as either Sibbet, Stafford or Luvaglio. Could they have come from the real murderer? It couldn't have been Dennis Stafford or Michael Luvaglio who waved on Mr Feather under Pesspool bridge at 12:45am as, at that time, they were in Newcastle at the Birdcage Club. The prosecution had spoken of anger, lust, jealousy and greed in the gaming-machine business, but an actual motive had not been established and neither had the murder weapon been found. Had a phone call been made to lure the Mark X Jaguar to South Hetton and then the collision staged? And had a hole been made deliberately in the Mark X radiator to look as if it had been forced to stop?

Finally, Mr Lyons pointed out, Angus Sibbet was over six feet tall and weighed over thirteen stone. It would not have been easy for Stafford and Luvaglio, who were not heavily built, to lug his body off the road and into the back of the Mark X. Yet improbably, no mud was found on either of the accused and no debris from the E-type had been found on Angus Sibbet.

The following morning, Tuesday, 14th March, Raymond Dean, QC for Michael Luvaglio, made his closing pitch to the jury. 'The prosecution does not prove that a man is a murderer by proving two cars collided,' he began. 'There are too many pieces of the puzzle missing and too many that don't fit.' Echoing the proposition floated by Rudolph Lyons, he observed that the murder had 'all the hallmarks of gang warfare'. Indeed, it had been shown that Sibbet was 'not content with the image of a mere collector' but was 'lavish' with money, went about in 'flashy cars' and gave the impression to many people that 'he was the big man of the organisation'. He momentarily seemed to infer that Angus had got what he deserved as he dwelled on his infidelities and how he'd 'mastered the art of deceiving his mistresses'.

Dennis Stafford, he implied, was just as bad, going to Majorca with a woman who was neither his wife nor his mistress. 'The whole thing, to most of us, is repulsive,' said Dean, before belatedly reminding the jury that they mustn't hold this against the accused, who were not 'on trial for their morals but for murder'.

He disputed the prosecution claim – their weakest link if more had been made of it – that the shooting must have happened around 11:45/11:50pm. If so, why had James Golden, cycling by, heard nothing, let alone five gunshots. He emphasised that no blood had been found on either man, except a speck inside the waistband of Michael Luvaglio's trousers, and he reiterated the point Lyons had made about the blood found on the Mark X transmission tunnel that didn't belong to either man. 'How and when did it get there?' he asked. 'Can it be written off as irrelevant?' And wasn't a busy road like the A182 an odd place to choose to commit a murder? In Dean's view, it was 'about as stupid as one can imagine'.

With the advocacy for both the prosecution and defence now complete, all that remained was for Mr Justice O'Connor to deliver his summing up. Worryingly for Michael and Dennis, he began in a similar tone to Henry Scott on the opening day, telling the jury that they must ignore what they might consider the 'very immoral way of life of the accused' but then proceeded to dwell on what he described as their 'repellent cheating' on their wives and mistresses.

The defence counsel, he continued, had said that 'suspicion is not enough' and had claimed that only two things were proved: Angus Sibbet was murdered on the night in question and, at some point during the night, there was a collision between Sibbet's car and a red E-type. But O'Connor insisted that a lot more than that had been proved. 'Evidence shows that the collision happened on the A182 near Pesspool bridge and that Angus Sibbet was shot on the A182 about six-tenths of a mile away,' he said. Ignoring the reservations that had been expressed about the precise time of death, the judge invoked a classical analogy, noting that it was 14th March – the Ides of March. Had not Julius Caesar, at the moment of his death, looked up in disbelief as his good friend Brutus plunged the knife in and uttered the famous words '*Et tu,* Brutus'? And seventy-five years later, had not one greater than Caesar been betrayed by Judas Iscariot with a kiss? Was Michael Luvaglio really a true friend of Angus Sibbet, O'Connor asked? Or was he a false friend and a good actor? Was Angus Sibbet the victim of gang warfare? Were there other killers beside the accused? And was someone trying to frame Vincent Luvaglio?

He referred to what he saw as four groups of witnesses: those who saw what occurred at South Hetton, those who saw what occurred in Newcastle, those who saw what occurred in Peterlee and those who could testify to what was found in the roads around South Hetton. The defence, said O'Connor dismissively, were saying all of this was 'circumstantial evidence'. But there was 'an alternative account for these facts. If you come to the conclusion that you are sure there was a collision between these two cars, shortly before midnight at this spot, then it must follow that Luvaglio and Stafford' – the libertines and gamblers – 'have not been telling the truth.'

O'Connor moved on briefly to the doubts that had been cast on the police and prosecution timescale of events. 'Does it take four minutes to shoot a man?' he wondered. 'It could be it doesn't take three minutes to clean out a car. It could be there was time to call at Chelsea Grove and still be at the Birdcage Club by twelve twenty to twelve thirty am.' He observed that 'the witness

Mrs Brady', who had testified about seeing the red E-type at the club, worked as a cleaner of Vincent Luvaglio's car. Was she a liar? he asked.

He concluded with a mention of the disputed time when the accused had supposedly left Westmoreland Rise. Police officers had testified on oath that Michael Luvaglio and Dennis Stafford said they left the house at 11pm. Other witnesses disagreed. 'Who was telling the truth?' he asked solemnly.

It was a simple question that went to the heart of the Crown's case – one with which the judge clearly appeared to sympathise. 'Who should the jury believe?' Officers of the law? Or the bandit men with the immoral lifestyle who had cheated on their wives?

On the afternoon of 15th March, the jury were sent out to consider their verdict. Anticipating a long wait, some of the press adjourned to nearby pubs, like the Crown Posada, having first recruited a court usher to come down and warn them when a decision was near. Others walked round the corner to the bar of the Royal Station Hotel, where Dennis Stafford's champagne was on ice, as ordered. Cheltenham races were on the television in the background and, as well as betting on the Champion Hurdle, some of the reporters were striking bets on the likely outcome of the trial. Acquittal was strongly favoured due to the mostly circumstantial nature of the prosecution evidence and some opening paragraphs for the next day's editions were being prepared and rehearsed accordingly. But the excitable end-of-trial atmosphere was punctured by some of the more experienced crime writers and locals, who urged caution, mindful that, despite Newcastle's hard-living, party-going image, there was an older Methodist element in the background too and a distaste for the bandit men and their hedonistic lifestyle. They were outsiders, after all: Londoners who had come up to the north-east and made a fortune, flaunting their flash suits and fancy cars, just as Mr Scott and Judge O'Connor had described them. With feelings running high, they warned, the 'Fancy Dans' would have done better if the trial had been moved out of Newcastle altogether.

The jury were out for four-and-a-half hours, and it was nearly five o'clock when they returned. Judge O'Connor ordered Michael Luvaglio and Dennis Stafford to stand up. Luvaglio was white faced but smiling at Pat Burgess and at his mother, who was sitting behind him. Stafford was staring straight ahead. The jury foreman rose to deliver their verdict.

Guilty. Both men. Guilty as charged.

Michael grasped the rail of the dock, looking as if he was about to feint. Dennis's expression was inscrutable. O'Connor told the prisoners that he was going to pass the only sentence that the law allowed. Less than three years before, that would have been death by hanging and, although capital punishment for murder had been suspended in 1965 (and would not be abolished until 1969), there was still a condemned cell and working gallows in Durham prison, where the two men were destined to return in the short term. The tenor of O'Connor's remarks suggested he'd quite like to have been donning the black cap and invoking the Almighty. As it was, he sentenced them both to life imprisonment.

There were audible gasps in the public gallery and tears from friends and relatives. Salena Jones and Pat Burgess covered their faces with their hands, while Frank Luvaglio wept on his wife Maud's shoulder before collapsing onto the floor. He was eventually taken away in an ambulance. Michael and Dennis showed no emotion as, handcuffed to a prison officer, they were taken back down the steps to the cells beneath the court.

Outside, a huge crowd gathered round the exit, including more than fifty pressmen and photographers, and police with dogs were deployed to hold them back when Michael and Dennis emerged about thirty minutes later. They were in a group of three police cars, Dennis Stafford in the second car, Michael in the third, each of them flanked by prison officers. Some of the people in the crowd shouted out comments and there were a few cries of, 'Good luck, Dennis.'

All the photographers wanted a picture of 'the Gentleman Gangster' and they ran after the cars as they drove up the slope to Castle Garth and turned left on to High Bridge. The rush-hour traffic halted for a moment and then the grim little convoy pulled away across the river and set off on the road back to Durham.

Some of the journalists were already on the phone in the Station Hotel ringing through their copy. But others had stayed behind at Moot Hall, where they were rewarded by the dramatic sight of Vince Landa standing theatrically at the top of the steps outside the courthouse. The great bridges of the city – road and rail – straddling the skyline behind him: the river Tyne beneath. Vince was wearing his trademark dark suit and coat, although not, at this moment, his dark glasses. He was *the* one-armed bandit – the gambling kingpin and chief symbol of Methodist disapproval who had vied with T Dan Smith for the title of Mr Newcastle. He was Vincent Luvaglio – the older brother of a convicted murderer who had been in Spain when Angus Sibbet was shot and who had been strangely silent throughout the committal proceedings and the trial. With his wife, Gwen, standing beside him and weeping silently, he remained outside Moot Hall for half an hour, answering questions and holding court.

Vince began by saying that he had been waiting to give evidence all along but had not been called. He speculated on whether the red E-type had been deliberately taken away from the Birdcage Club to fake an accident and implicate him. Or whether there had been two red E-type Jaguars on the Durham roads that night, which he thought would explain a lot of things. His father, he said, was very ill but he said nothing about the fate of his brother Michael or Dennis Stafford and had no words of condolence for the parents and relatives of Angus Sibbet. He seemed more concerned to emphasise that his own business career would continue going forward, no matter what, though he warned that Tyneside may have seen the last of him. 'I'm thinking of selling out and moving from the north-east,' he said. 'Other people can take over the companies and we may have completely fresh blood.' Unbidden, he revealed that he'd had a turnover of £1.7m in 1966 but that, since Michael's arrest in January, they had not been doing so well. His accountant, Murray Nathan, was coming up from London to Newcastle on the 16th, though, to sort out his affairs.

The reporters lapped up his comments and his presence enthusiastically, some of them preparing side bars to run alongside the main story. Vince Landa was news whatever he did. He sold newspapers. He got people talking. His every action encouraged rumours and speculation. But none of the journalists present that afternoon were prepared to ask him the big question: if not Michael Luvaglio and Dennis Stafford, then who did he think had really been responsible for Angus Sibbet's murder?

CHAPTER FIFTEEN

THE TRIAL MAY have come to an end but the show was not over yet. Far from it. On Friday, 17th March, the meeting with the accountant behind him, Vince Landa held another informal press conference, this time at his offices in Sunderland. There had been a change of heart, he told his audience, and, 'after long discussions', he had decided to stay on in the north-east 'for a while, at least'. He claimed to have been offered a £50,000-a-year job with a London company. But instead of taking it and relinquishing his interests in the region, he would continue to act as the chief executive of Social Club Services, his decision influenced by receiving nothing but messages of comfort since the convictions of his brother and Stafford. 'I've had my faith in humanity restored,' he declared. 'The people connected with the working-men's clubs have been particularly good.' He didn't specify which men or which clubs as he moved on to give an update about his father, Frank, whom he said was now 'resting at home. It isn't as bad as we thought, and he's been given pills by the doctor and told to calm down.'

Vince said that his accountant, Murray Nathan, had told him that SCS 'would do much better' with him at the helm for now and, with Gwen standing beside him again, along with Dennis Stafford's solicitor, Graham Andrews, he spoke a little about Angus Sibbet. He said they all knew that he had been 'living above his means', given that he'd been getting £50 a week plus expenses and commission amounting to maybe another £50 a week. There were still no direct expressions of shock or sadness or regret for Sibbet's death or his brother's plight, but he assured a columnist for the *Daily Mirror* that he would be tireless in his efforts to prove the innocence of the accused. 'I believe this killing was an attempt to get at me; to frame me and get me involved,' he said. 'Then, with me out of the way, it would be an easy job for the people concerned to move into the gaming-machine business I've built up.' He finished by saying that he'd hired four private detectives during the trial and that he shortly proposed to issue a private summons against the man who he believed had committed the murder.

It was bold talk but, with no name or identity supplied, Vince's claim of a breakthrough was soon lost amidst the scrum of gossip and speculation. The papers preferred to focus, with relish, on the fate of Dennis Stafford, 'the Playboy who turned murderer', who was now in prison for life. They were equally gripped by stories of Angus Sibbet's extravagant lifestyle, with some alleging that he had been skimming up to £200,000 from Social Club Services and spending it on up to eighty pairs of gold cufflinks and tailored suits. Was such a man worthy of public sympathy, people were asking? Or was his fate, and that of Michael Luvaglio and Dennis Stafford, a salutary reminder of the wages of sin?

As Michael and Dennis disappeared into the maw of the prison system, their lawyers began working on an appeal. But the background music continued to be unhelpful. On 10th March, the Home Secretary, Roy Jenkins, had announced that Dino Cellini, his brother Eddie and three other Italian Americans living in London were to be deported and would have to leave the UK by the 21st. Cellini was phlegmatic about his exclusion, just as George Raft had been before him, observing that it was the product of 'typical socialist moral disapproval of gambling'. Cellini's career was far from over and, in the 1970s, he went on to play a leading role with Resorts International in Atlantic City, where they opened the first legal casino hotel in the US outside of Nevada. He also turned up again in Europe, in Hamburg, in what was then West Germany, working with the Lebanese-born Freddy Ayub, who had run the Colony Club croupiers' school in Hanover Square. Once the subject of a possible Martin Scorsese/Robert De Niro screenplay, Cellini died in Miami in 1978.

George Raft, the former Colony front man and lifelong smoker, who had been barred from returning to Britain the year before, died of emphysema in LA in November 1980.

The decisions to kick out Raft and the Cellini brothers did little in the short term to change the status of the Colony Club, which continued to be a proxy Mob business owned by Meyer Lansky and Angelo Bruno, with British staff taking over the management. But the official acknowledgement of Mafia links with the UK gaming industry reinforced public perceptions that the men who worked in it were probably immoral and unscrupulous, especially if they had Italian surnames like Luvaglio.

Up in the north-east, there was a feeling of satisfaction within Durham Constabulary that at least two local bandits were no longer at large. More dangerous characters were removed from circulation on 12th April, when the four men accused of attacking

Above: Vincent Luvaglio, also known as Vince Landa. © *Mirrorpix*

Below left: Michael Luvaglio, Vincent's younger brother. © *Mirrorpix*

Below right: Angus Sibbet. © *Mirrorpix*

Right and centre:
A typical night at a
workingmen's club.
Elderly clientele get
the beers in, a scruffy
amateur band plays,
and things look a little
down-at-heel.

© *Getty / Homer Sykes*

Right: When the money
started flooding in,
Newcastle's club scene
took off. Tuxedo
Junction, pictured here
in 1979, was a favourite
of Dennis Stafford's.

© *Mirrorpix*

Above: The Kray Twins were no strangers to nightlife. Reggie Kray (pictured right) on a night out with Barbara Windsor (second left)…

© Getty / Larry Ellis

Below: But the Luvaglio brothers could match them for flashy company: Tom Jones (pictured here), joining Michael for dinner at Angus Sibbet's house, along with Angus's daughter Karen and Paddy Hallett. © *Mirrorpix*

Above: The Twins were keen amateur boxers and enjoyed the company of fellow pugilists. Pictured here with the World Heavyweight Champion, Sonny Liston. *© Getty / Evening Standard*

Below: And again with the former World Heavyweight Boxing Champion, Joe Louis, with whom they turned up at the Dolce Vita Club in Newcastle on a brief reconnaissance trip. *© Getty / Evening Standard*

Left: Dennis Stafford, pictured with his first wife, Pat Smithson, celebrating his release from jail in 1964. © *Keystone*

Above right: …and, as was sometimes typical, pictured with an unnamed woman in a nightclub. © *Mirrorpix*

Left: Dennis in Robert De Niro Goodfellas mode, 1964. © *Mirrorpix*

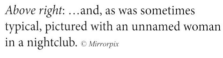

Right: The 'Gentleman Gangster' being escorted back to prison in a bespoke overcoat. © *Mirrorpix*

Above: The damaged Mark X Jaguar saloon.

© *Mirrorpix*

Left: Vince Landa's E Type and the Jaguar side by side. © *Mirrorpix*

Right: Pesspool Bridge, South Hetton, County Durham. January 1967.

© *Mirrorpix*

Above: Dennis Stafford, not ashamed to be seen as he's driven back to Dartmoor. © *Mirrorpix*

Below: Michael Luvaglio, head covered by a blanket, as he's driven away to Durham Jail. © *Mirrorpix*

Right and centre:
Michael Luvaglio
on Open University
graduation day, 1978,
receiving his BA
degree, at Alexandra
Palace in London.
He was allowed day-
release from prison to
attend. © *Mirrorpix*

Left: Dennis Stafford
and Michael Luvaglio
re-united for the first
time in thirty years.
London, 2008.

© *PA Images*

Paddy Hallett outside the Birdcage Club in February came up for trial at Moot Hall. The driver of the car, Robert Snowdon, insisted from the dock that he 'had nothing to do with this' but was found guilty and sentenced to five years' imprisonment. George Stewart, who had assaulted Hallett with a knife, also got five years. Robert McKenna got eighteen months and the teenager Malcolm Tully was sent to Borstal. 'I will make sure you don't grass,' Stewart had said to Hallett. But grass what? That he had been told to set up a fake appointment for Angus Sibbet with Michael Luvaglio on the night of 5th January and then warned not to accompany Sibbet to Shiney Row? But who by and why?

Detective Superintendent Ronald Kell felt that his job was still only half done and that it was time to focus on Vince Landa, Social Club Services and the whole one-armed bandit slot-machine business. On 13th April, the police spoke to a man called Angus Hamilton Earl, who was the managing director of North East Heating (Durham) Ltd, a central-heating company of which Vince was a shareholder. In the wake of the Angus Sibbet trial, Hamilton Earl had come forward to say that he had been an involuntary visitor to Dyderdale Hall, where he was accused of taking £1,300 worth of company stock. Under pressure 'during an intense meeting' with Vince and others, he had admitted fraud and put pen to paper 'out of fear for my family and knowing full well the circles that Landa moved in and the type of people he associated with.' He had since retracted his confession.

Earl's experience was just one of many things that Ronald Kell would like to have talked to Vince Landa about, but he wasn't an easy person to get hold of. Despite his assurances that he was remaining at the helm of his businesses, he was never at the Low Row office in Sunderland when the police called and he was never at home at Dryderdale Hall either. In May, his Social Club Services accomplice William 'Buster' Thompson, who had briefly been a director of the Piccadilly Club, reported that Mr Landa was, in fact, back in Majorca at his villa outside Palma. What's more, said Buster, he had a 'critical illness' and may have to be operated on.

At the time, Vince still officially owned 15 different companies employing between 150 and 180 people and servicing over 800 gaming machines in working-men's clubs. Buster explained that, in Vince's absence, his own role was like that of a 'company doctor', assuring everything continued to run smoothly until the boss's health improved and he could return to take charge. He also categorically denied reports circulating in the Newcastle and Sunderland papers that the police suspected Vince of being 'the regional kingpin of organised crime'.

On 16th June, Buster gave a further update, saying that Vince was in a private clinic and had been having several operations for 'malignant growths' at the base of his spine (which sounded more alarming than it was and would nowadays involve simple liquid nitrogen treatment for pre-cancerous solar keratoses caused by too much sun). Buster explained that he was flying out to Majorca at the weekend, as he had been every week since Vince had become ill, and he believed that Landa was hoping to come home by the end of the month. But despite Buster's valiant pretence, Vince didn't come back in June or in July, instead remaining at the clinic for further treatment, according to Thompson. Cynics wondered if his health was suffering because of worrying news that he was now officially wanted in Newcastle in connection with a fraud investigation into the sale and rent of one-armed bandit machines to working-men's clubs. And that wasn't all. He was also suspected of receiving stolen goods obtained during a burglary in Stockton-on-Tees, for which George Shotton, a notorious local villain and friend of the safe-cracker and future owner of Darlington Football Club, George Reynolds, was awaiting trial.

The gangster haven that became known as the Costa del Crime didn't come into being until the 100-year-old extradition treaty between Britain and Spain expired in 1978. If Vince Landa was really 'the regional kingpin of organised crime', he could have been extradited from Spain perfectly legally in 1967. But it seems he had influential friends in Majorca as well as north-east England and, as long as he could afford to pay them to ignore his presence, he wasn't leaving the island any time soon.

On 3rd July, Vince's brother Michael was moved from the high-security wing in Durham to Wakefield prison a hundred miles further south: a longer and more tiring journey for his parents when they wanted to visit him. Dennis Stafford was shipped down to Parkhurst on the Isle of Wight. Not quite Alcatraz but still Britain's 'Island Fortress' and the Home Office's prison of choice for some of the country's toughest villains. A fortnight before the transfers, the Director of Public Prosecutions, Sir Norman Skellhorn, had written to the Chief of the Durham Constabulary to congratulate the force on their detective work and handling of the One-Armed Bandit Murder case. The convictions of Luvaglio and Stafford, he said, would act 'as a warning to friends of all these men here and elsewhere.'

Detective Superintendent Kell's attempts to take down some of those friends and associates received a timely boost at the end of August, when the *People* newspaper began a series of articles on the slot-machine business designed to show how badly misled many club officials had been when acquiring bandits for their members to play on. 'One of the most ingenious of all fruit machine fiddles,' it reported 'is that of the rigged mechanical counter. How many times it's been used to swindle workingmen's clubs in the Northeast, it is impossible to establish. But it has certainly diverted thousands of pounds into unscrupulous hands.'

Ronald Armstrong, secretary of the Percy Main Social Club in North Shields, disclosed that, ever since January 1966, he had noticed that their share from the club's two fruit machines, which had averaged around £80 a fortnight for the first year, were down to more like £70 or less, despite them being as popular as ever with his members. So he and his committee had decided to set a trap to see if they could catch whoever was milking them.

On the Saturday afternoon of Whitsun weekend in May 1966, they emptied the machines of all the thousands of sixpences that had been fed into them during the previous two weeks, adding them up painstakingly to £70-18s-6d.

That evening, they were due to be officially emptied by a collector for Cam Automatics of Seaham, County Durham, from whom they were rented. As usual, the money was tipped out in the presence of the committee and fed into a mechanical counter brought by the collector. The total registered £73. But the machines had been in use for two hours since the committee had conducted their tally and there should have been more money in them. They got the club chairman to ask the collector to leave the room on the pretext that one of the machines needed looking at and then picked up the counter and shook it. It rattled.

There were coins in the base adding up to £40-1s-6d in what amounted to a false bottom. The committee at once complained to Cam, whose managing director, Robert Murray, went to the club and said he was 'flabbergasted' and knew nothing about it. An employee must have been responsible, he said, and, indeed, one was promptly dismissed and Cam paid the club £500 in compensation.

Cam Automatics were one of the local rivals to Social Club Services, although they operated on a much smaller scale. But the revelations about corrupt practices at Cam intensified speculation about what exactly had been Vince Landa's business model and the secret of his success. The Central Social Club in Gateshead offered a glimpse when their secretary William Burn, former chairman John Peden and treasurer John McGill revealed that Vince had regularly given backhanders to officials as a way of promoting sales of his fruit machines to their clubs.

Central had been offered two machines: one of them a Bally and the other a 'Mountain Climber' made by Keeney and Sons, another American firm that had been in business since 1916. They had both been imported from the US and reconditioned by Social Club Services, who then sold them as brand new. The Central Club paid £2,600 for them, unaware they were worth less than half that. They also bought a mechanical change-giver for £100 and a CCTV system for £2,400. They intended to do it all on HP, with a £1,700 deposit and monthly payments of £178 to guarantee takings of £400 per month for four years. To further encourage the committee, Vince Landa had said that he would pay them £600, to be shared by three officials, for their help and, on signing, write them a cheque for £225 to go towards their HP liability. He would also give £50 cash to the assistant barman to look after the machines during the day and an extra £25 to three other committee members to cover their 'expenses'.

The officials never received the £600 or the cheque for £225 and, shortly afterwards, in January 1967, Michael Luvaglio was arrested and charged with murder and William Burn and his Central Club colleagues felt that 'there was no point pressing the matter any further'. Burn defended their culpability in accepting the bribe by saying that £100 was 'a great temptation to any working fellow', and they thought 'there was no harm' in making a few quid for themselves. Instead, they had been 'badly misled'. SCS had defaulted on the £400 a month and there had been no payments from them since the start of 1967. The club now had a debt of £3,200 and still had to meet HP charges every month.

Years later, Vince Landa would admit giving cash inducements, which, as far as he was concerned, were a legitimate business practice, but he was dismissive of the idea that the clubs were all poor, exploited victims. If he was crooked, he said, the committee members were 'just as bent or could be bent very easily. When we tried to sell them a machine, there were very few who didn't automatically look for the cut. There had to be a payment for them to split amongst themselves. It was something I didn't want to do in the first place, but the committees forced us into it.'

Whatever part cash payments to club committees made, the One-Armed Bandit Murder and subsequent trial and conviction of Michael Luvaglio shattered Social Club Services' hold on the market in the north-east and, in September 1967, it was announced that the company had gone into liquidation. Visible confirmation of what, only a year before, would have seemed an unimaginable reversal of fortune came when a public auction of Social Club Services' property took place at the Low Row HQ in Sunderland to raise money owed by the firm for unpaid rates. The sale was conducted by the fast-talking Stanley Robinson, who pointed to a range of office equipment including executive desks, typewriters, radiators and curtains. One typewriter went for £28, a swivel chair for £8, Vince's cocktail cabinet for £20 and his teak desk for £35. There was also a locked filing cabinet on the market for £8. 'Find Mr Landa and he will give you the key,' quipped Robinson. Detectives from Durham CID mingled with the bidders, who comprised bandit operators from local firms and from London – and who didn't want to give their names – as well as Sunderland and Newcastle café and shop owners.

The police deduced that dozens of small firms were hoping to start up in the north-east in the hope of profiting from Vince's eclipse, which appeared to be entering a criminal phase. On 10th October George Shotton, who described himself as a trawler owner and car dealer, went on trial in Durham accused of burglary and receiving stolen goods and being an accessory after the fact. The prosecution alleged that Shotton, who had been involved with the Findlay brothers in the Battle of Percy Street in Newcastle in 1963, had 'bought' £10,000 in cash and other stolen articles – watches, jewellery and a gold piece – together worth £4,343, from the proceeds of a break-in at a house in Stockton. They also claimed that he had paid for the money and goods with £10 notes given to him by Vince Landa as repayment for a debt. The money had been drawn out of the bank by Vince's wife Gwen and then handed to her husband, who, in turn, handed it over to Shotton in the Royal Station Hotel. But Shotton denied ever having been at the hotel on the day he was meant to have received the cash and also denied any contact with the three men involved in the robbery.

Gwen Landa, who was noticeably not in Majorca with her mysteriously ill husband, was called as a witness and stuck doggedly to her story that the money was simply a debt that Vince owed Shotton and that neither she nor Vince had any knowledge of the robbery. She was accused of telling lies by the prosecution, who inferred that Vince had either alibied George Shotton or in some way set up the break-in and provided Shotton with the funds to acquire the stolen cash and other goods from the burglars. 'Did the money get to Mr Shotton or not?' asked the prosecutor, Mr Neville QC, as he addressed the jury. 'There is one person who could back Mrs Landa up – one person who could satisfy you – and that is Mr Vince Landa. He was suffering from ill health but he's well now. He is missing for a good reason . . . a classic case of *Hamlet* without the prince. I say Mrs Landa is covering up for her husband in some way.'

Neville had mounted a compelling case but, without the corroborative evidence to back it up, there was never much doubt that Shotton would get off. Yet, with more and more unanswered questions and negative publicity emerging about the one-armed bandit business, it was beginning to look doubtful whether Vince Landa would ever be able to return as a figure of substance in the north-east. Especially when, four days after the George Shotton trial, his wife Gwen revealed that Dryderdale Hall – their family home and the lair of the 'Mountain King' – was up for sale. She was unable to confirm whether she and her husband were still together.

CHAPTER SIXTEEN

IN NOVEMBER 1967, the Prime Minister, Harold Wilson, conducted a cabinet reshuffle and Roy Jenkins and James Callaghan swapped jobs, Jenkins becoming the new Chancellor of the Exchequer and Callaghan taking over as Home Secretary. In the wake of violent incidents like the Battle of Mr Smith's Club and the One-Armed Bandit Murder, the Home Office continued to have gambling in its sights, believing that further legislation was needed to stamp out racketeers and bring a wayward industry into line.

It was the liberal intellectual Roy Jenkins who had ordered the deportation of George Raft, Dino Cellini and their friends. Now it fell to Jim Callaghan, a right-winger and former trade-union official with no interest in gambling, to follow up and introduce a new Betting and Gaming Act, which had its second reading on 13th February, 1968. Callaghan told the House that the origin of his bill was 'the failure of the Betting and Gaming Act, 1960 to achieve its purpose.' It had been intended to prevent the exploitation of gaming by commercial interests but 'I regret to say that gambling in Britain has achieved a profusion of variety unique in Europe.' Callaghan admitted that the architects of the 1960 Act had 'never envisaged this development' and so there were no proper safeguards to control the clubs from becoming 'the haunt of criminals . . . and foreign interests of wholly undesirable origin.' But he wasn't just proposing measures to deter the owners of establishments like the Colony Club. He also told the House that 'serious abuses had developed' regarding the provision of gaming machines. 'I do not think that in 1960 there was a clear perception of just how profitable these machines could be.' In many cases, he said, the percentages of stakes that the machines retained had been 'quite excessive', benefiting less the clubs than the dealers, who had designed ingenious forms of contract to ensure they retained the lion's share of the profits.

Callaghan accepted that some members would like 'to suppress commercial gaming altogether' but believed that suppression would be ineffective, simply driving much of the activity underground and into the hands of the crooks and racketeers who had already battened on to it. Favouring rigorous control over full Cromwellian prohibition, he advised his honourable friends that gambling was 'a human weakness that has persisted through the centuries. It has never been stamped out. Like most other vices it does little harm in moderation, but it cannot remain uncontrolled.' The new measures, he said, were designed not just to cut back gaming but to 'thoroughly purge it'. Hard gaming, by which he meant high-stakes London gambling clubs like the Clermont, Crockfords and the Colony, would be subject to much stricter licensing and registration and have to satisfy an enhanced gaming board staffed by 'real experts' with widespread powers, backed up by police enforcement. Gambling in these clubs was, henceforth, to be rigidly confined to members who had joined at least twenty-four hours before playing.

The act was designed to be equally tough on the retailers of gaming machines, who would have to be certified by the Gaming Board as 'fit and proper', and installation of the machines would be restricted to clubs and miners' welfare institutes, which were specially registered for the use of machines alone. All clubs and suppliers would need proper authorisation, which could be withdrawn if abuses were found, and all the machines would have to state their minimum percentage pay-out and be liable to checks at any time, only to be emptied by the club authorities or employees, not by the retailers. It was a move that would have seriously impaired Angus Sibbet's nightly collections, and past events in Newcastle were clearly on Callaghan's mind as he warned that, 'in some cases', a link already existed between fruit machines in a club and 'robbery, violence, protection rackets and even murder'.

Callaghan's aim was to reduce the sum total of gambling in the UK and one of the other main planks of his strategy was to 'prevent the issue of gaming licences to night clubs', which would have potentially disastrous consequences for clubs like the Dolce Vita in Newcastle. The Labour MP for Wallsend, Ted Garrett, assured the Home Secretary that he was as eager as anyone to stamp out the 'evils connected with the supply and sale of one-armed bandits' but he felt that the Home Secretary had been 'governed too much in his thinking by concentration on London, with a little less on the provinces.' Speaking from his experience as a north-eastern MP, he said that he knew 'many clubs where gaming is the lesser of the entertainment provided. Many people attend these clubs principally to listen to and see top-class entertainers.' His point was taken up by the Accrington MP, Arthur Davidson (Labour), who told the House that, in night clubs in the north of England, about 'ninety per cent of the people are there for the cabaret and ten per cent for the gambling' but the clubs were unable to provide top-class entertainment without the gaming tables to finance it. 'This form of Saturday night out is not confined to compulsive gamblers,' he said. 'It's now part of the social scene' and the government should be careful to insure that 'an honest and respectable evening is not stopped because of what gangsters are doing in London.'

It was a cry from the heart that resonated on Tyneside, in Leeds and in Manchester. Was the Home Secretary really saying that there should be no more Tom Jones or Tommy Cooper? No Ella Fitzgerald or Billy Eckstein? It was not an issue that appeared to bother Callaghan's Conservative shadow, Quintin Hogg – he of the 1963 report on the north-east, which had long since vanished into the parliamentary mist. In a long and portentous speech, he welcomed the support for the bill by the Casino Association, seemingly unaware that it was essentially a cartel of the biggest players that envisaged its power being strengthened by the new restrictions. Gambling, declared Hogg, was 'wholly irrational' and not something he would ever encourage his family to participate in, but he nevertheless bemoaned the idea that Parliament imagined it could 'make people good by statute'.

Arthur Lewis, the Labour MP for West Ham and a proud supporter of his local dog track, was one of the few members to speak out positively on the subject of gaming machines. People invested on the Stock Exchange, he observed. So why not on greyhounds, football pools and the slots? 'Just make sure the one-armed bandit's pay-out is clearly marked on the machine,' he said. 'People don't have to go on putting in their sixpences and, providing the machine is fairly controlled and in no way rigged, I cannot see why we should protect these people from themselves.' Furthermore, he suggested, if 'we are to have one-armed bandits, let's make them in this country and help the balance of payments.' He said he'd been advised that British dealers were currently importing £4.5m worth of machines a year from the US – a figure that Bally and Phonographic Equipment would not have denied.

The Northampton MP Reginald Paget, an ex-Eton and Cambridge-educated barrister and, unusually for a Labour member, also the Master of the Pytchley Hunt, felt that, where gaming was concerned, the House brought 'to these subjects great respectability . . . and a lot of ignorance.' His contribution encouraged Albert Murray, the Labour MP for Gravesend, to suggest to the Home Secretary that he should arrange for roulette tables and games of blackjack to be set up in the House of Commons so that the more sheltered members could experience gambling for themselves. Alternatively, perhaps the Home Secretary would like to organise a group outing for them to the Playboy Club. All in the interests of research, of course.

Callaghan did not reply. But the consequences of his bill were unrelenting. The number of licensed casinos in Britain fell from 1,000 to 120 within a year and the casualties included the Colony Club, whose management, comprising the puppet frontman Alfred Salkind and Phonographic Equipment, still reported to Meyer Lansky and Angelo Bruno. They were unlikely to meet the new standards, especially after the Mafia's continuing connection to the club was exposed in January 1968 when Albert Dimes went to the Tavistock Hotel in Bloomsbury to collect a debt owed by the

Phonographic numbers man Max Fine to Tony 'Ducks' Corallo for gaming machines that had been ordered but not paid for before Gabe Forman was deported. Lansky didn't care for the publicity and he wasn't enamoured of the new British Gaming Board either. There was a conference in Miami in March 1968 at which Lansky and other Mob bosses concluded that the casino business in the UK had become 'overly regulated and exorbitantly taxed' and the Colony closed the following year.

Lansky ended up living quietly in retirement in Miami Beach and died there, aged eighty, in 1983. His former partners were less fortunate. Angelo Bruno was shot dead in Philadelphia in 1980 and Tony 'Ducks' Corallo, who had been instrumental in supplying reconditioned American bandits machines to UK suppliers like Vince Landa, was jailed for racketeering in 1987 and died in Springfield federal prison in the year 2000.

Exclusive clubs that survived the purge, like the Clermont and Crockfords, catered unashamedly to high-stakes gamblers – some professional, many compulsive – and, while their food and drink was the best, they never bothered laying on additional entertainment. But provincial night club owners who had depended on their gaming tables to subsidise the cabaret, as well as the bars and restaurants, were in serious trouble. Fortunately for the Levy brothers, in Newcastle they had been shrewd enough to sell the Dolce Vita to the Bailey group at the top of the market, and before the new act became law. They had sensed the public's unease about underworld menace and had the foresight to see the restrictions on gaming licences coming down the line. The sight of top American talent flying into Newcastle every week was over. Under new ownership, the fabulous Dolce – once the queen of the Tyneside clubs and the very epitome of Newcastle as the

Las Vegas of the north – embarked on a long slow decline and, by 1979, it's unique selling point was that it sold 'the cheapest beer on Tyneside' at 22p a pint.

If the new act was the death knell for many top nightspots, it was also a forerunner of even worse things to come for what remained of Vince Landa's Social Club Services and its employees. But that summer, the Luvaglio family – or at least all of them not in hiding in Majorca – were focused on the outcome of Michael's and Dennis Stafford's appeal, which was due to be delivered by Lord Justice Edmund Davies on 30th July. Since the end of the Newcastle trial, Michael, Frank and Maud Luvaglio had retained the services of the London solicitor David Napley, who, along with his partner Sydney Kingsley, had built up a distinguished reputation as a criminal practitioner and would go on to represent many famous clients, while also taking a lifelong interest in miscarriages of justice. Knighted in 1977, his most celebrated case began the following year, when he acted for the former Liberal leader, Jeremy Thorpe, who was charged with conspiring to murder his ex-lover, Norman Scott. The trial at the Old Bailey in May 1979 culminated with a coup de théâtre as the barrister, George Carman, instructed by Napley, tore the credibility of the chief prosecution witness, Peter Bessell, to shreds and Thorpe, although guilty, was acquitted.

Napley, who from 1968 combined his law practice with being chairman of the Mario and Franco restaurant group, pioneer owners of La Trattoria Terrazza in Soho, had a lifelong love of Italian food and described himself as 'a Disraelian Conservative', rather than a left-winger or anti-establishment firebrand. He and his colleague Dennis Goodwin had trawled exhaustively through all the Newcastle trial documents and spent long hours interviewing

Michael Luvaglio in prison, where they were impressed by his devout Catholicism. At the end of their first visit, he asked them to remember to tell the nuns who had been in touch with him, and who were praying for him and lighting a candle for him at nine o'clock each evening, that he would pray at the same time so that they all might pray together. As a result of these conversations, combined with the research they had done into the case, Napley became convinced of Michael's innocence. Dennis Stafford, who Napley was not representing, had maintained that he was innocent too. Napley described Stafford as 'a notorious figure of ill repute' and recognised that Michael's involvement with Stafford made him liable to guilt by association. He suspected that Stafford knew a lot more than he was saying about the circumstances leading up to the shooting, but the solicitor was convinced that his client was not guilty of the crime and should never have been convicted on the back of the evidence presented in court. As Stafford himself had said, Michael was the kind of man 'you wouldn't even take to a pillow fight', let alone a murder.

The crucial elements, as Napley saw it, were the ambiguity surrounding the precise time of Angus Sibbet's death and the implausibly narrow timescale within which the police and prosecution had alleged the murder took place. They had claimed that the defendants had left Peterlee at 11pm – which they denied – driven to South Hetton, encountered Sibbet, murdered him, cleaned up any incriminating evidence, dumped the Mark X under Pesspool bridge and then driven sixteen miles to Newcastle in severe weather, arriving at the Birdcage Club by 12:30am. If the time of Sibbet's death could be established more accurately and compared with the whereabouts of the accused at the same time, the whole prosecution case might fall apart.

Napley felt that the initial medical examinations of Angus Sibbet's body had been grossly inadequate. At the February 1967 committal proceedings in Peterlee, Dr John Seymour Hunter, the local GP, had made no mention of rigor mortis or anything he had done to determine if it was present when he inspected the body at 5.50am on 5th January. But at the trial, a month later, he said that, yes, he knew Sibbet was dead because of his general appearance, his pallor and the presence of rigor mortis. 'Did you move the body at all?' the prosecutor, Henry Scott, had asked him. 'I took hold of the left leg and raised it slightly to ascertain the presence of rigor mortis,' he replied. Yet Hunter made no effort to test or record the external temperature or ascertain whether there was any heat left in the body and his comments made no sense in the light of the statement given to the police by the miner Tom Leak, who had been the first person to discover the body in the car. Leak was emphatic that, when he looked, the left leg was lying straight along the rear seat. The police photographs taken half an hour later, at 5:45am, showed the left leg bent and hanging down in front of the rear seat, in which case Hunter couldn't possibly have detected the presence of rigor five minutes later. Rigor mortis, once broken down, cannot be re-established and the pathologist, Dr Ennis, said that rigor mortis was present when he carried out the post-mortem in Easington mortuary that afternoon.

In his report, Ennis had estimated that the time of death had been between midnight and 4am and, on that basis, other pathologists, like the hugely experienced Dr Francis Camps, whose assessment had helped to convict the serial killer John Reginald Christie and clear Timothy Evans, would have settled on the median time – 2am – as the most probable. But that would not have been helpful to the police and prosecution, who needed the murder to have taken place between 11:30pm and midnight to allow enough time for Stafford and Luvaglio to get back to the Birdcage Club in Newcastle and establish their alibi.

At the trial, under questioning by Rudolph Lyons for Stafford, the pathologist had wavered and agreed that twelve o'clock to one o'clock, or even twelve thirty, would have been a more reasonable time. The prosecution had made much of the police test run from South Hetton to the Birdcage Club, which had taken them forty-six-and-a-half minutes. If the Crown evidence was correct, the accused arrived at the club at 12:30 or 12:40am at the latest, the murder having taken place at South Hetton between 11:53pm and 12:03am. If Stafford and Luvaglio had taken the same time to drive back to Newcastle as the police, they would have had no more than six-and-a-half minutes in which to commit the murder, dump the body in the car and clean up, which Napley described as 'so fast as to be worthy of inclusion in the *Guinness Book of Records*. He also pointed out that, while a large number of people had come forward to say that they saw the two cars in South Hetton, not a single witness had seen a red E-type careering back from South Hetton to Newcastle on snowy and icy roads.

Napley was also struck by the fact that, while a lot of witnesses saw the Jaguar Mark X stationary under Pesspool bridge after 12:35am – and while it appeared to have become stationary between 11:50pm and 12:35am – one man saw an arm come out of the driver's side window at 12:45am and no witness saw a dead body in it until Tom Leak did at 5:15am. Had Angus Sibbet been forced to leave the car near the bridge, taken somewhere and then brought back later and shot? Or had he been shot elsewhere and his body thrown onto the back seat?

Then there was the question of the blood found on the transmission tunnel of the Mark X and on a page of the telephone directory in South Hetton, along with the evidence of Matthew Dean, the Birdcage Club doorman, which, if correct, indicated that a vehicle had definitely collided with the E-type outside the club, causing significant damage. Dean knew neither of the accused by name, only by sight, and nobody ever suggested that he was lying. Might the red E-type have been taken from outside the Birdcage between 12:35 and 2am? The judge, Mr Justice O'Connor, gave no direction or advice to the jury on these points at all.

In Napley's view, O'Connor's summing-up was unfair, unsatisfactory and 'fell far below the requirements of English standards. There was not a shred of evidence to suggest that Angus Sibbet and Michael Luvaglio were not good friends and what particularly appalled the solicitor was the judge's references to Julius Caesar and Brutus and to Jesus and Judas Iscariot. 'It was highly questionable whether the case should have been heard at Newcastle with a local jury at a time when feelings were already running high against those who, it was believed, had introduced an element of gangsterism into the local workingmen's clubs,' wrote Napley in his autobiography, *Not Without Prejudice*, published in 1982. 'If ever there was a case, therefore, which required the judge to avoid the introduction of any emotive material it was this, yet in almost fifty years association with the law I have never known a judge employ a more dangerous passage.'

Neither Angus Sibbet's brother James nor the shadowy minder, Thomas 'Paddy' Hallett, were prepared to have their original statements shared with the defence while the mother of Angus's mistress Doreen Hall said that her daughter's whereabouts were unknown and that, even if she did know, Doreen was 'emphatically not prepared to testify' again. Napley also had to reluctantly accept that, no matter how much 'ingenuity and thought' was brought to bear, it was impossible for the defence to provide 'a watertight explanation of the involvement of the red E Type Jaguar, which had been in the possession of Stafford and in which Luvaglio had never denied being driven, at a significant time.' He observed that the law imposed no duty on an accused person to establish their innocence; only on the prosecution to prove their guilt beyond all reasonable doubt. It was not for the defence to furnish an acceptable theory that exculpated their clients but Napley worried that their failure to do so, and the inability of Michael Luvaglio to explain away the scientific evidence, was bound to weigh on the Appeal Court judges' minds.

Napley briefed two of the most 'able and experienced advocates' he knew to present the arguments. The Irish-born James Comyn, QC, who was President of the Oxford Union in 1940 – beating the future Home Secretary, Roy Jenkins, by four votes – had a large and fashionable practice and had successfully defended the safe blower and prison escaper Alfie Hinds in his action against a senior Scotland Yard detective. He would take the lead with the criminal barrister, John Mathew, who was building a reputation of equal stature as his junior. Mathew was a Senior Treasury Counsel at the Old Bailey and, at that point in his career, spent most of his time prosecuting, rather than defending. But he had twice defended the Great Train robber Charlie Wilson, as well as holding a watching brief for Lord Astor in the Stephen Ward case. He also went on to represent David Holmes, one of the four co-defendants in the Jeremy Thorpe trial in 1979.

Mathew and Comyn were leading figures in that era of 'ebullient criminality', as it was described in Mathew's obituary in the *Spectator* in April 2020. A period when assorted gangsters, mavericks and over-reachers, who had refused to be constrained by the austerity of post-war British life, ended up in showpiece trials, sharing top billing with their briefs. Michael Luvaglio was a lucky man, explained Sir David Napley. He could not have wished for a better or more experienced team.

The two barristers conducted their own rigorous interviews with Michael in Wakefield prison, subjecting him to questioning on every aspect of the case. David Napley said they were unable to fault him and that Comyn came away with the firm belief that he was innocent. Mathew was unwilling to say that he was convinced Michael was innocent, but he was equally far from convinced of his guilt. Both barristers were 'abundantly satisfied' that, on the evidence presented, no jury ought to be satisfied either.

The Crown and Dennis Stafford were represented by the same counsel who had appeared for them at the trial – Henry Scott, QC, and Rudolph Lyons, QC – and the court consisted of Lord Justice Edmund Davies presiding with Lord Justice Fenton Atkinson and Mr Justice Waller, who came from Newcastle and had practised on the north-eastern circuit and was familiar with the area where the murder had occurred. Edmund Davies, who gave the judgement on behalf of all three on 30th July, was a miner's son from South Wales who had progressed from Mountain Ash Grammar School to attaining degrees at King's College London and Exeter College, Oxford. Called to the bar in 1929 and knighted in 1958, he had presided over the controversial murder trial of Gunther Fritz Podola, who was hanged for killing a policeman in 1959, and the trial of the Great Train Robbers at Aylesbury in 1964, where he handed down unprecedented thirty-year sentences to the principals. He'd been made an Appeal Court judge in 1966 and, in the same year, he was appointed chairman of the Aberfan Disaster Tribunal by the Secretary of State for Wales, Merlyn Rees.

David Napley had great respect for Edmund Davies and was 'totally lost in admiration for the brilliance and skill which he displayed' in upholding the convictions and dismissing the appeals, disastrous as it was for Michael Luvaglio. The hearing had begun with a lot of 'Alice in Wonderland' legal rigmarole about whether it was permissible to call four new witnesses, including Professor Francis Camps and another ballistics expert, who had been available at the time of the trial but not called then. To Napley's dismay, permission was denied.

Edmund Davies did accept three criticisms of Judge O'Connor's summing-up. He said that, in places, he could have 'expressed himself in more balanced terms' and that he was wrong to tell the jury that giving the accused the benefit of any reasonable doubt meant doubt for which they could provide a reason. He also felt that O'Connor would have been 'well advised' to omit the references to Caesar and Brutus and Judas and Christ. But then. with 'great clarity and persuasiveness', according to Napley, he homed in on what he regarded as the strength of the circumstantial evidence, listing the alternative theories put forward to explain the involvement of the two cars and demolishing them.

In particular, the judge mocked the notion that the red E-type Jaguar might have been taken from outside the Birdcage Club on the night in question and then 'courteously brought back' there ninety minutes later, where 'the enraged Luvaglio and the police might well be investigating its disappearance.' He gave equally short shrift to the idea that the Mark X could have been driven to the club and deliberately damaged there or outside Michael Luvaglio's house. The jury, he said, had arrived at 'the only possible verdict' and proof of the defendants' guilt had been established by 'a brilliant and patient investigation for which all concerned are to be highly commended.' He acknowledged that 'maybe another, or others, also participated' and that 'most certainly there are others who know far more about the killing than has yet emerged.' But the court believed that the evidence from the forensic experts as to the time of death and nature of the debris from the collision between the two cars was 'clear and convincing' and the conclusions drawn from it 'absolutely irresistible'. Not content with dismissing the applications to appeal, he also ordered Michael Luvaglio to pay £210 costs for transporting two Jaguars to London from the north, in the vain hope they would be accepted as evidence.

Compelling as Napley found the reasoning of Edmund Davies, the decision was still a bitter blow, and even more so for Michael and for his parents Frank and Maud Luvaglio, who had mortgaged their house to try to pay for their son's ongoing legal battle. By this point, Napley was so disturbed by the whole affair that he was prepared to go on acting on their behalf whether they paid him or not and, over the next few years, he continued 'burrowing away', as he put it, delving over and over again into the inconsistencies of the case. He was aware of the existence of the note that Angus Sibbet had left Doreen Hall on the night of 4th January, 1967, telling her that he had a meeting 'with Mick' at 11pm that night at Shiney Row. But he had since heard from Joyce Hall that, when she got back to her flat in Gateshead after 2am, she had thought that her bed looked as if it might have been 'used' or sat on. She had also been told by someone that, when Angus left the Dolce Vita, he had, in fact, returned to her flat in St Edmunds Road and that he'd had another girl in the car with him. Had the libidinous Angus cooked up the story about his appointment with Michael – at 11pm, not 12:30am, at the Birdcage – in order to conceal another liaison from his regular mistress? If so, it in no way helped the prosecution case.

Napley's aim now was to work towards an appeal to the House of Lords and the strategy he recommended to the Luvaglio family and their friends was to try to arouse wider interest in the case from parliamentarians, the press and TV. He would be greatly assisted in a few years' time by the publication of a book called *Most Unnatural: An enquiry into the Stafford Case*, written by Peter Hughman, who was then an articled clerk in a solicitor's office in Newcastle, and the journalist David Lewis. At the same time, Napley himself wrote a long article for the *Law Society Gazette*, calling for a full public enquiry. But while public sympathy for the plight of one Luvaglio brother may have been growing, it was distinctly lacking in regard to the former business empire of his older brother, who, as of November 1968, had reason to fear that he might soon join Michael in prison.

CHAPTER SEVENTEEN

AT THE END of 1968, Durham Constabulary, encouraged by the new Betting and Gaming Act and the damning comments in Parliament about one-armed bandit suppliers, resumed their investigation into Social Club Services with increased vigour. On 28th November, they arrested Vince's henchman, William 'Buster' Thompson, in Gateshead and the SCS sales director, William Edgar, in South Shields. The company's former general manager, George Wilson, was tracked down at Hedley Hope near Bishop Auckland, where he was running a small hotel, and Stanley Robinson, once a co-director of SCS, was detained by police in Sweden, where he agreed to return voluntarily to the UK. More shockingly, Vince and Michael's father, Frank Luvaglio, was arrested by Detective Superintendent Ronald Kell at his home in Newcastle and, along with the others, charged with 'acting under false pretences' in connection with the supply and operation of gaming machines. With Graham Andrews, the solicitor who had acted for Dennis

Stafford in 1967, representing them, all the arrested men were released on bail.

The big coup for DS Kell was the news that the elusive and seemingly untouchable Vince Landa had been arrested too by Spanish police at his villa in Majorca. Extradition proceedings were underway and, with bail denied, Vince was currently residing in a prison cell in Palma. But celebration proved premature. The Bandit King had always boasted of his contacts in high places – men like T Dan Smith, who had enlisted Landa's help to organise discreet private holidays for himself and senior politicians like George Brown, who was depressed and drinking heavily when he stayed at the Formentor hotel, Majorca, in 1966. Vince had also been careful to hold on to a generous supply of funds in case of emergencies and, in February 1969, he was suddenly released by the Spanish police without charge. Whether or not money changed hands, as suspected, he was helped by the coincidence that the British government was in the middle of one of its periodic spats with Spain over the status of Gibraltar and the local authorities were in no mood to hand over a wanted man.

Vince was said to be returning to his villa to live quietly with his wife and children. But he wasn't so naive as to bet his future on the diplomatic situation never changing and, on 18th April, several hours before the Guardia Civil came knocking at the door, he vanished.

Landa – like Harry Lime in *The Third Man* – may have been out of sight but he was not out of mind. On 6th June, the Social Club Services fraud trial began at Moot Hall in Newcastle and Vince's name and reputation was invoked continually throughout the thirty-six-day proceedings.

The five accused were all charged with Vince Landa and 'others unknown', with two counts of conspiring to cheat and defraud clubs by purporting to sell them new gaming machines that they knew were, in fact, old and reconditioned. They were also charged with defrauding Northwest Securities Ltd, who handled hire-purchase agreements on behalf of the working-men's clubs.

If gangsterism and racketeering had been a constant backdrop to the One-Armed Bandit Murder Trial in 1967, it was even more firmly lodged in the public consciousness two years later. In March 1969, the Kray twins had been convicted of murder at the Old Bailey and sentenced to life imprisonment with a recommendation that they should each serve a minimum of thirty years. Their elder brother, Charles, and six other co-defendants had also been sent to prison at the end of the thirty-nine-day trial, which had offered the public a detailed picture of the inner workings of the Firm. Rumours were circulating that, before their arrest, the twins had attempted to muscle in on the Newcastle club scene and, by implication, take over the north-east's lucrative slot-machine trade. Figures had been bandied around again about Social Club Services being valued at over £8m before Angus Sibbet was murdered and Vince Landa disappeared. But if the Krays or any other outside parties had been hoping to scoop a windfall from the break-up of Vince's business, they would have been sorely disappointed by the revelations that emerged during the fraud trial at Moot Hall. Stories of a fortune, once fabulous, had long since been engulfed by debt.

Mr Douglas Forrester-Patton, QC, for the prosecution, told the court about Coinamatics Amusements Ltd, a slot-machine supply company run by Vincent and Michael Luvaglio and

Derwent Finance, a London-based company run by Vincent and his father, Frank. The latter supplied clubs with the deposits to buy gaming machines from the former with the additional help of the HP firm Northwest Securities. But the deposits, like the ones involving the Central Club, were usually fictitious. The machines would be supplied to a club after a credit-sale agreement and based on a so-called 'guarantee contract' under which the takings from the machines belonged to SCS and, in return, they agreed to pay the club a monthly sum. These contracts, explained Mr Forrester-Patton, were illegal and worthless since the passing of the new Betting and Gaming Act. The clubs would also be invited to enter into an agreement with another of Vince Landa's companies, Social Club Engineering. Yet most of the work done at the SCE workshop in Sunderland consisted of disguising old American machines – bought from Phonographic Equipment in London who, in turn, were getting them from Bally in the US – as new ones so that they could be sold for around £1,250 each, when they were worth no more than £375. Worn parts were replaced or resprayed and sometimes whole machines were reconditioned.

It was a deceitful but extremely profitable enterprise, said the prosecutor, and, on the back of these fraudulent transactions, Vince Landa had become 'a legendary figure', living at Dyderdale Hall, mixing with fellow millionaires and owning a Rolls Royce and a fleet of American cars. For the first five years, the working-men's clubs and the HP provider, Northwest Securities, were happy but then, in June 1966, Northwest received an anonymous letter advising them of the fraud SCS were engaged in. Two of Northwest's managers, a Mr Wood and a Mr Guy, made no enquiries other than politely asking Vince Landa if there was any truth in the accusations. He assured them there was nothing to worry about and they were content to accept his word, 'which showed how persuasive he must have been,' said the QC.

In December 1966, a month before the murder of Angus Sibbet, there was more excited talk about the company soon being floated on the stock exchange. Whereas the truth was that it was already in 'dire financial straits' and all standing orders in favour of clubs under the company's guaranteed profits scheme had stopped. By July 1967, twenty-six clubs were owed large sums of money by SCS. By September, when the company went into liquidation, it was more like a hundred and it was clear that Vince Landa's empire had 'finally crashed'. Landa had long since abandoned the sinking ship, leaving the defendants, once considered his friends, as well as employees, to face the consequences alone.

The court heard how, in December 1966, the Roker Victory Club in Sunderland had been approached by George Wilson, who persuaded the club secretary, Matt Riddell, to buy three machines for £1,250 each, along with stereo equipment for use in the club disco. The deal was to be financed by Northwest Securities and a deposit of £1,000 was paid by Wilson on behalf of SCS, who also agreed to pay the club £600 a month to cover their HP repayments plus 'a little bit extra' to make up the club's percentage of the profits from the machines. The Roker committee belatedly realised, just as the Central Club in Gateshead had done, that they had paid way over the market price for their bandits and, while the supplier's reps were collecting £40/50 a week from the club's machines, nothing was ever paid into their account by SCS. There were also instances of unscheduled late-night visits from the money counters and collectors, who came armed with their own keys. When George Wilson was eventually confronted about the situation, he responded by saying, 'If you really want to know the position . . . the company is skint.' As to his view about the exorbitant prices being charged for reconditioned machines, he claimed there was nothing illegal in it. 'You could simply call it good business,' he said.

James Burke of the Skelton and District working-men's club in Yorkshire described a sequence of missed payments from SCS under their guaranteed profit scheme and another club that had taken machines on a fixed monthly profit deal was twice given cheques for £363-1s-7d, which bounced.

David Lambert, former secretary of the Clayton Street Club in Newcastle, related how takings from one of their machines 'began fluctuating downwards' during a period in 1966 when Angus Sibbet was the collector.

Officials from the Oxhill Central Club in Stanley, a colliery town south-west of Gateshead, said that they were 'persuaded' to get rid of two machines they were buying from another company and take three from Social Club Services instead. The total cost came to £3,750 and the club ended up with an HP debt of over £2,000 but they later discovered that SCS had been paid approximately £1,600 for the pair of machines they had so generously taken off the club's hands.

Kenneth Hope, a former car salesman employed by Social Club Services in 1966, said that he'd been given the job of visiting clubs to explain why the company had defaulted on their payments. He'd met Vince through Stanley Robinson who, before he joined SCS, had been the sales manager for a firm of Sunderland and Newcastle car dealers owned by Alderman WS Martin, Chairman of the Sunderland Town Finance Committee and an influential friend of Vince Landa. It was Robinson, he said, who had told him how Landa had got rid of James Sibbet, the boss of the SCE workshops in Sunderland, who was Angus Sibbet's brother. 'I don't know how it came about,' he said when it was suggested to him by the prosecution that James Sibbet had refused to collude any longer in Vince Landa's frauds. 'But I do know he went out.'

There were no appearances by Vince's most trusted friends and lieutenants like Ray Thubron and George Reynolds but the defence did call a few witnesses who testified that, as well as frauds and defaults, SCS had also showed high life and good times both to its employees and to club-committee men who bought into its schemes. George St Vincent Lee, a sales rep and secretary of the Stanley Central Working Men's Club, told of Vince inviting officials from his and other clubs to a big party in London and paying all their expenses, including hotel bills and loss of wages and laying on a coach to take them there and back.

Vince's biggest courtroom fan was Edward Foster, the ex-secretary of the Windy Nook and Carrhill working-men's club in Felling, who had been so pleased with the job that SCS had done redecorating the club for £7,000 which Foster felt had been money well spent. He, too, remembered the 'famous jaunt' to London and the night clubs visited and also the time Vince had wined and dined several hundred club officials at another party he threw at Langley Park Hall near Durham.

Opinion was divided as to how much tributes to Vince's generosity and flair were likely to help or hinder the accused in the eyes of the jury. But barristers for the defence, seeking to deflect guilt from their clients, kept returning to what they described as the almost mythical power and influence of the man who wasn't there. 'You must condemn these men only on any evidence,' said Mr RP Smith, QC, for Wilson, 'not because they worked for Landa. We have heard of the milking of company money. He was obviously getting it out of the country. We have heard of money being diverted to Vince Landa Consultants – £8,000 in just over twelve months and free of tax. It has all been Landa using other people as his dupes and tools. Mr Vincent Landa was a very persuasive gentleman, and his powers of persuasion were enormous.'

In his final speech, Rudolph Lyons, QC, who had appeared for Dennis Stafford at the murder trial two years before and was now representing Buster Thompson, described the case as '*Hamlet* without the prince' (a description that had also been heard at George Shotton's burglary trial the year before). The real villains, said Lyons, were not in the court. 'One member of the family is in exile, a second is in prison and a third came before this court before you were present and was discharged. Only the supporting players are in the dock.'

In his final address, Peter Taylor, QC, who was representing Wilson and had acted as junior defence counsel for Michael Luvaglio in the One-Armed Bandit Murder Trial, went so far as to claim that 'Vince Landa's technique was the same as Hitler's with his flamboyant attitude and the pressure he put on people by inviting them to his home.' Secretive Dryderdale Hall, Taylor implied, had been north-east England's equivalent of the Eagle's Nest in Bavaria, with dogs and armed guards patrolling the grounds. The ever more extravagant allusions seemed to affect Mr Justice Mars-Jones, who began his summing-up by talking admiringly of how Vince had moved from a council house in Horden to Dryderdale Hall (valued at between £75,000 and £100,000) inside four years. In that time, he had, indeed, 'become an almost legendary figure in his own field in the north-east' and there was no doubt in the judge's mind that the defendants were all equally susceptible to his powers. But he finished by warning the jury that 'irrelevancies' advanced in mitigation of the accused were 'no defence in a trial of this sort'.

The jury were out for two hours and, when they came back in, their verdicts were 'guilty' on both charges for all four men. Buster Thompson, who was unemployed and went bankrupt the following year with debts of over £23,000, said later that they had fully expected to go to prison. But Mars-Jones was minded to be lenient and the custodial sentences he handed down were all suspended for two years. It seemed that even a High Court judge found it hard to get out from under the shadow of the Bandit King.

Mercifully for Maud Luvaglio and her imprisoned son, Frank Luvaglio was discharged before the trial began – hence the courtroom reference by Rudolph Lyons – after Mr Justice Mars-Jones ruled that he had no case to answer. The decision confirmed the suspicions of the Luvaglio family that Frank's arrest and prosecution had been a deliberate and calculated move by the Durham police designed to increase the pressure on Vince and make him return to the UK. If that was their strategy, it failed but, with Frank's health getting worse and Michael Luvaglio now entering the third year of his sentence, David Napley intensified his efforts to arouse public interest in Michael's case.

In July 1971, Napley was helped by Michael's former constituency MP, Geoffrey Rhodes, who led an all-party group of MPs signing a commons motion calling on the Conservative Home Secretary, Reginald Maudling, to set up a public enquiry. As the Labour member for Newcastle north-east, Rhodes shared the mounting sense of unease about the scale of corruption in the region and his fears were intensified when he received an anonymous letter, posted in Leeds, warning him to 'not interfere in this matter. There are very big fish involved. It is nothing to do with an MP.' Similar threats were made to members of a BBC *Twenty-Four Hours* team who had gone up to Newcastle to investigate the One-Armed Bandit Murder and question the convictions. The late-night current-affairs programme, which started broadcasting in 1965 and lasted until 1972, had a number of experienced presenters, including Kenneth Allsop and Cliff Michelmore, who had previously introduced *Tonight*, and reporters on the ground included Julian Pettifer, Tom Mangold and Michael Parkinson. They spent a month up in County Durham trying to find out more about the death of Angus Sibbet. During that time, some of them were tailed on foot and by car and one received a threatening phone call telling him to back off. Some of their hotel rooms were ransacked and informants with inside knowledge of the slot-machine trade were threatened and tape recordings tampered with.

Maybe the newspaper headlines were right. Maybe the Mafia had come to Newcastle. The image of a fun-loving city and its population enjoying late-night clubs and entertainment on the one hand and a harmless flutter on the gaming machines on the other was dissolving in front of David Napley's eyes. In its place appeared a much darker world, replete with amorality, violence and possible police malpractice. To his astonishment, he had discovered that no fewer than seventy witness statements taken by Durham Constabulary in January and February 1967 were first shown to the junior prosecuting counsel, Richard Castle, by a 'visibly agitated' DS Kell on the opening morning of the One-Armed Bandit Murder Trial. Of this batch only twelve were given to the defence before the proceedings began.

When Napley and his colleagues, Derek Goodwin and Christopher Murray, went through the seventy statements and got in touch with some of the witnesses, they found that a total of thirty-seven of them, mostly miners, had passed a Mark X Jaguar saloon under Pesspool bridge at some point between midnight and 2am on 5th January, 1967, and had seen neither damage to the car nor a body in the back. But none of them had been called to testify at the trial, partly because the defence had not been aware of their existence. Napley had also contacted another automobile expert, who reckoned that by no means all the damage to the E Type had been caused by a collision. In his estimate, some of it might have been faked.

On the back of the new evidence, Napley wrote to the Home Secretary Reginald Maudling, who had been appointed after the Conservative general election victory in 1970, demanding that the case be made the subject of a full public enquiry. He had high hopes of Maudling, who had replied sympathetically to letters he had received from Michael Luvaglio in prison and was perceived as relatively moderate and easy going compared to some of his Tory predecessors, like the homophobic David Maxwell-Fife. A genial, intelligent man who got a First in Greats at Oxford and had an exuberant actress wife, Maudling had been a rising star in the Conservative Party in the 1960s until losing out to Ted Heath in the 1965 leadership election. Perhaps he didn't want the top job badly enough, but he possessed a certain louche charm and had once turned up to an evening cabinet meeting sporting a midnight-blue dinner jacket, which led the then Prime Minister Harold Macmillan to comment that 'Reggie looks as if he's off to play the drums at the 100 Club.'

In his autobiography *A Bag of Boiled Sweets*, the Tory

backbencher Julian Critchley described Maudling as a compassionate, civilised man who was never happier than when he was contemplating a plate of hearty nursery food like the plum duff they served for pudding in the House of Commons dining room. Unfortunately, he was also hungry for greater financial reward than a Cabinet Minister's salary and, in pursuit of his 'little pot of gold', as he called it, he accepted remuneration from a series of dubious financial enterprises. It began with Rolls Razor, the washing-machine firm owned by the entrepreneur John Bloom (whose chairman, the Conservative MP Richard Reader Harris, was a friend of Vince Landa), which was forced into liquidation in 1964. Then there was his role as President of the Real Estate Fund of America and advisor to the Peachey Property Corporation, whose chairman, Sir Eric Miller, a leading Labour Party benefactor and supporter of Harold Wilson, ended up being accused of embezzlement and committed suicide.

Maudling's downfall would ultimately come about through his association with John Poulson, the Yorkshire architect and corrupter of T Dan Smith, who had amassed a huge network of useful contacts, political and financial, in both London and the north of England and was now looking to expand overseas. In 1966, Maudling accepted the post of chairman of Poulson's company, Construction Promotion, later adding positions with Open Systems Building and Industrial Technical and Construction Services, and used his connections as former Shadow Commonwealth Secretary (1965/66) to try to persuade the Maltese government to award one of Poulson's companies a £1.5m contract to build a hospital on Gozo.

By 1972, the potential fall-out from Poulson's and T Dan Smith's activities was building in the atmosphere like the pressure from an impending thunderstorm. But on 3rd March, safe for the moment, the Home Secretary announced that, in response to representations from the solicitors for Michael Luvaglio and Dennis Stafford and 'the grave concerns of many responsible people', including members of parliament, he was referring the One-Armed Bandit case back to the Court of Appeal.

It was not the enquiry that Napley had wanted but it was a victory of sorts. Except that it came too late for Michael's father. In November 1971, Frank Luvaglio had died of a heart attack. He was sixty-five years old. His funeral took place at St Teresa's Roman Catholic Church in Heaton, Newcastle, and at Heaton Cemetery, and Michael Luvaglio was allowed out of Wakefield prison for the day to attend. The drive back to Newcastle briefly transported Michael into a very different city to the one he'd known during the heyday of Social Club Services, the Piccadilly Club and the Dolce Vita. The Swinging Sixties were already a distant memory. The Beatles had broken up in 1970 and, that same year, Jimi Hendrix had died from accidentally choking on his own vomit after a drug overdose. The 1971 Christmas number one would be Benny Hill's 'Ernie (The Fastest Milkman In The West)'. The optimism and excitement of the 1960s had been replaced by mounting unease about inflation, oil price rises and industrial strife, which would culminate in the three-day week and the Heath government's monumental clash with the miners' union in 1974.

As the car conveying Luvaglio and his escort arrived at the cemetery, press photographers were out in force, just as they had been at Angus Sibbet's funeral in 1967. The next day's papers all had pictures of the convicted murderer wearing a dark suit and a dark overcoat and tie. When the committal was over, Michael saw his mother, Maud, back into her car and kissed her goodbye. Then he was seen weeping as he got into the back of the black Austin Princess, in handcuffs, and was whisked away back to prison. There was no sign of his brother Vincent. It was now four years and nine months since Michael had gone down. He still had eight more years to go.

James Comyn, who had led for the defence at Michael's first appeal in 1968, was not available the second time. John Hazan, QC, who served with David Napley on the Home Office Criminal Law Revision Committee, took over, with John Mathew acting again as junior. Bryan Anns and Lewis Hauser, QC, in Napley's view 'an able advocate but one liable to go on for too long', came in for Dennis Stafford. The Crown were now represented by the leader of the north-eastern circuit, John Cobb, QC, who, in the chummy and incestuous world of the Bar, was both an acquaintance of Napley's and a fellow member of the Garrick Club.

The defence team's biggest fear was that the three Court of Appeal judges would refuse permission to call extra evidence, citing arcane procedural reasons. But to Napley's relief, they appointed Mr Justice Croom-Johnson to sit first as an examiner and then report back to them. Croom-Johnson sat for sixteen days from 14th November to 30th November, 1972, and sixty-three witnesses, many of whom had never 'been heard before by any court concerned in the matter', appeared before him. The written record of their testimony ran to six thick volumes.

Unfortunately for the defence, the hearings occurred two months before an edition of the BBC current-affairs programme *Midweek* cast further doubt on the police and prosecution case. *Midweek*'s host was Ludovic Kennedy, the esteemed investigative journalist who had exposed the miscarriage of justice that led to the wrongful execution of Timothy Evans in 1951 in his book *Ten Rillington Place*. On 17th January, 1973, *Midweek* featured an interview with a Scottish petty criminal and getaway driver called John Tumblety, who had convictions for armed robbery on Tyneside in the 1960s. Tumblety, who was known to supply guns to criminals, claimed that, on the night of 4th/5th January, 1967, he was at the Birdcage Club in Newcastle when he received a phone call asking him – or was it telling him? – to go and pick up a man in South Hetton. For whatever reason, the request was one that Tumblety felt he couldn't refuse.

When he got to the Durham village, Tumblety discovered that his passenger was a man with a London cockney accent, whose left trouser leg was torn and left sock soaked with blood. Tumblety said that he drove the man back to the Birdcage, as requested, and that, after that night, he never saw him again. But he was convinced that the man he'd picked up was either Angus Sibbet's killer or had been a party to the killing. Was it possible that it was this man's blood that was the unidentified sample found on the transmission tunnel of Sibbet's Mark X Jaguar? Blood had also been found in the telephone box in South Hetton, which was the only place the man could have rung from, but whoever it belonged to had never been traced by the police.

Forty-eight hours later, with the story of Angus Sibbet's murder national news and Michael Luvaglio and Dennis Stafford in custody, Tumblety was warned by a man called 'Mike' Tully that he should forget everything that had happened that evening, including their conversation. And if Tully's name was brought up by the police at any point, Tumblety was to 'clear him'. Might Mike Tully have been one and the same as Malcolm Tully, the young offender who was involved in the attack on Angus's minder, Paddy Hallett, supposedly to prevent him grassing at the committal hearing in Peterlee in February 1967?

Midweek also interviewed Matthew Dean, the doorman at the Birdcage who had been called to give evidence at the trial at Moot Hall but only asked about the condition of the red E-type. He said he remembered Tumblety receiving a call at the club on the night of the 5th and going off and returning with another man about an hour later. Dean said that both men signed the club book when they got back to the Birdcage and that the book would also have recorded Luvaglio's and Stafford's times of arrival and departure. But the book was never taken away and used in evidence by Detective Superintendent Ronald Kell. Perhaps because it would have conflicted too much with the theory that Kell was trying to prove.

None of *Midweek*'s findings were later requested by the Appeal Court judges, who could easily have asked to see the programme, or referred to at any point by the three men who were about to decide Luvaglio's and Stafford's fate. The panel this time comprised the Lord Chief Justice, John Passmore Widgery, Lord Justice James and Mr Justice Everleigh and it was the sixty-one-year-old Widgery who delivered their verdict on 26th February, 1973. The Lord Chief Justice, who headed the first inquiry into Bloody Sunday in 1972, whitewashing the armed forces and laying the blame for the deaths at the door of the organisers of the civil-rights march and the IRA, was also the senior judge who, in 1976, dismissed the first appeal of the Birmingham Six against their wrongful convictions for the Birmingham pub bombings. (Patrick McCarthy O'Connor, who had presided at Luvaglio and Stafford's trial at Moot Hall, was one of the judges who rejected the second appeal in 1988.)

Widgery continued in his role until his reluctant retirement in 1980, despite visibly being afflicted with dementia for the last eighteen months of his term.

The Chief Justice began by accepting that part of the new evidence tended to show that more than one car had been put under Pesspool bridge that night, which, he said, introduced 'a very strange feature in an already strange case. But he then went on to say that the court still believed that the Mark X Jaguar stopped there involuntarily and the fact that none of the new witnesses 'saw either the damage or the body in the back' didn't surprise 'the members of this court in the least.' And why weren't they surprised? The explanation, according to Widgery, was that the witnesses were honest but mistaken. They had been expecting to find a drunk or sick man sitting at the wheel and had not seen the dead body because they weren't looking for one. Napley, sitting in the court and listening in disbelief, wrote in his autobiography that 'it occurred to me that had I, at that moment, with or without the aid of Tommy Cooper, suddenly turned into a large buck rabbit that would not have surprised any of them either.'

A further defence witness had been found who could testify to seeing the red E-type Jaguar parked outside Michael Luvaglio's house in Chelsea Grove at midnight on 4th January, which would have made it impossible for him and Stafford to have been in South Hetton ten minutes earlier as the police and prosecution claimed. Widgery's comment was that the jury at the 1967 trial had not been persuaded by the evidence of the other two witnesses who said they saw the car at Chelsea Grove at that time and 'you do not necessarily improve the strength of your evidence merely by multiplying the numbers.'

Dr John Seymour Hunter was recalled and admitted that,

contrary to what he'd said in 1967, when he saw Angus Sibbet's body at 5:50am on 5th January, 1967, there was no rigor mortis present and that the police had specifically told him not to move anything. Lord Widgery said that, in the circumstances, no one could have accurately predicted the exact time of death, although he did accept that the defence had now shown it was 'probable' that Sibbet's death had occurred after midnight, rather than before. When it came to the fact that neither dirt nor blood – excepting an infinitesimal trace – had been found on either Luvaglio or Stafford, the Chief Justice admitted that 'we do not find any sort of explanation from the evidence before us which explains why.'

Yet, when it came to his conclusion, Widgery maintained that the prosecution case had not been sufficiently knocked about to 'make it impossible to say that the verdict remains safe and satisfactory.' And just as David Napley had suspected, the most damning point remained the 'extraordinary difficulty' of accepting any kind of alternative explanation put forward for the damage done to the E-type Jaguar and 'the disposition of the Perspex which undoubtedly came from it.' Michael Luvaglio, Dennis Stafford and their counsel were unable to account for how the collision must, or could, have happened in their absence and therefore the Appeal Court judges, ignoring all the inconsistencies in the crown case, were upholding the original convictions. 'We find the inference of guilt is irresistible,' said Widgery. 'There are improbable features on both sides of the case, but they are insufficient to say that the jury's verdict was unsafe or unsatisfactory.'

As Widgery reached the end of his summation, Maud Luvaglio shouted out, 'My Lords, as God is my judge, my son is not guilty of this', and then collapsed sobbing as the three judges turned and left the bench. Outside the court, Dennis Stafford's mother, Maggie, also burst into tears, crying, 'My boy is innocent. Who can I get at in there? How can they dismiss the appeal? Call this British justice?'

David Napley sought leave to appeal to the House of Lords, which was granted in April. Five law lords, led by Lord Dillhorne (the former Attorney General, Reginald Manningham-Buller), heard the case that summer but their verdict, delivered in October 1973, unanimously dismissed the appeal on 'substantially the same kind of reasoning' as Widgery had done eight months before.

If the parents of Luvaglio and Stafford were distraught, David Napley was profoundly depressed by his and his colleagues' failure to achieve a positive outcome. He continued to believe whole-heartedly that Michael was innocent – a belief based in part 'on the nature and personality of the man himself. He is not and never was a killer.' To think of him returning to the cramped confines of a prison cell was unconscionable. Napley's concern would not have been eased had he known at the time that, straight after the failure of the appeal, all the forensic evidence in the case held at the Northern Forensic Science Laboratory, including fingerprints and blood samples taken from the cars, was destroyed on the instructions of Detective Superintendent Ronald Kell.

In retrospect, the second failed appeal seems all of a piece with other cause célèbres that occurred throughout the 1970s. The Troubles in Northern Ireland were slowly poisoning society in insidious ways, including police cover-ups and fabricated evidence, like the cases involving the West Midlands Serious Crime Squad and the Birmingham Six, whose 1975 sentences of life imprisonment wouldn't be overturned for seventeen years.

Corruption was rampant in local government too and, if it's

true that the fish rots from the head down, the gangsterism and fraud perpetrated by the bandit men in Newcastle and the north-east had taken its cue from the men in power like T Dan Smith and Alderman Andrew Cunningham. And now the full extent of their corrupt dealings with John Poulson was about to be revealed.

CHAPTER EIGHTEEN

AT HIS UNASSAILABLE peak between the two Labour general election victories in 1964 and 1966, T Dan Smith had been flying down to London from Newcastle at least twice a week. His accountant, Bill Kirkup, a Tory politician who had been chairman of the Newcastle Housing Committee in the mid-1950s, was running Smith's PR companies in the capital and he'd formed a close relationship with Foley-Brickley and Partners, an advertising agency with offices in Kensington. Suitors would queue up for a meeting there with Smith or at the House of Commons, where he was feted by admiring MPs. It was through Foley-Brickley that one of Smith's companies, Fleet Press Services Ltd, became involved with the deputy leader of Wandsworth borough council, Alderman Sidney Sporle.

The alderman, a railway porter's son who left school at fourteen but rose to become Mayor of Battersea, was initially seen as a dynamic and idealistic character, not unlike Smith and similarly committed to slum clearance and redevelopment.

He and his wife lived in a flat on the Peabody estate and enjoyed a lavish lifestyle, despite Sporle despite having 'no visible means of support', as it was later described in court.

In December 1965, Sporle met T Dan Smith at the Royal Station Hotel in Newcastle and Smith offered him a consultancy with John Poulson's company, Open Systems Building, at £1,000 a year. The following month, Wandsworth's general-purposes committee awarded an exclusive contract for PR work for the council to Fleet Press Services Ltd, of which Smith was the chairman.

In November 1966, another Wandsworth councillor, Brian Bastin, met Smith in London and was told that he, too, could be on the payroll. Bastin was tempted but then had a change of heart and, in 1967, he went to the Metropolitan Police, alleging corruption. Smith was interviewed by Detective Chief Superintendent Gordon Mees at Bill Kirkup's house in St John's Wood in December 1968 and maintained that he'd had no personal involvement with Sporle in relation to the Wandsworth PR contract. A few days later, T Dan had a private meeting with the Home Secretary, Reginald Maudling, who advised him that 'all was not financially well' with John Poulson's companies but that he should be in the clear as regards the Wandsworth affair. He then cautioned him to pretend that their meeting had never taken place.

In January 1970, Sporle and Smith were both arrested and charged with bribery under the Public Corrupt Practices Act. In March 1971, after a five-week trial at the Old Bailey, Sporle was found guilty on seven counts of corruption involving council-housing contracts and sentenced to six years' imprisonment, later reduced to four on appeal.

T Dan Smith, whose defence was led by yet another acclaimed barrister, Jeremy Hutchinson, QC, who had defended Penguin

Books at the Lady Chatterley trial in 1960, was tried separately at the Old Bailey in June and July 1971. Smith claimed that he'd been unaware of payments made by Bill Kirkup on his behalf and was acquitted (although he never got round to paying Hutchinson for his services). But Maudling had been right about John Poulson's finances and, as more details emerged about his companies' web of Masonic practices, Smith was compelled to resign all of his political offices. But not before the brutal concrete imprint of his many 'visionary' schemes could be seen all over Newcastle and the north-east.

Smith was proud of Newcastle's new Civic Centre, which was part of a twelve-storey office block, complete with an underground car park, overlooking the A1. At one time, he had hoped that the renowned Danish designer Arne Jacobsen would take on the project but, in the event, it was designed by Newcastle City Architect George Kenyon and opened in 1968 by King Olav of Norway. There was a striking Nordic influence to the new council chamber, with walls of Norwegian slate offset by walnut and marble interiors and the aged, copper finishings of the exteriors. Kenyon and a local sculptor, David Wynne, designed the 'River God Tyne' – a sixteen-foot-high bronze statue that stands outside the council chamber – and Wynne also designed the 'Swans in Flight' sculpture in the inner courtyard, the five swans representing the five Scandinavian countries of Norway, Denmark, Sweden, Finland and Iceland.

Work on the Tyne Metro began while Smith was leader of Newcastle City Council and he worked hard to persuade various local authorities to co-operate in cleaning up the river Tyne and help turn Newcastle Airport into an international air terminal. But few of the other construction projects he forced through were either popular or architecturally distinguished. Swan House was an ugly multi-storey office block on stilts on top of a roundabout with the new Central Motorway, built between 1963 and 1969, running underneath it. In 2002, it was converted into apartments and renamed '55 Degrees North' after the Earth's circle of latitude that runs through the city. Even uglier was Westgate House, a 150-foot-high twelve-storey office block opposite the station on the eastern end of Westgate Road. It was supposed to be a 'gateway' to the city and confident symbol of the new economic era but, to the journalist Christopher Booker, writing in 1978, it was a 'monstrous and overpowering concrete block utterly out of scale and context with the nearby fine Victorian buildings.'

Brooker was yet more appalled by the redevelopment of John Dobson's 1824 masterpiece, One Eldon Square. He described the first phase of the reconstruction, which opened in 1976, as 'perhaps the greatest single act of cultural vandalism in Britain since the war.' Only one side of the original square was to remain, the rest dominated by 'an astonishingly brutal shopping centre put up by Capital and Counties.'

One of the most sensitive projects, as far as T Dan Smith personally was concerned, was Cruddas Park in Scottswood, where several hundred new high-rise flats had been built by Wimpey, using a Swedish pre-cast modular design very similar to the one deployed by Ohlsson-Skarne. The tower blocks were designed and built by Leslie and Co, a Bovis company, and named after George Cruddas, a founder member of the nearby Vickers-Armstrong armament works.

When work on the flats began in the early 1960s, they were a source of great pride among Labour politicians and excitement among local people. 'Isn't it wonderful?' said a schoolteacher.

'Newcastle is getting a Manhattan skyline.' But five years later, the residents discovered that the much-vaunted Swedish pre-fabrication techniques had resulted in damp, badly constructed and poorly executed buildings with high maintenance costs. With unemployment rising and reduced funding available for social housing, the reality of high-rise and new-town living, which was nowhere near as sociable as the old mining communities it was intended to replace, seemed a far cry from T Dan Smith's idealistic image. After 1969, no more contracts in Newcastle or Peterlee and Aycliffe new towns were awarded to Ohlsson-Skarne or other companies employing the Scandinavian model but the legacy left by their defective houses and flats inflicted lasting damage to Smith's reputation.

It wasn't only Cruddas Park that became synonymous with Newcastle's desecration. The city's most notorious brutalist landmark was Trinity Square multi-storey car park in Gateshead on the south bank of the Tyne. It was designed by Rodney Gordon for the Owen Luder partnership, which, like Poulson, favoured massive, bare concrete forms denuded of cladding or decoration. The persistent rain and damp of the north-eastern winters soon turned them a shabby shade of brown and grey, streaked with marks where the rainwater had run down the sides. The car park would have its moment in cinematic history, becoming a favourite stop-off on cult tours of the city. But in other respects, it was every bit as desolate and ugly as the buildings that Poulson himself had designed, like Forster Square in Bradford: a grey, lime-streaked eyesore housing offices and shops. Or the Castlegate Centre in Stockton, the Horsefair flats in Pontefract and the drab new façade, complete with multi-storey office block on top, at Cannon Street station in London.

BANDIT COUNTRY

The financial meltdown of Poulson's over-stretched empire, which required so many bribes and backhanders to keep going, had begun at the end of December 1969, when he stepped down from day-to-day control of JGL Poulson and Associates, and accelerated in November 1971, when he filed his own bankruptcy petition. In a surreal twist to the story, he was still acting as an Inland Revenue commissioner in Wakefield when the hearings into his case got underway. As more and more revelations seeped into the public realm and a Metropolitan Police inquiry was announced, the scandal accounted for Reggie Maudling, who resigned as Home Secretary in July 1972, his links to the Gozo hospital contract and the three Poulson companies exposed. The following year, Granada Television broadcast a hard-hitting edition of *World in Action* entitled 'The Rise and Fall of John Poulson'.

The producer, Raymond Fitzwalter, was the former deputy news editor of the *Telegraph & Argus* in Bradford and had conducted an earlier investigation of Poulson in print. Before transmission, the programme makers had to face down the unease of some members of the ITA board, who had come under pressure from government sources anxious to protect the reputations of Maudling and other politicians linked to Poulson's firms.

But by now, cover-ups were too late. The police and the IRS had gone through all those notebooks and ledgers Poulson had compiled to prove to himself and the world just how superior he was to his rivals when it came to finessing deals. On 22nd June, 1973, the sixty-three-year-old was arrested and charged with corruption in the awarding of building contracts and, on the same day, George Pottinger, a senior civil servant at the Scottish office, was arrested in Edinburgh. Pottinger had been delegated to work closely on the new Alpine-style leisure complex in Aviemore, which was intended to bring more tourism to the Highlands. Poulson won the contract and, in the process, was alleged to have given £30,000 to Pottinger in bribes, as well as a new car, tailor-made suits and foreign holidays. One of Poulson's companies even designed and built a house for Pottinger – a bungalow called 'Pelicans' – overlooking Muirfield golf course. Pottinger was at a black-tie dinner at Muirfield on the evening of the 22nd in the company of two sheriffs and a High Court judge. They had just reached the brandy-and-cigars stage when Detective Superintendent Kenneth Everidge, deputy head of the Fraud Squad and renowned in Scotland Yard as 'a good thief taker', made an unwelcome appearance.

On 9th July, another of Poulson's friends and one of the biggest fish in the north, Alderman Andrew Cunningham, was added to the charge sheet. 'Back Handy Andy', or the 'Godfather', as the trade-union baron was also known, was arrested at his solicitor's office in Newcastle after a warrant was issued by Scotland Yard Deputy Assistant Commissioner James Crane, the head of the Fraud Squad and the man who had arrested Poulson. The accusation against Cunningham was that he and Poulson had conspired to ensure that he 'corruptly received gifts or considerations as inducements in relation to diverse public bodies and their building projects.' As well as being chairman of the Durham Police Authority, Cunningham had been on a dozen important and influential local government and political bodies in the north-east. Power had coursed through his hands as if he was directly connected to the National Grid and projects promoted or dashed according to his patronage. The alderman resigned as Police Authority Chairman the day after his arrest and after two GMWU officials stumped up £5,000 each to get him out on bail.

BANDIT COUNTRY

What was now the biggest corruption inquiry in British history, finally and inevitably caught up with T Dan Smith, the one-time Mr Newcastle and driving force in the north, who was arrested for the second time in October 1973.

The Poulson case culminated in a fifty-two-day trial at Leeds Crown Court in February and March 1974, at a time when the country was still in the grip of the three-day week and the miners' union was on its collision course with the Conservative government. The proceedings cost £1.25m, with 100 witnesses called and 500 documents presented as evidence. In his summing-up the judge, Mr Justice Waller, who had been one of the three Appeal Court judges who had dismissed Michael Luvaglio's and Dennis Stafford's appeals in 1972, described how Poulson's 'web of corruption' had amounted to bribes worth £500,000 and encompassed 23 local authorities and 300 individuals. On 15th March, Poulson and Pottinger were both found guilty. Waller sentenced Poulson to five years' imprisonment, later increased to seven. Pottinger got five years, reduced to four on appeal.

In April, they were followed into the dock at Leeds by T Dan Smith and Alderman Andrew Cunningham. Appearing as a character witness for Cunningham was Lord George Brown, who had enjoyed that free holiday in Majorca in the 1960s, courtesy of Smith and Vince Landa. The one-time Foreign Secretary and Deputy PM described Back Handy Andy as 'outstandingly forthright, courageous, solid and loyal' and the alderman's wife, Freda, said that her husband had always 'loved what he was doing', but the jury were not impressed. Smith, who had pleaded guilty, and Cunningham, who had not, were both sent to prison. T Dan got six years, reduced to five on appeal, and Cunningham four years, later reduced to three.

Reginald Maudling and his fellow MPs and Poulson bene-ficiaries, John Cordle, Conservative, and Labour's Albert Roberts, wriggled off the hook, claiming parliamentary immunity. It wasn't until July 1977, after several years of obfuscation and delay, that the report of a parliamentary inquiry into the conduct of the three MPs was finally published. In a 'Save Reggie' ploy, not dissimilar to the Owen Patterson affair in 2022, Tory MPs were whipped to 'take note' of the report's findings, rather than endorse them. They voted accordingly and no punishment was imposed, although, given the sentences handed down to Poulson, Pottinger, Cunningham and Smith, the corrupt trio were extremely lucky not to go to prison. Maudling had been briefly rehabilitated by Margaret Thatcher, who appointed him Shadow Foreign Secretary in 1975 but sacked him a year later, but he never did get his pot of gold, succumbing to alcoholism, along with his wife, and dying of kidney failure and cirrhosis of the liver in 1979.

The big men who had run the north-east in the 1960s had been brought down. But what of Vincent Luvaglio, the self-made gambling magnate and supposed kingpin of organised crime, who had become rich during the Smith and Cunningham years? What had become of him, and would he ever be brought to book? It hadn't escaped comment that the supremo of the Durham Police Authority during the one-armed bandit boom and the Angus Sibbet murder trial had been the now publicly disgraced Alderman Andrew Cunningham. There was widespread suspicion that Masonic corruption may have extended to members of the police force too, who must have been aware of Cunningham's activities but chose to ignore them. If Scotland Yard hadn't intervened, would the locals ever have fearlessly and rigorously investigated their own boss? Or were they too busy receiving backhanders like everyone else? In those circumstances, could the same plain-clothes detectives like Detective Superintendent Ronald Kell and his team be trusted to have conducted an honest inquiry into the Dennis Stafford and Michael Luvaglio case?

That was the question asked by the writer CP Taylor when his play *Bandits* was produced by the RSC in 1977. In a world of clubs filled with punters, slot machines and easy money, he portrayed a cynical, despairing and world-weary police superintendent whose feeling is 'What does it matter if men are wrongly convicted of a particular crime if they would have been guilty of something else anyway?' The superintendent's view of the murder and subsequent convictions is that, consequently, 'that's three bandits less in the world. Best thing they've ever done in their lives.' In Taylor's narrative, the evidence is deliberately manipulated to get the verdict that 'righteous citizens' will find acceptable with the proviso that the racketeers in sharp suits were no more immoral than the politicians and developers whose respectable images and affluent lifestyles were supported by widespread white-collar crime. It made for a compelling drama but, as Michael and Dennis would have been the first to point out, the white-collar fat cats like Poulson and T Dan Smith still got off relatively lightly in terms of jail time: three- or four-year terms being very different to life.

As audiences queued up to watch Cecil Taylor's play at the Donmar Warehouse, the real-life bandits were still locked away in Yorkshire and on the Isle of Wight. News had emerged that Dennis Stafford, the self-styled Gentleman Gangster and Count of Monte Christo, was continuing to have problems with authority. With the aid of his fellow Parkhurst inmate, the Russian spy Peter Kroger, he had drawn up a petition protesting his innocence and sent it to various people whose names and addresses he'd found in *Debrett's* and *Who's Who*, both of which were surprisingly available in the prison library. He had also complained that, on the orders of the Home Secretary, he was not allowed to have a personal radio in his cell or other little conveniences permitted to other maximum-security prisoners and could only watch television for entertainment, which meant no Open University courses. Neither could he take lessons from an outside tutor in subjects like law or business studies because the Home Office would only pay for a teacher to come in if there were at least two prisoners in the class, and nobody else in the special unit in Parkhurst wanted to join in.

Behind these protestations, Stafford was nonetheless perceived to be deploying all the old skills and knowledge of how to survive prison life that he'd acquired during his previous stints in Wormwood Scrubs, Dartmoor, Port of Spain and Armley jail in Leeds. As a Category A inmate, he was in the company of men like Charlie Richardson, the train robber Charlie Wilson and the Kray twins, whom he believed were over-rated. Reggie Kray had a similar view of Stafford, who nonetheless claimed to have seen a gentler side to Ronnie than the rest of the world ever saw.

By comparison, Michael Luvaglio, a first timer with no old friends or accomplices on the inside, was finding life behind bars a much tougher experience. He'd become ever more religious since his conviction and was commended as a model prisoner by the governor of Wakefield. He'd also taken up painting and done a series of portraits of the Bishop of Wakefield, Richard Hare, who came to visit him on a fortnightly basis. Otherwise, Michael's days and nights continued to be dominated by the endless and, so far, abortive attempts to have his case re-opened, and worrying about the health of his widowed mother, Maud. 'Please God, I will be justly released from my prison while my mother is still alive,' he wrote to David Napley.

Michael made no mention in any of his letters of his missing brother, whose fate, like the disappearance of Harry Lime in *The Third Man*, still continued to grip the imagination of the north-east.

CHAPTER NINETEEN

VINCE LANDA'S OLD house, Dryderdale Hall, was no longer empty. In December 1972, it had been bought by Dr Ananda Chakrabarti, a thirty-year-old Indian geologist and tin-mine owner whose English wife, Jane, was born in Sherburn, four miles east of Durham. The couple had three children and said they were . enjoying spending about a month at a time, four times a year, in their £70,000 property. 'It was really going down the drain' when they moved in, said Dr Chakrabarti, but he had installed fountains and floodlights in the grounds and was planning to build an indoor heated pool and sauna. He wasn't bothered by who had lived there before, he said, and knew very little about him.

Chakrabarti may have been cheerfully ignorant of Vince Landa's life and whereabouts but the big constituency who had followed the Bandit King's story avidly for the past fifteen years or more were eager for news. Finally, in 1977, ten years after Michael's conviction and Vince's disappearance, they got it. The Newcastle *Evening Chronicle* received a tip-off that Landa had been arrested in Sicily, having apparently spent the last decade living a double life worthy of Tom Ripley, the charming, amoral anti-hero of Patricia Highsmith's series of novels. A reporter flew out to Malta and then to Sicily and discovered that the 'runaway gaming boss', as the paper called him, had reinvented himself as George Rowe, a wealthy British yachtsman with property interests in Italy, Malta and Greece.

The agreeable Mr Rowe had told members of the Royal Malta Yacht Club (RMYC) in Valletta that he was planning to go into business supplying oil rigs in the Red Sea. Vince had arrived in Malta from Spain in early 1977 and promptly sold the boat he had sailed over in and bought a 129-tonne yacht that had been moored in Valletta for the past decade. It had an English captain, Charles Smith, from Exeter, and Vince applied for it to be registered in Colchester in the UK under the name *Joy of Lee*. The RMYC berthing master, Larry Darmanin, got to know the Englishman well, or thought he did. Mr Rowe, he said, was often accompanied by his eighteen-year-old son – who was, in fact, Dean Landa – or one of his daughters but Darmanin hadn't 'the slightest inkling' about his Tyne Tees past. 'We've never had any complaints about him,' said Darmanin. 'I've met him socially at the RMYC and he's a charming person to talk to.'

Vince had spent £10,000 refitting his new yacht and had insured it for £45,000 the day before it set sail for Sicily on a trial run. But he wasn't on board. He had gone on ahead by plane, telling Darmanin that he had to 'meet some oil people there' to arrange a contract. It was about 200 nautical miles from Valletta to Messina – a well-worn route – and the weather and sea conditions were favourable, but the *Joy of Lee* never arrived in Sicily. On 1st December, it suddenly and mysteriously sank off Messina, leaving its three-man crew – two Italians and one Maltese – to struggle ashore.

Arthur Garbutt, the Lloyds agent in Messina who interviewed the crew, was baffled. 'It's very strange,' he said. 'Just before the yacht left it had a complete refit and was in good order. They had spent a lot of money on her and it's very unusual that she sank when the weather was so good, and the sea was calm.' So, was it just another unfortunate accident that could have befallen anyone? Had the propeller caught in a fishing net, as Vince claimed? Or was it a suspiciously convenient incident for an owner in need of cash and anticipating collecting the insurance money (as some people believed had been the story behind the Piccadilly Club fire in Newcastle in 1966)?

The Sicilian police shared Garbutt's suspicions, especially when they discovered that 'George Rowe' was better known as Vince Landa and was on Interpol's wanted list. The *Joy of Lee*'s crew were interviewed but could offer no clues as to the causes of the sinking and claimed ignorance of the real identity and location of the owner. But when the retrieved yacht was towed ashore and searched, large amounts of dollar bills were found along with a false passport in the name of Rowe, showing that Vince had recently spent time in Florida.

With the aid of a tip-off from the *Joy of Lee*'s skipper, Charles Smith, who had stayed behind in Malta, the elusive George Rowe was tracked down at the Hotel Jolly Maritimo in Catania and placed under arrest. Under questioning, Vince confessed to his true identity and described his primary occupation as 'sailor'. He admitted that he'd been running an illegal ferry service between Spain, Malta and Italy, flying the Red Ensign, the flag traditionally flown by British merchant ships, and said that he'd also made business trips to the US and had visited Britain several times during his decade on the run. The UK trips had been mainly to see his children but hadn't involved his first wife, Gwen, who had left him some years before and gone back to Edinburgh, where she was living under her maiden name, Gwen Sinclair.

While the Sicilian authorities contemplated what charges they were going to bring against him, Vince was brought before local magistrates, who refused bail and ordered him to be detained in Syracuse prison. News of his capture travelled fast. NORTH'S MR BIG ARRESTED IN SICILY, proclaimed the Newcastle *Evening Chronicle* on 4th December. Reminding their readers that Landa was suspected of being behind a £3m one-armed bandit fraud, the paper contacted the now retired DS Ronald Kell at his home in East Horrington near Sunderland, where he talked of how he had spent nearly three years 'trying to break Landa's racket' back in the 1960s. Kell shared the frustration of Neville Trotter, the Conservative MP for Tynemouth who, in the House of Commons on 12th December, demanded an explanation from the Attorney General, Sam Silkin, as to why Vince had not been found and extradited long before?

The answer to Trotter's question appeared to involve the money Landa had sent out of the country during the boom years of Social Club Services: an escape fund that had provided him with the means to buy the silence of police and foreign powers in Majorca, Malta and Italy for ten long years. But now the money was running out, which was why he'd resorted to the yacht fraud in an attempt to regain some liquidity.

Vince's sixty-seven-year-old mother, Maud, living alone in a small village in Dorset, was contacted and asked for her thoughts. If she'd been honest, she would have said that she was much more excited about soon being reunited with Michael, who, along with Dennis Stafford, now had a pre-release day job. Stafford was living in a Pentonville hostel, while Michael, who had been transferred from Wakefield to Wormwood Scrubs the previous year, was in temporary accommodation, address not disclosed. As to her eldest son's sudden reappearance, Maud said she was 'very surprised' to hear about it. She said that he had offered to come home three months after his father, Frank, died in 1971 but that she'd had no idea where he was. 'He just went abroad, and I didn't hear any more from him. As regards to coming back now, he'll have to please himself. I would like to see him but it's up to him entirely.'

It probably wasn't entirely up to Vince, who spent another year in and out of jail in Sicily, trying on the one hand to pay off Italian prosecutors – who were not unfamiliar with bribes given their long experience of dealing with the Mafia – and on the other to negotiate with the British authorities the possible terms of his return to the UK. On 6th December, 1978, his concerns seemingly allayed, he finally flew back to London, hired a car and drove up to the north-east. The next day, accompanied by a solicitor, he walked into Chester-Le-Street police station in County Durham and gave himself up. He had lost none of his gift for charm and fast talking and, within forty-eight hours, he was out again on bail on fraud charges and, by January 1979, he was living in a remote country cottage in the Yorkshire Dales and waiting for his day in court to come around.

Vince's timing was propitious. On 5th January, 1979, his brother Michael and Dennis Stafford were released on licence. If the months they'd been held on remand in early 1967 were included, Michael and Dennis – who were now forty-two and forty-five years old, respectively, had been in prison for twelve years. The terms of Michael's parole stipulated that he should have no contact whatsoever with anyone on a criminal charge. So of his older brother he saw nothing and he didn't speak to him on the telephone either. Refusing requests for interviews, he declined to comment on the rights and wrongs of his conviction. He just slipped away into south London and reunited with his mother, who had moved back up from Dorset and was living in a house in East Dulwich.

Vince felt less constrained and, on 26th March, 1979, he gave an interview to the Newcastle *Evening Chronicle*. He didn't explicitly say he thought his brother was innocent and appeared to have forgotten his boast outside Moot Hall in March 1967 when he said he had four private investigators working on the Angus Sibbet case and was planning to bring a private prosecution against the guilty man. He said that he had not yet spoken to Michael because of his own impending trial, which clashed with the conditions of his brother's release. But Vince's twenty-one-year-old son, Dean, who lived in London, had seen him.

I understand that Michael is very well, and I think it's a very remarkable achievement to have stood up to twelve years in jail. I was locked up for five months in Majorca and in that short time I began to miss birds, flowers and everyday things. Michael was locked up as a young man and has come out middle aged. Those years are irreplaceable. As a convicted killer he was kept with other convicted murderers and has known no kindness from his fellow prisoners. Anyone who knew Michael will know that he cared for other people. I believe he wants to do social work in the future.

Whatever the future had in store for Michael, the day of reckoning for Vincent Francis Luvaglio had been scheduled for 22nd February, 1980, at Teeside Crown Court. It was the first time that the One-Armed Bandit King had been seen openly in the region for thirteen years and the public areas and press benches were full to capacity. The forty-eight-year-old Landa, who arrived with his new nineteen-year-old fiancée, Julie Hamblin, a former waitress, and his daughters Diane, aged twenty, and Claire, aged seventeen, cut a rather different figure to the man who had held court on the steps of Moot Hall at the end of his brother's trial. He'd put away his dark glasses and his hair was longer, blow dried in the fashion of the time, and he was sporting a Zapata moustache.

Instead of attempting to field an elaborate and expensive defence, Landa effectively threw himself on the mercy of the court, pleading guilty to seven charges of fraud involving gaming machines he'd supplied to north-eastern working-men's clubs. It was roughly the same indictment as at the Social Club Services trial in 1969: Vince had signed up clubs to buy new gaming machines but supplied them with old ones. He had guaranteed them a £40-a-month profit but had collected all the takings plus a forty per cent rake-off from the HP company. The verdict was never in doubt but, to Landa's evident surprise and delight, and the disbelief of many onlookers, he was sentenced to pay a £2,750 fine and £1,000 costs and that was it. There was to be no prison time. No ride in handcuffs in the back of a black Austin Princess to Durham or Armley or Wakefield prison. No sojourn on the Isle of Wight or reunion with his old adversary Reggie Kray and other murderers and psychopaths. No porridge. No slopping out. The London boy who had gone north to make his fortune, ending up living like a titled squire and then fleeing the country to spend more than a decade cruising the Mediterranean, had got away with it again. 'I feel as if I've hit the jackpot,' Vince told reporters. 'I am guilty. I don't think I should have gone to jail, but I thought public opinion would send me there. If I'd known that the police would be so fair, I'd have given myself up much earlier. But I was deeply shocked when Michael and Dennis were given life and I thought it might happen to me too. I've been the biggest loser of all until today.'

Toasting his freedom with a double Scotch in a hotel bar, Vince itemised all the blows he had suffered. His business empire had long since gone into liquidation. He'd had to sell Dryderdale Hall and his yacht had sunk off Sicily and, so far, the insurance company had refused to pay him a penny. But now he was back in the region to stay and living as a divorce at Beechfield in Newton Aycliffe. He had got a new job too, as director of a firm converting cars from petrol to natural gas. 'Now I'm going to make another million,' he said, before adding, modestly, that it could 'take me until the end of next year.'

By no means was everyone convinced that Vince's losses were comparable to the experience of his brother, who had been locked up for twelve years for something he had said repeatedly he didn't do. There was also some scepticism about the 'surprisingly fair' Durham police, as Vince described them, and speculation that they and the judiciary might have been bought off at some point. But over the coming days, there were also tributes to Landa's entrepreneurial skills by assorted local friends and associates, politely described as 'colourful' by the press. His old dog and horse-racing companion Ray Thubron, who had first introduced him to the world of the working-men's clubs in 1959, was emphatic. 'He's a fabulous man,' he said. 'A genius. Of course, there was fiddling but that's life.'

George Reynolds, orphan turned safe cracker and future owner of Darlington Football Club, said that Landa had 'educated Northeastern clubland. They didn't know what a one-armed bandit was until he came here. Now I feel sorry for him. They've just put it [corruption] all down to Vince.'

A similar view was taken by George Shotton, who had been acquitted of burglary and receiving stolen goods in the October 1967 trial in which Vince was implicated. He, too, believed that Landa had been made a scapegoat. 'A lot of people in this area, businesses and prominent people, have feathered their nests,' he said. In the process, they had acquired their money crookedly 'and their only way to get away with it was to make out that Landa was the arch villain.'

In all the speculation about Vince's next move, there was still a notable lack of regret or explanation from him about the circumstances that had led to Angus Sibbet's death and his brother's imprisonment. Three hundred miles away in south London, Michael had started working with a charity that helped mentally handicapped young people. But he was still determined to clear his name and he had not yet lost faith in the appeal process. He had high hopes of a two-part BBC documentary entitled *The One-Armed Bandit Murder* that was broadcast in March 1980 and in which he and Dennis Stafford were both interviewed by Stuart Prebble, another experienced investigative reporter. Michael said that he was sure that, if the jury that had convicted him watched the programme and learned about the witness statements and files supposedly lost in the Home Office archive, they would have serious doubts about the safety of their original verdict. His aim, in co-operation with Sir David Napley, as he had become, was still to persuade the government to set up a full public inquiry.

Alas, the government of the day, now headed by Margaret Thatcher, with William Whitelaw as Home Secretary, declined to respond. A climactic moment in the story was on its way. But not quite in the form that Michael Luvaglio and his supporters would have hoped for.

CHAPTER TWENTY

WHEN DENNIS STAFFORD came out of Gartree prison in Leicester in 1979, he had £12 in cash and a 'useless suit', which no longer fitted him and, even worse for such a dapper dresser, it was in a style that had gone out of fashion.

After such a long time away, Dennis might have been expected to go back to London to see his parents, Joe and Maggie, and to catch up with his good friend Wally Birch at the Londoner and the other West End clubs they used to frequent. But instead, he went in the opposite direction and headed, for the third time in his life, right back to the north-east, where his estranged wife and daughter still lived and where he had acquired a certain kind of fame that would be hard to live down.

Newcastle was no longer T Dan Smith's city. Unemployment in the region was rising and traditional mainstays like coal and steel looked in peril from a Conservative government that was intent on a radical departure from the economic policies of the past. The Newcastle club scene had changed too, and the Dolce

Vita was not the only famous name from the 1960s to have closed down or changed hands. The taste for softly lit interiors and men in dinner jackets and women with teased-up hair had been replaced by the disco craze, exemplified by Slooopy's, the new discotheque the Bailey Group had opened on the top floor above the old Dolce. Other clubs now featured regular 'stag nights' with 'exotic dancers'.

Mike Jeffrey's A'Gogo had closed in 1968 – Jeffrey was killed in a plane crash five years later – and the site of Vince Landa's former Piccadilly Club, gutted by fire in 1966, was briefly acquired by Bob Monkhouse in partnership with a local entertainer. They called their new club Change Is and the theme was meant to be excitingly unpredictable, with different music, menus and line-ups each night. Monkhouse, who later admitted he knew nothing about being a club owner or licensed victualler ordering food and drink and hiring staff, ploughed around £40,000 of his own savings into the venture and lived to regret it. His business partner was a part-time hypnotist called Ronnie Markham who went under the stage name of 'Romark' and, one day in 1970, Monkhouse discovered that Romark had hypnotised all the funds out of their joint account and made off to South Africa. Conceding defeat, Monkhouse sold up at a loss and the next owners transformed the club into a discotheque called Bloomers.

The one exception to the slide downmarket was Tuxedo Junction in Market Street, which combined lavish restaurants with three dance floors including a disco and light show that was proclaimed to be the best in the north. It was owned by the Tyneside businessman Michael Quadrini, whose company Absolute Leisure went on to open the floating night clubs the Tuxedo Royale and the Tuxedo Princess on converted ferry boats on the river Tyne.

After more than a decade in prison, Dennis Stafford's sex drive was as strong as ever and a glitzy night club like Tuxedo Junction, complete with willing hostesses and attractive young women on the town, was exactly the kind of place he felt comfortable in. In the winter of 1979/1980, Stafford made regular appearances at the club with his latest girlfriend, Lorraine Brown, a model he'd met one night at the Oxford Galleries dance hall on New Bridge Street, where she had won the Miss Variety Club of Great Britain contest. Described as 'a raven-haired beauty' by the compere, Bobby Pattinson, the nineteen-year-old Lorraine came from Longhorsley, near Morpeth in Northumberland, where her parents ran a restaurant.

Stafford meeting and seducing an attractive young woman in a night club was an old, familiar story. So was the response that his name engendered. When Lorraine's mother and father discovered who he was, they warned their teenage daughter that she would either have to end the relationship or move out of their house altogether. She chose to stick with Stafford, who had been temporarily staying with his ex-wife, Pat, and her daughter, Paula, near Durham but that couldn't last. The man who came to Dennis's aid and who had been with him that night at the beauty contest was none other than his old employer and business associate, Mr Vincent Landa. In a weird reprise of the arrangement in Peterlee fifteen years before, Vince once again used his local contacts, whom he had remained in touch with, to help Stafford and his lover find a £16,000 three-bedroom house in Newton Aycliffe, the same County Durham town where Vince was living with his young fiancée, Julie Hamblin.

In the 1960s, Aycliffe and Peterlee had been joined at the hip, both under the stewardship of the new town corporation represented by T Dan Smith and Alderman Andrew Cunningham. In 1966, Vince had used his connections there to get the house for Stafford and Salena Jones in Westmoreland Rise in Peterlee – the address from where Dennis and Michael Luvaglio had set out in the red E-type on their fateful drive to the Birdcage Club on the night of 4th January, 1967. Now Stafford was back on the same patch and seemingly involved with Landa again in some way that suggested a bond existed between them, perhaps pertaining to a secret that had yet to be revealed.

When he walked out of court at the end of his trial in February 1980, Vince talked about having a new job as the director of a company trying to covert cars from using petrol to liquefied natural gas. The business in question was the Washington Car and Carriage Company, run out of Washington, County Durham, by a friend of Vince's called John Baxter, who also owned garages and supermarkets. In his autobiography, *Fun-Loving Criminal*, published in 2004, Stafford claimed that Vince introduced him to Baxter and that, in turn, the enterprising Dennis won a contract from a company in Italy to market liquefied natural gas in the UK.

With prospects looking up, Stafford and Lorraine Brown decided to go down to London, where they moved into a flat in Shootup Hill in Cricklewood, but they weren't alone. In the summer of 1980, Vince Landa's seventeen-year-old daughter, Claire, came down to join them and somehow Lorraine and Claire got themselves into a spot of trouble, stealing a Barclaycard and a Diners Club card from the jacket pocket of an accountant called Terence Bland, who Stafford was meant to be working with on the natural gas project. Bland had an office in Stanmore and, while he was in another room, possibly in a meeting with Stafford, the girls took the cards from a jacket, which was hanging on a chair, and went off to buy over £250 worth of clothes in Oxford Street stores. The theft was quickly discovered and the police arrived at the Cricklewood flat to talk to the girls but not before Stafford had disappeared.

Brown and Sinclair appeared at Marlborough Street Magistrates Court on 22nd August, where they both pleaded guilty. Brown, now twenty-one, was fined £250 and Claire £200. The defence solicitor, Peter Hughman – who co-wrote the 1971 book *Most Unnatural* about the Angus Sibbet murder – told the court that Brown would be moving out of Stafford's £35-a-week flat and returning to live with her mother in Northumberland, while Claire would be going back up to County Durham to live with her father. The court was also informed that Scotland Yard would very much like to talk to Dennis Stafford about the frauds but had been unable to find him, which was not surprising as the fun-loving criminal, in knowing breach of his parole and also on the run from a drink-driving charge, had already left the country.

In his autobiography, the lustful Dennis said that, when he was back in London, he had run into Salena Jones again, which would have threatened the longevity of the Lorraine Brown liaison even without the credit-card fiasco. He also said that, despite the big deals meant to be in the air with Baxter and the Italians and liquefied natural gas, he badly 'needed to make some money somehow'. He'd come up with a plan to drive a Rolls Royce to Greece for a rich client and then sell it and return to the UK by boat. But, just as this delicate deal 'reached a crucial stage', wouldn't you know it, he was confronted by 'a very pushy journalist working for the *News of the World*' who was desperate for an angle. Dennis was 'in a difficult spot'. He suspected the journalist was going to run a story about him and Lorraine Brown whether he co-operated or not. So, for a fee of £12,000, he decided, in a spirit of blamelessness and with the best of intentions, to 'fabricate a story that could later easily be proved to be complete rubbish.' But was it?

Even by the standard of regular 'News of the Screws' exclusives, Stafford's account was explosive and they gave it the full front-page treatment with banner headlines on Sunday, 7th September, 1980. 'I Pulled the Murder Trigger' was the caption beneath the picture of a grinning Dennis, pulling the lever on a one-armed bandit. He confirmed that Angus Sibbet's death had been the result of a dramatic early-morning shootout on a snowbound road and that, despite all the pleas of innocence, the TV programmes and allegations of police malfeasance and the articles in esteemed publications demanding a public inquiry, he had been guilty all along. And what's more, Michael Luvaglio – the devout Catholic – while not a participant, was present at the scene of the crime.

In the course of his 800-word confession, Stafford – who was said to be holed up in an unnamed European hideaway – pulled the rug out from under all the people who had worked so tirelessly on his and Michael's behalf, including his parents, Maggie and Joe, and seemed inordinately proud of the extent to which they had nearly got away with it. 'We managed to cast so much doubt on the verdict because it just didn't happen the way the police and prosecution described it,' he said. 'Very early on the police had a theory of how we managed to do the murder and any evidence that was produced had to be measured against the time schedule they had created for themselves. In fact, I killed Sibbet about four hours later than the time they said. It was because of their own pig-headed narrow mindedness that we nearly got off.'

The libidinous collector, Angus Sibbet, had become greedy, said Stafford, and had been stealing from the firm's fruit-machine takings. He was 'getting involved with some people from Glasgow' and could no longer be trusted. 'In Newcastle they may have thought he was something big, but he was nothing. He was given £100 a week and a company car' and, as well as skimming, he was attempting to blackmail a clubland boss over a car crash some years before where a woman had died. It had been decided that the over-mighty servant should get, at least, a 'bloody good hiding' and Stafford believed it was 'eighty per cent certain he would have gone anyway, even if he did ease up.'

Sibbet had been wary of Stafford from the outset and his suspicion that the 'mystery man' had been recruited to do more than just manage the Piccadilly Club and book acts was well founded. 'When I went up to the North-east, I had a certain reputation. He didn't know what I was up to and felt a little insecure having me around.' Angus might have felt even more insecure if he had known that Stafford had a gun – a Walther PPK with a magazine of eight bullets – which he'd acquired in London and kept in a clip by the steering wheel of the white Mercedes that Vince Landa had given him and Salena Jones.

If what Stafford said was true, Sibbet had tried to pre-empt any trouble that was coming his way and had fired shotgun pellets at a dustbin outside Stafford's and Salena's house in Peterlee and had even tried to poison their milk. Once the 'Mr Big' – who Stafford didn't name – had decided that Angus 'had to go', a meeting was set up between him and Stafford at the Birdcage

Club at midnight on 4th January, 1967, with Michael Luvaglio going along too as the unwitting bait. Sibbet had turned up at the meeting but never went inside the club and the initial damage to the red E-type had been caused by Sibbet's car bumping into it while it was parked outside.

Stafford and Luvaglio left the Birdcage at closing time, which was more like 3am than 2am, and, on their way back to Peterlee, they encountered Sibbet's dark-green Jaguar Mark X parked on the left-hand side of the road under Pesspool bridge in South Hetton. According to Stafford, the collector had 'some sort of place in South Hetton where he hid his loot' and he had been waiting for them there and planning an ambush in the hope that he would get in the first blow. He wasn't alone either. Stafford claimed that there were two people in Sibbet's car and that another man got out and looked like he was running to the phone box, where he made a quick call. He reckoned that the Mark X had been there for some time with the lights out.

Stafford put his foot down and drove on down the A182 towards Easington and Sibbet followed him, flashing his lights. The Mark X bumped into the E-type once, trying to force it off the road, and then, about half a mile from Pesspool bridge, it hit it again, causing the E-type to spin round and come to a halt on the grass verge. Stafford grabbed his gun and got out of the car and allegedly saw that the other unidentified man had got out too and was holding a sawn-off shotgun. As the other gunman tried to take cover, Angus Sibbet came out of his driver's side door holding an automatic pistol. Stafford, standing in the middle of the road with his Walther PPK and fearing that he was about to be killed, shot first and Sibbet went down. When Stafford looked up, the other man had disappeared (perhaps he was running back to the South Hetton telephone box to call John Tumblety?). All the while, a terrified Michael Luvaglio was sitting in the red E-type, shaking with fear, but he had nothing to do with the shooting.

With Sibbet dead, or dying on the ground, Stafford got Michael to get out of the car and help him to lift Sibbet's body into the back of the Mark X. Then, with Michael following him in the red E-type, Stafford drove the Mark X another 400 yards to the right turn into Pesspool Lane. 'I wanted to get off the main road,' he said. 'I didn't know what to do so I left Sibbet there in his car and drove home with Mike in the E Type. I told Mike to keep his mouth closed and he did. I conned my mum and dad. But what could I do? Tell the truth? Mike and I had decided there was very little we could do to cover it up. We just had to take our chances.'

When the pair got back to Westmoreland Rise, Michael was 'feeling a bit shaky' and went to bed but Salena Jones and Pat Burgess didn't know a thing about what had happened. The next morning, Stafford said that it was 'Mike who rang Mr Big' and told him about the shooting and that he was 'over the moon' at the news of Sibbet's death. Later that day, Stafford took his Walther PPK and Sibbet's Beretta, which he had picked up off the road, and drove to the Byker bridge in Newcastle and threw them into the Tyne.

Stafford ended his tale with a mixture of bitterness at the way he had been treated by the prison service and regret that the 'dead straight and very good living' that he and his fellow bandits had been making from selling machines to the working-men's clubs had been derailed. But he left readers in no doubt that he blamed Angus Sibbet's greed for their collective downfall, rather than his own actions that night in South Hetton and Pesspool Lane.

Not the least shocking aspect of Stafford's statement was that he had depicted Michael Luvaglio as, if not an accessory to murder, then at least a witness to events he had spent thirteen years denying. Stafford said that Michael was 'only sent down' because he alibied him and wouldn't change his story. But questions of loyalty aside, the inference that Michael had been lying too was seen as a potentially fatal blow to his attempts to get his conviction overturned. On the weekend that the confession came out, Michael was in Germany with his mother, watching – along with thousands of other pilgrims – the Oberammergau Passion Play in Bavaria, which takes place once every ten years. When he returned to Britain, he made no direct comment about the article other than to repeat that he had nothing to do with the killing, while his cousin, Tony Hewison, informed the press that Dennis Stafford had 'made several attempts to see Michael again but Michael has wisely avoided any contact whatsoever.'

Maggie Stafford said that she and Joe were shattered by their son's revelations. 'It was very wrong of him to trick his dad,' said Maggie. 'He is ill, and this shock has really got him down.' The retired Detective Chief Superintendent Ronald Kell, however, felt vindicated and described how he had been 'grossly libelled' down the years by what he called 'publicity-seeking members of parliament and sharp practice lawyers'.

Michael's lawyer, Sir David Napley, a past president of the Law Society, winced at the imprecation that he could have been involved in any kind of sharp practice. He studied Stafford's confession with care and immediately decided 'it was phoney' as it didn't fit certain known and indisputable facts, such as the sightings of the Mark X and a red E-type Jaguar progressing together through South Hetton *before* midnight on 4th January, 1967. He spoke to his client and was assured that, while Michael 'could not express a view' about the parts of the article concerning Stafford, the parts relating to him were quite untrue and the account that he had given throughout was the correct one.

Napley invited David Mertens, the journalist who wrote the article, to come and see him and pressed him to reveal what level of payment the *News of the World* had offered Stafford to tell his story. Unsatisfied by the answer, he concluded that the confession was 'not the whole truth' but just a sensational version to raise money for the cash-strapped ex-convict. But he stopped short of dismissing it altogether.

In a long statement printed in *The Times* and other papers on 23rd September, Napley returned to the 'lack of precision' revealed at Luvaglio's and Stafford's trial regarding the exact time of Angus Sibbet's death. The time scale advanced at the committal hearing in Peterlee in February 1967 had been midnight to 4am, yet – as Stafford pointed out in his article – at the trial at Moot Hall, it was changed to 11pm to 2am. If, therefore, as Stafford was now claiming, he had killed Sibbet at a much later time than the prosecution alleged, it fell within the original pathologist's estimate and raised the possibility that the murder occurred *after* Michael Luvaglio had been driven home to Westmoreland Rise and had gone to bed. It was a hypothesis backed up by a witness statement from a uniformed police officer that Napley and his team found when they were preparing Michael's appeal. The local constable, PC Maurice Cluer, said that, when he arrived on the scene at 5:30am, blood was still dripping from Angus Sibbet's body. Yet that evidence was never presented at the trial.

As the collective legal head-shaking continued, writers with contacts in the milieu heard that it wasn't just Dennis Stafford's parents who were unhappy with his behaviour. Some of the prominent underworld figures he had been in Parkhurst and Gartree with – Richardson gang members like Frankie Fraser, train robbers like Charlie Wilson and other career criminals – felt that, in his quest for money, Stafford had needlessly and selfishly compromised Michael Luvaglio's efforts to clear his name.

If an empty wallet was the cause, Stafford had already espied another money-making opportunity and, on 28th September, he turned up in the *Sunday People* with his second tell-all confession in three weeks. 'It's all lies,' he said about the earlier *News of the World* story and said he had only done it for the money and to honourably 'show that newspapers will print anything'. It was widely assumed that he had been well paid by the *Sunday People* too – maybe another £10,000 or £12,000, although the sums were not revealed at the time. Either way, the *Sunday People* did not get an awful lot for their outlay, with Stafford merely asserting that all the evidence from the 1967 trial had shown 'that Sibbet had been killed before midnight', which was a direct contradiction of what he had said in the *News of the World*.

In his 255-page autobiography, published in 2007, Stafford devoted all of three paragraphs to his confession and subsequent retraction, claiming again that he had skilfully cooked up the first account knowing it could easily be discredited later and proved to be 'complete rubbish'. But was it really all lies? What if Stafford had gone out again on his own after Michael went to bed and had shot Angus Sibbet in the snow in South Hetton around 4am? Was that so unlikely? Sir David Napley certainly wondered if part of it could be true and felt that Stafford only had himself to blame if people were beginning to wonder whether the true explanation was that 'he knew a lot more about it than he would have had us believe. If a man, for money or for any other reason, is prepared to admit that he committed a murder then someone ought to look closely at it.'

Despite the time that had now passed, Napley stuck by his view that it was 'outrageous' that there had never been a full public inquiry, untrammelled by legalistic considerations, and believed that 'the latest turn of events made it even more desirable and essential' if justice was to remain a central part of 'our heritage and tradition.'

CHAPTER TWENTY-ONE

ANY ATTEMPT TO set up a public inquiry into the One-Armed Bandit Murder in the wake of the two Sunday-newspaper articles would have needed to do without personal appearances by Dennis Stafford. Following the drama and publicity that attended his confessions, along with the unwelcome drink-driving charge, he had gone to ground in Europe, but not before the Home Office had contacted Interpol, who issued the equivalent of a 'Get Stafford' notice to police forces in six countries.

With Stafford nowhere to be found and Michael Luvaglio preferring anonymity as he immersed himself in charity work in south London, the spotlight reverted to their former partner and Michael's older brother. Vince Landa was continuing his efforts to re-establish himself in the north-east and had declined to comment about Stafford's confession in the *News of the World*. But on 29th September, the day after the retraction was printed in the *Sunday People*, the Bandit King announced that he was embarking on an exciting new project. In a change of tack, he was venturing into the hospitality business and sinking £150,000 (more like £650,000 in 2022 and seemingly an indication that he still had access to capital) into buying the Castle in Durham. A former pub near the Market Place in Claypath, in the city centre, the Castle had closed in the summer of 1980 after a drugs raid and Vince said that he had 'snapped it up' for half of what the previous owner had paid. He was planning to turn it into 'a top-class restaurant and function centre' and it would be run as a joint concern in tandem with his fiancé and wife-to-be, Julie, and his three daughters.

Landa explained that he had been 'looking for some time for a business for my family. Newcastle has plenty going for it. Sunderland is a dormitory town at the moment, but Durham is the ideal spot. It's a beautiful city.' The ambitious makeover would see the new Castle catering for 120 diners with a wide range of food on offer, 'including vegetarian, health food and North African dishes', and there would be rooms for conferences, business meetings and council gatherings. In the evenings, the lighting would change and part of the bar area would be transformed into a disco, and he also intended to install a sauna and solarium for the comfort of his guests. One potential source of custom he wanted to focus on was American servicemen and their families. There were still a number of US military bases in the area and the north-east region's links with the American Air Force went back to World War II. 'Too many people wait for business to come to them,' said Vince, bullishly. 'I believe in going out to get it.'

It was bold and optimistic talk but bad luck seemed to stalk the project from the outset. On the night that Vince completed his purchase, gales blew the roof off, the main sewer collapsed and the basement was flooded. It was expensive to fix but fix it they did. But then, in July 1981, barely six months after opening, a fire broke out in a back room only a couple of hours after closing time. It was the weekend of the Durham Miners' Gala, the annual celebration of the history of the Durham Coalfield and its trade-union heritage and culture. Thousands of miners and their families paraded through the city streets behind brass bands and the banners, all colourfully illustrated, of the various NUM lodges before congregating at the Old Racecourse to hear speeches by prominent Labour Party and trade-union figures, which included that year the rising star Neil Kinnock, MP for Islwyn in South Wales.

The theme of the day may have been the usual blend of socialism and solidarity tinged with Christian principles in the face of Margaret Thatcher's Conservative government, but there were plenty of miners and staunch socialists present who had been active on welfare committees and in working-men's clubs that had bought one-armed bandits from Vince Landa in the Social Club Services boom in the early 1960s.

When the speech-making was over, the city's pubs began to fill up and, by closing time that evening, the Castle was packed. When the fire began, there were still about 150 customers in the bar, who all managed to escape unhurt, while two guests who were staying in the hotel got out over the roof and two members of staff used another rooftop exit. The blaze was confined to the disco but thick smoke belched into other rooms and damaged the entire building. Vince Landa, despite not having an oxygen mask, accompanied the firemen as they scoured the rooms looking for any trapped guests. 'The place was black with smoke, but I said I'd go with them because I knew the way,' said Vince afterwards.

Fortunately, everyone who had been in the building got out and Vince took satisfaction from the fact that his investment in smoke detectors and fire alarms had paid off. He said that some vandals had been in the bar earlier in the evening, trashing the gents' lavatory and ripping a phone off the wall, but he did not think they were connected and reckoned the fire was more likely to have been caused by an electrical fault. He didn't know how much the damage would amount to but feared that the rewiring alone would 'cost thousands' and said that the hotel would remain closed until the whole place had been made safe.

It was not quite fifteen years since fire had gutted the Piccadilly Club in Newcastle. Whether the blaze at the Castle was another attempted insurance scam or just an unfortunate accident was not explained but the hotel never re-opened.

If Landa had taken a hit from the failure of the Castle, he showed no outward sign of it and, a couple of years later, he was front-page news again when he and Julie Hamblin tied the knot at St John's Methodist church in Ashbrooke, Sunderland. There was a champagne lunch for family and friends at the Barnes hotel, followed by an evening party for 300. The celebrations and toasts to the future happiness and good fortune of the bride and groom mirrored that great evening in Sunderland back in 1963 when the newly minted Bandit King hosted his first big bash. The Charity Gala at the Rink Ballroom had announced Landa and his company on the north-eastern stage at a moment when clubs throughout the region were clamouring to buy his gaming machines and his income was soaring by the month. Whatever the disparity between his wealth then and his superficial prosperity twenty years later, the north-east as a whole was entering a period of deep and traumatic change.

The Thatcher government, which was re-elected in a landslide two months later, was intent on pursuing an uncompromising free-market ethos with industrial and trade-union reform at its core. In the move towards a service economy, traditional but increasingly unprofitable nationalised industries were in the firing line. The mercilessly unsentimental Scottish-American businessman Ian McGregor had already undertaken a drastic slimming-down of British steelmaking on the government's behalf and, in March 1983, he was appointed head of the National Coal Board, with a brief to conduct a similarly radical overhaul of coal mining. In early 1984, he announced an initial list of twenty uneconomic pits that were to close, precipitating the bitterly divisive miners' strike of 1984/85, which left wounds that would take years to heal.

At the start of the strike, there were still 174 deep coal mines in Britain, 18 of them in the Durham Coalfield, employing 171,000 miners and a total workforce of more like 220,000. Within ten years, ninety per cent of that workforce would have gone and it felt as if a whole culture and identity went with it, ripped out and smashed by de-industrialisation. South Hetton Colliery had closed at Easter 1983 after a working life of 152 years and the last section of the railway line that ran over Pesspool bridge was dismantled nine years later. The mine in Horden, where Vince Landa had lived when he first moved to the north-east in 1959 and where he sold his first one-armed bandits, closed in 1987, dooming the community to years of high unemployment and deprivation.

At the end of the strike, there weren't many working-men's clubs left that could have afforded to buy 'reconditioned' American gaming machines at the old prices, even if Vince Landa had still been in the business of selling them. But by then, the Bandit King had a new project. Since their wedding, Vince and Julie had been living in Southwick, a suburb of Sunderland on the north bank of the river Wear, but, in 1985, Landa spread his wings again and moved to Stanhope Castle in Upper Weardale, no more than ten miles away from his old home, Dryderdale Hall. The castle – which was built in 1798 – was originally owned by the Quaker mine owner and director of the Stockton and Darlington Railway, Henry Pease, who was also briefly MP for Durham South. His descendants had continued to live there until World War II but, from 1941 until the early 1980s, it had been turned into a remand home for delinquent boys.

Vince Landa, still perceived by many in the north-east and elsewhere as a very bad boy, reformed or otherwise, set about converting the lodge that adjoined the main building into a luxurious house for himself, his wife and children. But an air of flightiness, of dodgy dealings and cheques in the post continued to cling to him. In June 1986, the recorder at Teeside Crown Court ordered him to pay £6,000 of unpaid fees to his former financial advisor in relation to pub and hotel services at the Castle in Durham. Just as he had at Moot Hall in Newcastle in 1967, Vince stood outside the courtroom as the verdict was announced but this time there was to be no impromptu press conference and he left without comment.

The impression was growing of a man struggling to conceal mounting financial difficulties but then, in May 1987, the old flamboyant, big-spending Vince returned briefly centre stage with the announcement that he had taken control of the bankrupt Sunderland shipyard, S and S Marine Ltd, after agreeing a payment of £100,000 to the official receiver. The deal was intended to be part of an ambitious scheme to revitalise Sunderland Floating Dock PLC, which was suffering grievously from the closure of the neighbouring coal mines and general industrial decline. But only five days later, Landa pulled out. Alf McDonnell, who was going to run the new business, took control of the yard instead. 'Vince has stepped down because he believes it's in everybody's interests,' said McDonnell, hinting at political and shareholder unease. 'He has kept his word to me from an agreement we made ten years ago. He said if there was any problem with his name being involved in a company we were running he would automatically pull out. Vince has been accepted everywhere in the world but is not as soon as he is involved in the North-east.'

Whether he liked it or not, and regardless of McDonnell's generous tributes, Vince's fate was to be forever associated with and tainted by the One-Armed Bandit Murder and the fraudulent dealings at Social Club Services. In 1989, he applied for planning permission to build six houses at Stanhope Castle. He was proposing to convert some old classrooms and a pottery workshop that had not been in use since the reform school closed seven years before. He was also attempting to convert some of the spacious apartments in the castle into flats. But the hoped-for profits from the two schemes didn't come in time to save him from public humiliation and insolvency.

On 4th June, 1992, Vince was served with a bankruptcy petition at Durham Crown Court. It was brought by Allied Irish Bank and heard in his absence. At the time, he was fortuitously away in the US, staying at a property he owned at Daytona Beach in Florida, which seemed to imply he wasn't quite done with yet. When contacted by the authorities in Britain, he claimed that he was 'stranded' in America for the time being due to ill health and therefore unable to return. Three weeks later, police and firefighters were called to Stanhope Castle to investigate a suspicious blaze, which had severely damaged the ground floor of the lodge where Vince and Julie had been living. Again, Vince protested over the phone from Florida that he was unable to travel because of ill health but alleged that he had been told by the firemen that the house had seemingly been broken into via the bar area and the conflagration started deliberately using a 'high-value solvent'.

Another fire, like the ones at the Castle Hotel in 1981 and the Piccadilly Club in 1966. Another severe illness, just like the one in Majorca in 1967, rendering it impossible for the apologetic Mr Landa to be present in person. It wasn't just members of the press and the Durham Constabulary who were shaking their heads and exchanging knowing glances. When Vince did finally come back the next year, it was to attend his bankruptcy examination but also to relate details of the bizarre scam that he said had reunited him with his old associate from London: the mystery man himself, Dennis Stafford.

When the fun-loving ciminal disappeared after his two newspaper confessions in 1980, it was assumed that he was still in hiding in Italy. But for the best part of a decade, he had been 5,000 miles away, accumulating wealth and living another double life in South Africa. Stafford's nerve and guile had never been in doubt and he had used them to good effect. He had a spell of legitimate employment as a town engineer in Alberton, not far from Johannesburg, and, at one point, was running a restaurant called Daddy's Yacht. He had married and then divorced Lorraine Brown and moved on to wife number three: a beautiful Indian woman named Merle with whom he had bought a house in Johannesburg. But Dennis being Dennis, he was also attracted by a series of scams ranging from diamonds to a bank fraud he said he was co-opted into by his fellow Englishman Stuart Pegg, a former Slater Walker employee. Stafford succeeded in obtaining a management position for three days with the Trust Bank of Johannesburg, which was long enough for him to nimbly award himself £12m worth of Krugerrands in gold coins.

Stafford's plan was to fly the coins, which were VAT exempt, to the UK and then melt them down into gold ingots and sell them back to the bullion houses, charging them VAT on the transactions. He took a plane to London and checked in to the Royal Garden Hotel in Kensington under a false name – Dennis Scott – and using a false passport. What he didn't know was that the former President of the Soviet Union, Mikhail Gorbachev, was in London at the same time and staying at the Soviet Ambassador's residence in Kensington Palace Gardens. Members of the Russian delegation were staying at the Royal Garden Hotel and the police and security services had conducted a check on all the guests who were registered there. Stafford's fake passport was discovered and his real identity established, and he was arrested. There was no extradition treaty then between Britain and South Africa but, although he avoided being sent back to Johannesburg, he didn't escape prosecution in the UK. He was sentenced to two years' imprisonment for breaching the terms of his parole in 1980 and then got six more for being part of a counterfeiting fraud and attempting to print false passports and American Express cheques. And there was still a further twist to come.

Within a month of the fire at the Stanhope Castle lodge in June 1992, Vince Landa – once the 'nearly mythical' gaming magnate and Bandit King – was declared bankrupt with debts of over £1m. At his examination at Durham Crown Court in November 1993, he said that his affairs had been thrown off course due to his unwise entanglement with Dennis Stafford. According to Landa, his old Piccadilly Club booking manager had tried to persuade him to go to South Africa on his behalf, pick up £300,000 worth of the Krugerrands and take them back to London. He also inferred that he and Stafford were involved in a dispute over the ownership of Stanhope Castle and accused Dennis of deliberately attacking him and being behind the arson at the lodge.

Vince admitted having debts of £400,000 but maintained that, if ownership of Stanhope Castle – which he had been in the process of converting into flats – was included, his assets amounted to £1.78m. Stafford's version of their mutual transactions, as described in his autobiography, was that he was Landa's biggest creditor, having put up nearly fifty per cent of the asking price in the deal to buy the castle back in 1985, and that he was owed £100,000 but never got a penny.

What was not fully explained was why Vince Landa had gone into business with Stafford again or why Stafford had gone back to the north-east for a fourth time. Was it just mutual convenience? A case of Landa needing money to buy and develop the castle and Stafford being able provide it with the promise they would both be in profit when the property was sold. Or was there also some other reason – something in their past; some bit of business – that was forever yoking them together?

What was not in dispute was that neither Vince's evasions about his bankruptcy nor the spectacle of Stafford reverting to his former career as a conman and professional criminal were likely to help either his or Michael Luvaglio's long-running attempts to convince the world they were innocent of Angus Sibbet's murder.

CHAPTER TWENTY-TWO

IN 1980, MICHAEL Luvaglio had an operation to remove a brain tumour from the left side of his cerebrum. A year later, it was disclosed that he also had a tumour on the right side and that it was being treated with drugs to try to shrink it. Despite his misfortune, Michael's condition had not stopped him from throwing himself into the job of production manager with the team at Share – Self Help and Rehabilitation for Employment – which had started in the borough of Wandsworth in 1972.

The charity's expressed aim is to help disabled people who need assistance and support 'in order to achieve their potential and realise their dreams and aspirations'. It provides training, employment advice and 'well-being resources' for people with a wide range of disabilities, from learning issues to physical and sensory impairments and from autism to mental-health needs. Since its foundation, Share has expanded across London from Croydon, Tooting and Merton in the south-west to Lambeth and Southwark in the south. The charity, whose patrons include (Lord)

Alf Dubs, the former Battersea MP, and the actresses Geraldine James and Patricia Hodge, now works with between 120 and 250 people each year, liaising between 'students' and social workers and families. It operates two social enterprises – Share Nurseries, which grows and sells plants and Share Catering, which provides catering services for meetings and events – both designed to offer students the 'chance to work in a safe and supported environment' and gain 'valuable work experience'.

Michael Luvaglio ended up spending twenty years working with Share – the deeply rewarding second act of a shattered life – and, when he retired in 2001, he was presented with the Wandsworth Civic Award and told that, had it not been for his time in prison, he would have been recommended for an OBE. He also received a degree in Humanities from the Open University. It was a world away from the life he had once led with his older brother in the north-east in the 1960s but, whatever sense of personal achievement or atonement he may have felt, it still didn't diminish his passionate longing to have his murder conviction overturned. He never stopped pursuing the case in any way he could and intermittently encountered others who wanted to assist him.

In January 1987, Tyne Tees Television broadcast a twentieth-anniversary re-examination of the One-Armed Bandit Murder, which resulted in five new witnesses coming forward with testimony that contradicted the prosecution's version of events. The independent Durham Crown Prosecution Service (CPS) found the witness statements sufficiently disturbing to merit sending them to the Director of Public Prosecutions in London. Simultaneously, detectives from Durham Constabulary began an investigation into some of the new evidence that had been unearthed. It was essentially a case of the Durham police investigating themselves, which is never satisfactory, and their findings, which were not made public at the time, offered little encouragement to Michael Luvaglio and Dennis Stafford.

The most serious of the new claims was the story told by Tom Fellows – a freelance paint sprayer who rented space in the Fleet Buyers Garage in Whessoe Road, Darlington –which was owned by Colin and Stuart Dunne. The brothers were known to the police as friends and associates of Vince Landa, and Colin Dunne had accompanied Angus Sibbet on some of his rounds collecting 'the harvest' from the machines. Fellows said that, at around 8am on the morning of 5th January, 1967, he was at the garage when 'an agitated man in his early thirties, speaking in a cockney accent, came into the garage and demanded to speak with the owner.' The man, who said his name was Darren Reynolds, was holding an automatic pistol and had a badly injured right leg, which was bleeding as a result of being crushed between his car and the Mark X Jaguar belonging to Angus Sibbet.

According to Fellows, the Londoner told him that he'd had orders to 'frighten Mr Sibbet' but, fearing that he was about to be attacked himself, had shot him dead. The man did not want an ambulance. He had been told to go to the garage if there was any problem and just wanted to know 'where the hell' Colin Dunne was. He was so shaken up that he loosed off a shot into the asbestos cladding around some piping running along the garage wall. A few minutes later, Colin Dunne arrived and led the gunman away, warning Tom Fellows 'that man's never been here'.

Fellows didn't go to the police in 1967 because he was fearful for his own safety. But when he read that Luvaglio and Stafford were coming up for appeal six years later, he went to Darlington police station and reported what he had witnessed, only to be told by a detective that he was wasting police time and sent home. Detective Chief Superintendent Eddy, who looked into Fellows' story, was equally dismissive, reporting back to Durham CPS that he believed it to be 'a total fabrication from beginning to end'. Fellows, he said, was himself an associate of Colin Dunne, who had worked for Social Club Services and was linked to Vince Landa and, in view of Dunne's role as 'a front man in various illegal property deals, his story may well be the result of a conspiracy to spread doubt over Michael Luvaglio's conviction.' Eddy cited the testimony of Ronald Hine, a small-time bandit supplier who said that his machines had been smashed by Angus Sibbet and that he had been subjected to frequent harassment by Dunne and the Luvaglio brothers. A hint that it wasn't just charm that had persuaded clubs to do business with Social Club Services and that more threatening methods may also have been involved.

DCS Eddy didn't buy the idea that a professional hitman – if that is who 'Reynolds' was – would reveal so many details of the killing in front of a complete stranger, ignoring the possibility that the gunman was in a state of shock because of the injury to his leg. Regarding that injury, Eddy pointed out that no blood had been found on the front of the Mark X Jaguar, only red paint samples. Neither was it disputed at the trial that the shots that had been fired at Angus Sibbet were from the rear and side of the car, not directly in front and through the windscreen as Tom Fellows was told.

Eddy was suspicious of the gunman's name too: real or an alias? A Darlington woman called Violet Bowers had informed the police that her husband, Joseph – now deceased – had been told in 1967 that Sibbet's murderer was George Reynolds of Shildon, County Durham, acting as a hitman for Vince Landa. But there was only one George Reynolds in DCS Eddy's book and that was the notorious local villain who was, indeed, a friend of Vince Landa's but was in prison for safe-breaking in January 1967 and not released until fourteen days after the murder.

Eddy seemed to share the sentiments of the fictional superintendent in CP Taylor's play who was satisfied that his enquiries had resulted in 'three Bandits less in the world' so why try and stir things up any further. Yet, despite the Detective Chief Superintendent's negativity, efforts to establish Michael Luvaglio's innocence continued, albeit with longer gaps each time between new discoveries on the one hand and official dismissals on the other. In January 1993, a Mrs Walpole came forward to testify that she not only saw a red E-type outside Michael Luvaglio's house in Chelsea Grove at 12:10am on the night of the murder but that she also saw Michael himself standing in the window. In which case, he couldn't possibly have been in South Hetton with Dennis Stafford twenty minutes earlier.

Stafford's return to fraudulent cons and scams, and the prison terms that followed, did not help to enhance his claims that he, too, was innocent of Angus Sibbet's murder. But in May 2002, his lawyers went public with their view that a conviction based on the evidence presented in Newcastle in 1967 would have been inconceivable in any British court room thirty-five years later.

By now, the One-Armed Bandit Murder and all the stories that surrounded it had become north-east England's version of the 'Who Killed Jimmy Hoffa?' scenario in the US and the answers were no clearer on Tyneside than they were in Detroit. The noirish drama and the wintry setting in a Durham mining village gripped the imagination of Dire Straits founder Mark Knopfler, who grew up in Blyth, near Newcastle. The singer and lead guitarist was seventeen years old when the murder took place and remembered it 'figured very big when I was a young teenager. The body was in a huge Jag' and discovered by a pitman coming home from night shift on his bicycle on a frozen morning.' (Tom Leak, who found the body, was on foot and Knopfler may have been confusing him with his fellow miner, James Golden, who was on his bicycle when he was passed by the red E-type and the Jaguar Mark X.)

Knopfler's 2004 solo album *Shangri La* featured an image of a one-armed bandit on the front cover and the opening track was a haunting guitar ballad entitled '5.15am' after the time that Angus Sibbet's body was discovered. It touched on the irony of men whose natural habitat was places like the Dolce Vita and the Birdcage Club meeting their end in the dark, netherworld of a mining village and contrasted the lives of the cockney gangsters who brought the gaming machines to the north-east with the painful history of communities like South Hetton, where so many pitmen had lost their lives in the previous century.

It was hoped by Michael Luvaglio's supporters that Knopfler's song would add to the pressure they were trying to bring on the authorities in 2004 as they grasped what felt like one last chance to prove his innocence and applied to the Criminal Cases Review Commission (CCRC) to refer the case back to the Court of Appeal. An independent public body, the CCRC was set up in 1995 and began its work two years later. Mindful of the numerous high-profile instances of police misconduct and false confessions in the 1970s, the Commission is empowered to investigate possible miscarriages of justice. It can review cases where people feel they have been wrongly convicted and send their case back to the Appeal Court judges in the event of 'strong new evidence' or 'an argument that makes the case look different'.

The Commission is based not in London, like so much of the legal establishment, but in Birmingham and employs around ninety staff, forty of whom are case reviewers and aim to complete their case studies within twelve months of receiving an application. The decision on whether or not to proceed is then up to the twelve commissioners, who are a mix of senior barristers and solicitors on the one side and lay figures on the other, ranging from experienced board members to an ombudsman manager, a 'resilience advisor' and a facilitator. The service is free.

Between March 1997 and February 2022, the CCRC received 28,474 applications, out of which just 782 were referred back to the Court of Appeal, with only 538 of those appeals being successful. The appeal of Michael Luvaglio and Dennis Stafford was not one of them. The Commission's lengthy report, culminating in a provisional judgement in December 2005, said that Luvaglio and Stafford had failed to reveal any new evidence with which to challenge the verdict and that they could see 'no real possibility' of the convictions being quashed. The case reviewers felt that the question of the 164 unused witness statements that were never shown to the defence in 1967 had been considered at the second appeal hearing in 1973. It was also their view that Judge O'Connor's summing-up and references to Caesar and Brutus and Christ and Judas Iscariot, along with his description of the 'unsavoury' private lives of Luvaglio and Stafford, living with women who were not their wives, had made no difference to the jury's decision.

Michael Luvaglio had pinned his faith on the forensic evidence – or lack of it: namely the blood found in the Mark X and in the phone box at South Hetton, which belonged to neither himself nor Stafford. If it could have been subjected to modern-day techniques of DNA testing, it would surely have revealed the identity of the killer or his accomplice. The trouble was that, as the CCRC observed, all of the forensic evidence had been destroyed on the orders of Detective Superintendent Kell in 1973, and the Commission declined to speculate on what modern testing might have uncovered.

Michael's solicitor, Sir David Napley, had died in 1994 but he had always identified what he felt was another weak point of the trial judge's summing-up when O'Connor admitted that at least one other person, identity unknown, might have been involved in the killing. There has been much speculation that a hitman was sent up from London – perhaps by the Kray twins – and, in the 1987 Tyne Tees documentary, the petty criminal and getaway driver, John Tumblety, said again, on camera, that he had picked up a man in South Hetton that night and driven him back to the Birdcage Club and that he believed he was the real killer. He also said that the man was neither Michael Luvaglio nor Dennis Stafford. But when he was interviewed by the CCRC team, Tumblety had retracted his statement and claimed that he had signed something when he was in Armley prison in Leeds without reading it.

Tumblety's volte-face effectively sealed Luvaglio's – and Stafford's – fate every bit as much as the Newcastle jury's verdict in 1967. Stafford's solicitor, Michael Purdon, described the Commission's decision as 'ungenerous to a fault' and Michael, who was said to be 'distraught' at the outcome, sought a judicial review of the ruling in the High Court. But when it eventually came in April 2008, the 100-page decision by Mr Justice Maddison concluded that he could not overturn the CCRC decision or send the case back to the Appeal Court as there was 'no reasonable prospect of a successful outcome'.

Nine years later in March 2017, another senior judge endorsed Maddison's decision.

While all the official channels may appear to have been exhausted, speculation continues relentlessly among the case's ardent followers, who refuse to accept the legal verdicts and remain determined to expose what they believe to be the truth. None have trawled through the evidence in greater detail or put it more closely to the test than Peter Hughman, no longer an articled clerk but an experienced and highly respected consultant solicitor and expert in criminal law. In their two exhaustively researched books on the subject – *Most Unnatural* and *Sibbet: A Body Under The Bridge* – Hughman and his co-writer, David Lewis, focused on the numerous anomalies and inconsistencies in the prosecution's case, while offering three possible alternative scenarios as to what might have happened.

Their most persuasive points revolve around the paucity of forensic evidence linking Luvaglio and Stafford with Sibbet and the Mark X Jaguar. By contrast, there were numerous clues to suggest that at least one other person was present at the crime scene, but these were ignored. It wasn't just a case of the bloodstains found on the transmission tunnel of the Mark X or in the phone box at South Hetton either. The Durham police found fingerprints on both the rear doors of the saloon where they might have been opened to bundle a dead body into the back but none of the prints belonged to the accused men.

Then there was the box of Bahama cigars found on the dashboard of the car and visible in several of the official police photographs. Neither Sibbet nor Stafford nor Luvaglio smoked cigars, only cigarettes. So where did the cigars come from? Perhaps someone on Sibbet's rounds of the working-men's clubs had given them to him as a belated Christmas or New Year present but the box's existence was never mentioned in court.

The single most incriminating issue on the prosecution side was the seemingly incontrovertible evidence that the red E-type Jaguar – which Stafford and Luvaglio admitted driving that night – and the Mark X had been in a collision on the A182. As the leading prosecution counsel Henry Scott had said in his closing statement in 1967, 'if that accident happened on the A182, then these two men committed that murder. There is no other way out of it.' The collision was at the heart of Lord Justice Edmund Davies's dismissal of the first appeal in 1968, when he scorned the idea that the damage to the E-type was done outside the Birdcage Club and that the killers had borrowed the car while Luvaglio and Stafford were inside and then politely returned it, undetected, ninety minutes later. It was also what prompted Lord Widgery's description of 'an irresistible inference of guilt' at the second appeal in 1973.

But Peter Hughman had a theory. Suppose there had been two red E-type Jaguars involved that night? One of them Vince Landa's car, driven by Luvaglio and Stafford and which remained parked outside the Birdcage Club from 12:30am until closing time; the second E-type a so-called 'Judas Jag' driven by the real killers and intended to lure Angus Sibbet deep into the Durham countryside under the impression that he was heading into the company of friends. The killers had to have compelling bait to lure Sibbet away from the Dolce Vita and Joyce Hall at 11:15am on a dark and bitterly cold night, especially as he was travelling alone and without protection. The note found by Hall in which Angus said he had to go to a meeting with 'Mick' at Shiney Row at 11:15pm may provide the explanation, even though it wasn't presented in court. Either an unwitting Michael Luvaglio or, more probably, Sibbet's Irish ex-boxing trainer and minder, Thomas 'Paddy' Hallett, was responsible, which would explain why Hallett was attacked and nearly killed in Newcastle a month later, to prevent him from giving evidence at the committal hearing.

At least four witnesses testified that they saw a red E-type and a Mark X Jaguar travelling slowly and in convoy south of Shiney Row and in the direction of South Hetton around 11:35/11:45pm on the night of 4th January. Peter Hughman envisaged Sibbet, having found no one at Shiney Row, carrying on south in the direction of Peterlee, expecting to bump into Luvaglio and Stafford on their way back up to Newcastle. A red E-type was, indeed, waiting for him along the way and, when it pulled out, he followed on behind. It was impossible to make out the exact identity of the driver and his passenger in that light but Sibbet assumed that it was Michael and Dennis.

The cars progressed onwards through South Hetton, seen by the miner Henry Johnson while waiting for his bus and other witnesses, and then the E-type accelerated along the A182 before suddenly turning right into Pesspool Lane, which was where the two cars collided. When two men got out of the red E-type who were not Michael Luvaglio and Dennis Stafford, one of them a complete stranger, Angus Sibbet realised he was in danger and tried to reverse his Jag and turn back towards the A182, which is when his car hit one of the assailants, injuring his leg. Thinking that he was being attacked, the wounded man pulled out his gun – a Walther PPK supplied in Newcastle by the Scotsman John Tumblety – and shot Sibbet dead. The gunman – or 'Darren Reynolds', as he called himself in the version reported by Tom Fellows – and his accomplice then heaved Sibbet's body into the back of the Mark X, leaving their fingerprints on the car doors. The pair spent a couple of minutes in anxious discussion about what to do next and then the accomplice got back in the red E-type, or Judas Jag, and drove it away to a garage – probably Dunne's in Darlington – where it could be repaired. The gunman, meanwhile, drove the damaged Mark X in a circle up to Haswell and then back round to South Hetton, where the car packed up under Pesspool bridge. The man got out and went to the village phone box and rang John Tumblety at the Birdcage Club and told him to come out and collect him. In the process, he left traces of his own and Sibbet's blood in the phone kiosk and on the telephone directory.

As it was a freezing-cold night, the man decided to go and sit in the Mark X to keep warm and lit one of the cigars he had in a box in his overcoat to distract him from thinking about the pain in his leg. Which is why the witness Tom Feather said that he saw an arm come out of the stationary saloon and wave him on when he passed it at 12:45am. Tumblety eventually arrived and the hitman got out of the Mark X, forgetting his cigars, which he left on the dashboard. Abandoning the Jaguar, the hitman was driven back to the Birdcage and then, early the next morning, Tumblety took him down to the Fleet Buyers garage in Darlington, where he encountered Tom Fellows and then Colin Dunne, who looked after him and arranged his passage back to London.

It's an ingenious, if highly speculative, theory. But, if an outside hitman was involved, who was he and who sent him? Hughman had suggestions about that too. Jan Szymczuk – a Geordie with Polish parents, who grew up in Northumberland and spent thirty years working for the Metropolitan Police – retired in 2009 as the senior detective police artist. In 2013, Szymczuk sat down with Tom Fellows and listened to his description of the man posing as

'Darren Reynolds' who came into the garage in Whessoe Road, Darlington, at 8am on that bleak, winter morning in January 1967. The image Syzmczuk compiled, complete with slicked-back hair, a broken nose and a widow's peak, bore an uncanny resemblance to Albert Donoghue, one of Reggie Kray's lieutenants and a leading member of the Firm.

If Tom Fellows is to be believed and Syzmczuk's illustration is correct, it was the Krays who set up Sibbet's murder, with the intention of implicating Vince Landa and breaking up his one-armed bandit empire in the north-east. With Sibbet dead and Landa in prison, they would then step in and take over. But whether or not Albert Donoghue was involved in the killing, there are elements of the theory that don't stack up. The twins were arrested in London by Detective Chief Superintendent Leonard 'Nipper' Read in March 1968 (and Donoghue was one of those who turned Queen's evidence and testified against them at their Old Bailey trial the following year). But in the interlude between Sibbet's death and their own undoing, there is no evidence to suggest that they assumed any kind of controlling role in gaming-machine and clubland business in the north-east. As Ray Grehan said, after their 1966 visits to Newcastle, they were lost away from home and repeatedly rebuffed in their attempts to make an impact in both Manchester and Newcastle.

If not the twins, there have been suggestions that the One-Armed Bandit Murder involved the Scotsman Arthur Thompson, a brutal, violent man who ran protection rackets and loan sharking in Glasgow and dealt ruthlessly with rivals and disloyal subjects. Maybe Thompson, who owned a Mark X Jaguar, had been co-opted by the twins, the theory goes, and agreed to assist in putting Vince Landa out of business on the understanding that he would acquire a share of the gaming-machine proceeds once Social Club Services had gone under. It's another intriguing theory but a hard one to prove, whereas there is a third, much more likely, explanation that lays the responsibility for Angus Sibbet's death not at the door of the Kray twins or the Richardsons or the Mafia but points directly at Angus's old friend and colleague and Michael Luvaglio's older brother, Vince Landa.

Michael, loyal to a fault, said to both Durham police and to his lawyers that he could not believe Vince was in any way involved in the killing. Not least because he was meant to be announcing the big public offering of SCS shares in the New Year and to be in any way connected to a shooting in the run-up would have been financial suicide. But the supposed launch of SCS on the stock market was a sham. By late 1966, the company was haemorrhaging money, as the fraud trial would show three years later, partly due to the amounts Vince Landa was transferring to himself and sending out of the country. Transactions that included the interest in the business owned by Michael, who was visited – just the once – by his brother in Durham prison before the trial and persuaded to place his shares in Vince's hands for safe keeping. Michael never saw a penny of that paper wealth again.

Angus Sibbet had been skimming off the top of SCS for several years, justifying it as a legitimate bonus he was entitled to for his role in assisting the rise of the Luvaglio family. Some of his actions were acceptable to Vince if they meant spreading tips or bribes around to keep club stewards and officials happy. But by Christmas 1966, with his own financial position deteriorating, Vince decided that Angus was costing him too much and had to be stopped. He couldn't just reprimand him or fire him, though, because Angus Sibbet knew a dirty secret from Vince Landa's past.

He had attempted to blackmail him about it once before and there were veiled hints that he might do so again.

In 1961, the impatient gaming-machine entrepreneur had been involved in a hit-and-run accident near Ryhope on the north-east coast. His car knocked over and killed a woman called Vera Stamp and Vince neither stopped at the time of the accident nor came forward afterwards to admit responsibility. Sibbet had found out about it and, at one point, forged a letter purporting to be from Durham CID and threatening action. Vince discovered the letter was a fake and that his collector was behind it but he was wary of confronting him. Angus badly wanted to be the 'company director' and 'gaming chief' he was flatteringly described as after his death and, if Vince didn't comply with his ambitions, Angus would remind him he possessed the knowledge to bring him down.

In Dennis Stafford's confession in the *News of the World* in September 1980, he described how Sibbet had been discussed during that Christmas and New Year break in Majorca and how it had been decided that 'he had to go' and was 'eighty per cent certain to go', even if he toned down his act. Stafford's account was backed up by the testimony of Winifred Reed, who ran a typing and facsimile service in London and typed up the petition Stafford wrote while he was in Parkhurst in the 1970s. She said that Stafford's mother, Maggie, had told her all about the Majorca conference, adding that Vince Landa – the 'gangland Mr Big', as Stafford euphemistically called him in his confession – was overjoyed when he was telephoned on 5th January, 1967, and informed of Sibbet's death.

Perhaps Vince's frustration with his greedy collector had been expressed a bit like Henry II's exasperation with his 'turbulent' archbishop, Thomas à Becket in the twelfth century. Perhaps he never intended Dennis Stafford or Albert Donoghue or anyone else to actually kill Angus Sibbet any more than the Plantagenet king expected his knights to go off and assassinate his friend Becket. Was it meant to be just a punishment beating or 'bloody good hiding', as Stafford called it, to deter him from any more skimming and blackmailing threats? Alternatively, maybe Vince Landa was perfectly capable of ordering a cold-blooded killing, complete with a hitman from London, and then fleeing the country for thirteen years. Leaving his hired gangster and 'mystery man' Dennis Stafford and his hapless brother, the friend who had been unwittingly used to draw Sibbet into a trap, to take the fall.

Michael's Newcastle solicitor, Henry Mincoff had said that, on two occasions – once while Michael was in custody in January 1967 and once again during the trial – Detective Superintendent Ronald Kell told him that the police knew Michael was innocent and that, if he stated that Stafford had left him for a period of time on the night of 4th/5th January, he could walk free. Michael, doing as Stafford had told him and keeping his mouth shut, refused the offer, maintaining that he and Stafford had been together throughout that day and night. But were they?

Documents in the National Archives relating to Stafford's and Luvaglio's case show that, in 1972, Detective Chief Superintendent Jack Collinson interviewed a man called William Mulvenna who had been a fellow inmate with Michael in Wakefield prison. Prompted to speak out by the reports of Michael's impending appeal, Mulvenna said that Michael had told him that Dennis Stafford was not at the Birdcage Club from 12:30am until closing time. He left the club 'at one point without giving any reason' and didn't come back 'until the early hours of the morning'. Mulvenna was never called to testify to Mr Justice Croom-Johnson because, after his release from prison, he was suffering from depression and receiving electro-shock therapy.

Peter Hughman did not refer to Mulvenna's statement in his book and he barely mentioned Stafford's confession. But has Stafford 'anyone but himself to blame', as Sir David Napley put it in his autobiography, if an irresistible inference of guilt clings to the fun-loving criminal regarding Angus Sibbet's murder and suspicion that 'he knew more about it than he would have had us believe.' We can only speculate about Albert Donoghue. But Stafford admitted keeping a Walther PPK in a clip in his car. He was the professional brought up from London by Vince Landa and he and Sibbet began sparring soon after his arrival in Newcastle in 1966, with the collector sensing that the newcomer was a serious rival who had Landa's ear and a maybe even a licence to kill.

Some of the highly coloured details in Stafford's confession about Angus Sibbet having a hideout in South Hetton and a sidekick that night wielding a sawn-off shotgun sound fake. And, if Stafford is to be believed and the murder took place several hours later than the police maintained, an explanation has to be found for who was driving a red E-type in convoy with the Mark X Jaguar in South Hetton, as seen by several witnesses, in the run-up to midnight on 4th January. But other aspects of the story seem all too plausible. There was surely at least one other man involved who was never charged. It could have been Donoghue or another professional that Vince had hired in London or, more likely, it was one of the gang of four involved in the attack on Paddy Hallet in February 1967 and one of those men sustained a bloody leg and was picked up afterwards by John Tumblety.

When Stafford's article in the *News of the World* came out in 1980, it angered a lot of the men who had been in prison with him in the years before. Nick Davies, writing in the *Guardian* on 9th September, 1980, reported that one of 'the chaps' who had been in Parkhurst had said that 'Stafford told all of us inside that he'd killed Sibbet' but that he shouldn't have sold his story to a newspaper. His confession not only compromised Michael Luvaglio's long campaign to get his conviction overturned but also messed up the attempts of other prisoners to get their cases reviewed. Who was going to believe them now when Stafford had just popped up after thirteen years of protesting his innocence saying, 'Oh, by the way everybody. I did it all along.'

The men in Parkhurst weren't the only ones Stafford may have confided in either. Almost a decade later, in June 2009 – and now going under the name of Dennis Scott – he appeared in court in Bishop Auckland accused of threatening to set fire to a neighbour's sports car at Stanhope Castle apartments. In the course of the hearing, 'Scott' denied admitting to Gordon Witton, a café and ice-cream-van owner, that he had murdered Angus Sibbet.

Many have campaigned for Dennis Stafford and mourned for Michael Luvaglio, the innocent caught in the crosshairs, and deplored the loss of twelve years of his life. But not so many have mourned for the victim of the One-Armed Bandit Murder. Bearded, bespectacled and promiscuous Angus Sibbet. Who wept for him or his wife Brenda or his young daughter Karen or his parents or his brother and sister? All of them victims just as much as the men who were rightly or wrongly sent to jail for his killing.

Angus's brother James – and his minder, Paddy Hallet – refused permission for their witness statements to be shared with the defence at the time of the appeals. And, in 2004, James sent a statement of his own to the CCRC – one that he hoped they would weigh in the balance as they considered Luvaglio's and Stafford's plea.

In the 1992 western *Unforgiven*, there is a scene in which Clint Eastwood, playing the ageing gunfighter William Munny, looks back honestly at his violent past. 'It's a hell of a thing killing a man,' he tells the naive wannabe, the Schofield Kid. 'You take away everything he's got . . . and everything he's ever going to be.'

'Yeah – well I guess they had it coming,' the boy replies.

'We all have it coming, kid' says Munny.

There are echoes of that exchange in the anguish and pain James Sibbet expressed about the actions of Vince Landa, whom he believed was the catalyst behind the murder and the man who had ruined the lives not only of his brother but of his parents and relatives. They were the real victims, he argued. Not Luvaglio and Stafford.

Was Angus really stealing from the company? Or was he simply taking as much money as he felt entitled to? Why would Landa and his brother, supposedly running a legitimate multi-million-pound business, need to employ a life-long criminal like Dennis Stafford? A man who had never held a proper job. A man who had the ability to kill, including two convictions for possessing firearms and a lifetime's absence of morality. Michael Luvaglio, James reasoned, had been 'an essential lure'. The supposed close friend whose word would be enough to entice Angus out into the country and not far from the sea where his killers had hoped to get rid of the body. James was not convinced by the image of Michael as a gentle and saintly innocent adrift among thieves. He had been to a good school. He'd had a further education about life in the RAF. He must have known that deceit and sharp practice was a crucial part of his brother's sales technique with the clubs and the gaming machines. Yet he was quite happy to be a co-director and enjoy the good times and the riches. And how did this devout Roman Catholic suddenly become the bosom pal of Dennis Stafford and always be in his company in and out of office hours?

Despite the phone calls Michael made to check on Angus's whereabouts on the night of 4th/5th January, 1967, there was no evidence of any enquiries by him or Dennis Stafford the following day. By 5pm on the 5th, Michael had been told that something terrible had happened to Angus but neither he nor Stafford had tried to contact Angus's wife that evening, or Joyce or Doreen Hall, or offer their sympathies and ask if there was anything they could do to help. Neither did they call the police to inform them of Angus's failure to keep their appointment at 12:30am the previous night.

The only person who could have testified on oath that Michael and Dennis went to Chelsea Grove at midnight before going on to the Birdcage Club was Michael's cousin, Brian Ginger, who was living there, but he was never called as a witness in their defence. Neither was Vince Landa called to testify whether he had meant to ring Chelsea Grove at 1am Spanish time. Also, there was no corroborative evidence – other than Michael's word about a telephone call to Angus at 5pm on the afternoon of 4th January – that the Birdcage was to be the scene of a late-night meeting. Angus's regular club was the Dolce Vita and the defence never asked his wife Brenda to confirm whether he had said anything about a call from Michael and was going to see him and Stafford at the Birdcage at 12:30am.

James was exasperated by the theory that the collision of the two Jaguars had happened outside the Birdcage and incredulous that a highly experienced solicitor like Sir David Napley could ever have believed that Angus's spectacles and other debris from the accident was then taken sixteen miles away and scattered on the A182 in order to frame Luvaglio and Stafford.

Vince Landa was not at his brother's side once he was arrested, James pointed out. He seemed to keep as far away from him as was humanly possible. And Michael Luvaglio and Dennis Stafford, supposedly joint victims of a miscarriage of justice, didn't speak to each other again for years afterwards. (In fact, they met for the first time in thirty years at a London hotel in 2008.) That was hardly the picture of 'blood brothers' coming together to right 'an horrendous wrong'.

Maybe – just maybe – the Durham police had been right all along and it *was* Dennis Stafford and Michael Luvaglio travelling in the red E-type behind the Mark X at 11:45pm on the night of 4th January, 1967. Maybe the two cars did collide as described on the A182 and, despite the baffling absence of convincing forensic evidence, Michael did sit terrified in the E-type as Stafford, assisted by another, unknown, assailant who was already on the scene, opened fire on the collector.

Whichever way it happened, James concluded, the real-life sentences were the ones inflicted on the relatives. 'Our mother never had one day free of heartache for the rest of her life. I don't believe Mrs Luvaglio would've had either.'

CHAPTER TWENTY-THREE

THE POLITICIANS AND developers who framed, in more ways than one, the north-eastern background to Vince Landa's world, never returned to public life. John Poulson was released from prison in 1977. Discharged from bankruptcy and claiming to be 'more sinned against than sinning', he wrote an autobiography called *The Price* and died in 1993.

Alderman Andrew Cunningham was paroled from Ford open prison in 1976 and lived to be 100, dying in 2010. His son, Jack, had entered Parliament in 1970, aged thirty-one, taking the safe Labour seat of Whitehaven when Handy Andy was still a big power in the north. In 2005, he was elevated to the House of Lords as Baron Cunningham of Felling, his father's old Durham stronghold.

T Dan Smith, the one-time visionary and party boss whose passion to get things done had seemed so exciting before the fall, was released from Leyhill open prison in 1977. The East End gangster Eric Mason, who got to know Smith inside, described him in his biography as an imposing figure who worked tirelessly to support the resettlement of fellow convicts and was a leading light in prison activities, especially amateur dramatics and the debating society. Smith, who wasn't readmitted into the Labour Party until 1987, spent the last act of his life living in a shoddy council flat on the fourteenth floor of Mill House in Spital Tongues, one of the archetypal Newcastle tower blocks he had been synonymous with in the 1960s. He served on the executive of the Newcastle Tenants Association and died of complications following a heart attack in 1993.

The passionate, vibrant and cultured Newcastle of the twenty-first century is far removed from the concrete brutalism of T Dan Smith's city, although he would surely have admired many of the developments that have taken place there since his death. But, thanks to the skill and imagination of a director and cameraman fifty years ago, an unforgettable portrait of Newcastle and the north-east in the T Dan Smith and Vince Landa era exists on film. When *Get Carter* was first released in Britain in 1971, some reviewers and critics deplored it for its violence and the shocking amorality of the central character, played by Michael Caine. Five decades later, its brilliance is recognised, and not only as a classic of the gangster genre. In 2004, *Total Film* magazine polled twenty-five film critics for a survey of the top fifty British films of all time and *Get Carter* was voted number one ahead of Michael Powell's and Emeric Pressburger's *A Matter of Life and Death*, Danny Boyle's *Trainspotting* and Carol Reed's *The Third Man*.

The script was loosely based on the novel *Jack's Return Home* by Ted Lewis, which was first published in 1970. It is the story of a London gangster going back north to unearth the truth about his brother's unexplained death. Lewis, who is credited with inventing the British school of neo-noir crime writing, grew up on

Humberside and his book is set in the north-east, mainly around Scunthorpe. The film rights were acquired by Michael Klinger, who had produced Roman Polanski's lauded psychological thrillers *Repulsion* and *Cul-de-Sac*, and it was his decision to hire as screenwriter and director the then thirty-nine-year-old Mike Hodges for what would be his first feature film. It was an inspired choice. Hodges, who had directed two TV thrillers, had also been a documentary maker with *World in Action* and he decided to transplant the action from Scunthorpe to Newcastle, a city he remembered well from his time doing National Service on a Royal Navy minesweeper in the North Sea.

Hodges loved the Los Angeles-set novels of Raymond Chandler and Hollywood B-movie thrillers like Mickey Spillane's *Kiss Me Deadly*, and he understood the importance of a sense of place. He saw in Newcastle's hard-edged urban landscape, with its mixture of river and rail, high bridges, old industries and ugly modern concrete, a kind of British version of Chicago or Detroit, which he felt would be the perfect visual accompaniment to Ted Lewis's source material. But Hodges also chose Newcastle as his setting because he had been researching the One-Armed Bandit Murder and, the more he learned about the story, the more he realised how much the crime epitomised 'the sleaziness and corruption festering in the city's underbelly'.

Hodges began systematically working locations and themes from the Angus Sibbet/Vince Landa story into the film's narrative. As cinematographer, he recruited another experienced documentary maker, Wolfgang Suschitzky, who, in 1963, had photographed *The Small World of Sammy Lee*, starring Anthony Newley as a struggling hustler, which, in scene after scene, captured unsentimental black-and-white images of the old East

End. Now Hodges and Suschitzky set about doing the same for the wharves, pubs, clubs and mean streets of 1970 Newcastle, albeit in muted colour, rather than black and white. They were aided and abetted by an outstanding cast that included Ian Hendry, star of 1962's *Live Now, Pay Later*, as the villain Eric Paice and a smooth and sinister performance by the softly spoken playwright John Osborne as the Newcastle mob boss, Cyril Kinnear. But out front throughout and giving the performance of his life – better than in *Alfie*, better than in *The Ipcress File*, better even than in *The Man Who Would Be King* – was Michael Caine as the ruthless avenger and anti-hero, Jack Carter.

Over forty years before Cillian Murphy's Tommy Shelby appeared on TV screens in *Peaky Blinders*, Carter was breathtakingly hard, cold and real. 'I knew him well,' Caine said when referring to his south-London upbringing in an interview in 2002. 'He's the dead-end product of my own environment. He is the ghost of Michael Caine.' Along with Mike Hodges, the actor wanted to dispel the cheery cockney myths in English movies where 'gangsters were either stupid or funny. I wanted to show that they're neither. Gangsters are not stupid and they're certainly not very funny.'

Caine's Carter, in his sharply cut dark suit and trench coat, long hair curling over his collar, moves through the film like a deadly gunfighter in a western. And, from the outset, Hodges threads the subtext with acknowledgements to the One-Armed Bandit Murder beginning as Carter gets off the train at Newcastle Central and we see a newspaper headline in the background: GAMING WAR ROCKS CITY.

The theme continues with the character of Cliff Brumby, the portly one-armed bandit supplier played by Bryan Moseley, who

Carter first tackles at his home with the memorable line: 'You're a big man but you're in bad shape. With me it's a full-time job. Now behave yourself.' Later, when the extent of Brumby's complicity in his brother's death becomes clear, Carter infamously throws Brumby off the top level of the Trinity Square car park in Gateshead, which subsequently acquired iconic status. When it was finally pulled down in 2010, the council sold off commemorative pieces of concrete in especially decorated £5 tins.

The Las Vegas, the sleazy boarding house where Carter sleeps with the landlady, Edna, has telephone sex with Britt Ekland and is then confronted the next morning, naked apart from a shotgun, by the London villains Conn and Peter the Dutchman, was in Pelaw only a street away from Joyce Hall's Gateshead flat.

Hodges went even further when it came to depicting the lair of his fictional crime kingpin, Cyril Kinnear, filming those scenes in the then empty and abandoned Dryderdale Hall, formerly the home of Vince Landa and his family. Hodges said that filming in the 'grim Gothic house' – the hall of 'the demon king', as Geraldine Moffat's Glenda says to Carter – made the cast and crew all feel uneasy as they looked at its empty gun case and locked safe. The drawing room, where Kinnear fleeces the racegoers at cards, still had all the original wallpaper and furnishings in place. It was a room, said Hodges, that 'reeked of alcohol, money and women'. The director used the lake in the grounds as the place where the unforgiving Carter leaves the body of his brother's treacherous wife, Margaret, having tipped off the vice squad about Kinnear's pornographic film racket. And when the police are seen raiding the house at the end and arresting Kinnear and his crew, many of the guests and extras rounded up were played by Vince's real-life friends and associates.

Ian Hendry, who played Eric Paice – Kinnear's hard man and Jack's brother's killer – was a fine actor and was briefly considered for the leading role. The problem was that, by the 1970s, he was unfit, unreliable and beginning a slide into alcoholism. But he was ideal for Paice – who resents the intruder from London almost as much as Hendry resented the more successful Caine in real life – and the antagonism between the two of them ripples through their scenes together, from the first exchange at Newcastle races to the final, brutal early-morning denouement on Blackhall Colliery beach. It was another inspired setting: bleak, dark and pitiless and only seven miles from South Hetton. The colliery closed in 1981 but, back in 1970, the spoil from the pit was still winched up on an aerial ropeway and dropped into the North Sea, which is how Carter disposes of Eric Paice. Again, Hodges chose the site because of all the suggestions that the real One-Armed Bandit Murderers had intended a similar fate for their victim if the killing had gone smoothly.

In the final scene, Carter throws away his shotgun and starts to walk off the beach, trench-coat collar turned up and his job done, and then he is suddenly shot in the head by a distant sniper. As the gunman packs up his rifle and walks away, we see that it is the same anonymous figure who was seen sitting smoking in the corner of Carter's first-class compartment on the train up from King's Cross at the beginning of the film.

So Jack Carter was killed by a London hitman.

Will we ever know the truth about who killed Angus Sibbet?

POSTSCRIPT

'LET ME DIE a youngman's death', wrote the poet Roger McGough in 1967, and '... not a clean and inbetween the sheets holy water death ... Let me die a youngman's death / not a free from sin tiptoe in / candle wax and waning death / not a curtains drawn by angels borne / "what a nice way to go" death.'

Vincent Francis Luvaglio might have expected to die a young man's death. A dramatic finale like Jack Carter, perhaps. Mown down on a beach or on the steps of a church like James Cagney in *The Roaring Twenties*, or assassinated in a barber's-shop chair. But his end was solitary and grim. In July 2011, he was found dead in a flat in Chelmsford in Essex. He had died of a pulmonary embolism and it was estimated that his body had lain there alone for three weeks. Vince was seventy-eight years old, and he had seven children and six grand-children. His youngest son, Ben, paid tribute to him, saying that his father's younger years 'like many were touched by the fallout from the Second World War and the effect this had upon his friends and family.

However, this experience served to credit Vincent with the spirit and determination to succeed and live life to the full. He will be greatly missed by all who loved him.'

In November 2017, an eerie memento of Vince Landa's life came up for auction at the Imperial War Museum in Duxford, Cambridgeshire. It was the Carmine Red E-type Jaguar 4.2 roadster that Michael Luvaglio and Dennis Stafford were driving on the night of 4th January, 1967. It was acquired by an anonymous buyer for £135,000.

Michael Luvaglio did not attend Vince's funeral and said that he had not talked to his older brother for over forty years because he had no respect for him. Michael died of heart disease in 2020. He was eighty-three years old. He failed in his desire 'not to die as a convicted murderer' but his family and friends continue their efforts to try to clear his name.

Dennis Stafford, then eighty-eight years old, said on hearing of Michael's death that he 'was a very gentle person. He was not capable of murder.' In 2017, after the failure of their second attempt to get the CCRC to refer their case back to the Court of Appeal, Stafford – or Dennis Scott, as he is called now – said that he had given up the fight to clear his name. He had fought it for many years but now he was tired, and he just wanted to go to Asia, find a beach and 'make the most of the time I've got left'.

In his autobiography, Stafford claimed that the character of Jack Carter – sharp dresser, womaniser, killer – was based on him.

Vince Landa's legacy continues to proliferate throughout Newcastle, Sunderland and the north-east, with countless slot-machines and gaming lounges sitting alongside the nail bars, Turkish hairdressers and tattoo parlours. Many of the sites are owned by Admiral, a British gambling company with 233 high-street venues in the UK and a huge online presence. They are owned, in turn, by Luxury Leisure, a subsidiary of Novomatic, a global gaming concern with an estimated worth of £5bn. There is a twenty-four-hour Admiral casino on the site of the old Dolce Vita in Grainger Town in Newcastle and a similar Aspers casino opposite where the Birdcage Club once stood. Phonographic Equipment, which morphed into Associated Leisure, ceased trading long ago but some of the machines in British gaming parlours are still imported from the US, where Bally was acquired by the Hilton Hotel Group in 1996. But the brand lives on in the shape of the gaming manufacturing company Bally Technologies and the name still headlines half-a-dozen big casinos in America, including in Las Vegas, Reno and Atlantic City, New Jersey.

Nucky Johnson's belief that slot machines wouldn't exist 'if the majority of people didn't want them' is as true today as it was in 1929. But what he didn't say is that the real winners are not 'the people' pulling the levers and spinning the reels. The winners are the house. The gaming-machine magnates and their collectors.

The bandit men counting the harvest.

CAST OF CHARACTERS

THE BANDIT MEN

Vincent Luvaglio – Also known as Vince Landa.

Michael Luvaglio – Vince's younger brother.

Dennis Stafford – Londoner, Lothario and professional criminal.

Angus Sibbett – Collector for Social Club Services.

Albert Ginley – Angus's driver.

Thomas 'Paddy' Hallett – Angus's minder.

Ray Thubron, Dennis Richman, William 'Buster' Thompson, George Wilson, William Edgar and Stanley Robinson – Employees of Social Club Services.

George Stewart, Malcolm Tully, Robert Snowdon and Kenneth McKenna – Assailants.

John Tumblety – Petty criminal.

LOVERS, WIVES AND FAMILIES

Gwen Luvaglio, nee Gwen Sinclair – Vince's first wife.

Claire Luvaglio – One of Gwen and Vince's five children.

Julie Hamblin – Vince's second wife.

Frank and Maud Luvaglio – Vince and Michael's parents.

Brenda and Karen Sibbet – Angus's wife and daughter.

Alfred, Joan, James, Sheila and Alan Sibbet – Angus's mother and father, brother, sister and nephew.

Joe and Maggie Stafford – Dennis's parents.

Pat and Karen Smithson – Dennis's first wife and daughter.

Lorraine Brown – Dennis's second wife.

Salena Jones – American jazz singer and Dennis's lover.

Maxine Lee, aka Eileen Cook – Dennis's lover.

Pat Burgess – Michael Luvaglio's lover.

Doreen Hall – Vince's secretary and Angus's lover.

Joyce Hall – Doreen's sister and Angus's lover.

THE NIGHT CLUBS

Morris Levy – Owner, along with his brothers Norman and David, of the Dolce Vita.

Joe Lisle – Owner of Club 69.

Stan Henry – Co-owner of the Bailey Group and the Cavendish.

Mike Jeffery – Owner of the Club A'Gogo.

Ray Grehan – Co-owner of the A'Gogo and Whitley Bay gaming magnate.

Harry Sibley – Owner of the Blue Parrot Country Club and the Pear Tree Garage.

John Bowden – Manager of the Birdcage Club.

Matthew Dean – Doorman at the Birdcage Club.

Tom Jones and Billy Eckstein – Top of the bill performers at the Dolce Vita.

Eric Burdon and the Animals – House band at the Club A'Gogo.

Jimi Hendrix – Star turn at the A'Gogo, March, 1967.

THE POLITICIANS AND DEVELOPERS

T Dan Smith – Leader of Newcastle City Council, 1960-65 and Chairman of the Northern Economic Planning Council, 1965-70.

Alderman Andrew Cunningham – Leader of the Northern General and Municipal Workers Union (GMWU), Member of the Labour Party National Executive and Chairman of the Durham Police Authority.

John Poulson – Yorkshire architect.

Alderman Sydney Sporle – Wandsworth Borough Council.

Dennis Vosper (Conservative) – Joint Under-Secretary of State at the Home Office, 1959-60.

Quintin Hogg, Lord Hailsham (Conservative) – Cabinet minister and Tory emissary to the North-east, 1962, and Shadow Home Secretary 1966-70.

Roy Jenkins (Labour) – Home Secretary, 1965-67.

James Callaghan (Labour) – Home Secretary, 1967-1970.

Reginald Maudling (Conservative) – Home Secretary, 1970-72.

THE MAFIA

Meyer Lansky – Co-owner of the Colony Club Casino in Berkeley Square.

Angelo Bruno – Philadelphia mob boss and co-owner of the Colony Club, the Victoria Sporting Club and the Pair of Shoes in Hertford Street.

Dino Cellini – Manager of the Colony Club.

George Raft – Ex-Movie star, charmer and greeter at the Colony Club.

Tony 'Ducks' Corallo – New York-based supplier of slot machines.

David 'Gabe' Forman – Corallo's man in London and boss of Las Vegas Coin.

Herb Itkin – FBI informant.

'Italian Albert' Dimes – Soho Godfather and Lansky and Bruno's British partner.

THE LONDON ANGLE

Ronnie and Reggie Kray – East End twins and heads of 'The Firm'.

Albert Donaghue – Kray gang member.

Dickie Hart – Kray brothers associate.

Eddie Richardson – South London gangster and brother of Charlie.

Frankie Fraser – Richardson gang member.

Billy Hayward and Peter Hennessy – South London villains.

Wally Birch – Dennis Stafford's friend and owner of Winston's Club.

Cyril Shack, Max Fine and Michael Green – Managing Director, Chairman and Sales Director of the Phonographic Equipment Company Ltd.

THE POLICE

Detective Superintendent Ronald Kell, DS John Collinson, DS Arthur Chapman – all Durham CID.

Detective Sergeant Frank Morgan – Major Incident Unit, Aycliffe.

Detective Chief Superintendent Eddy – Durham Constabulary.

Superintendent Harry Lockerbie – Peterlee police.

PC Maurice Cluer – South Hetton.

Jan Szymczuk – Senior detective police artist.

Dr Jack Ennis – Official police pathologist.

Dr John Seymour Hunter – Local GP.

KEY WITNESSES

Tom Leak, Leslie Marshall, James Golden and Henry Johnson –
South Hetton miners.

George Wells – Retired Peterlee miner.

Nora Burnip – Farmer's wife.

Lillian Bunker – Dennis Stafford and Salena Jones's housekeeper
and cleaner.

Thomas Feather – Bus driver.

George Price, Norman Lee and Stanley Denton – Ballistics and
forensics experts.

Tom Fellows – Paint sprayer.

THE JUDICIARY

Mr Justice Patrick McCarthy O'Connor – Trial Judge, Moot Hall,
March 1967.

Henry Scott, QC – Chief prosecution counsel.

Rudolph Lyons, QC – Counsel for Dennis Stafford.

Raymond Dean, QC – Counsel for Michael Luvaglio.

Graham Andrews – Dennis Stafford's solicitor.

Henry Mincoff – Michael Luvaglio's Newcastle solicitor.

David (later Sir David) Napley – Michael's London solicitor.

James Comyn, QC, and John Matthew, QC – Michael's London
barristers.

Peter Hughman – Author and criminal defence lawyer.

Lord Justice Edmund Davies – Appeal Court Judge, 1968.

Lord Chief Justice John Passmore Widgery – Appeal Court
Judge, 1973.

ACKNOWLEDGEMENTS

I HAD HOPED to be able to give a copy of *Bandit Country* to Mike Hodges but, sadly, Mike died aged ninety in December 2022. He was one of the finest yet most under-appreciated of British film makers and, as his BFI obituary put it, from 'his earliest television dramas he explored the recurring themes of honour, revenge... and the corrupting nature of wealth and power'. RIP Mike.

I am grateful to my editor James Hodgkinson and the team at John Blake for bringing the book to fruition. I should particularly like to thank my agent Maggie Hanbury for all her help and encouragement. I am also indebted to Ian and Mo Wiles. Were it not for their kindness and generosity, my attempts to research the story might never have got off the ground.

Once again Jan Hollway kindly provided me with a London base while I was working at the British Library and in the National Archives, and numerous old 'faces' with experience of the milieu advised and directed me at various points and I am grateful to every one of them. I should also mention Peter Hughman's books

Most Unnatural and *A Body Under the Bridge* which are essential reading for anyone interested in looking further into the case.

I also recommend *Not Without Prejudice: The memoirs of Sir David Napley*, *T Dan Smith: Voice of The North* by Chris Foote Wood, *Crying with Laughter* by Bob Monkhouse, *Eric Burdon: Rebel Without A Pause* by Philip Payne, *Wild Thing* by Philip Norman and *Fun-Loving Criminal* by Dennis Stafford.

Finally, I can not thank my wife Sara enough for her love, tolerance and support. As ever, there would have been no book without her.

ABOUT THE AUTHOR

JAMIE REID IS the author of the non-fiction books *Doped*, the true story of the 1960s racehorse doping gangs which won the 2013 William Hill Sports Book of the Year Award, *Blown* and *Monsieur X* – which was short listed for the 2018 Daily Telegraph Sports Biography of the year. He is also a journalist and has written for the *Guardian*, the *Independent on Sunday*, *Private Eye*, *Money Observer* and the *Financial Times* colour supplement *How To Spend It*, or *HTSI*, for whom he wrote the 'Smart Money' column from 2006 to 2016.